TRANS GENDER PERSONS

AND THE LAW

2ND EDITION

Ally Windsor Howell, LL.M.

FOREWORD BY THE HONORABLE
PHYLLIS RANDOLPH FRYE

Cover design by Monica Alejo.

The materials contained herein represent the opinions of the authors and/or the editors, and should not be construed to be the views or opinions of the law firms or companies with whom such persons are in partnership with, associated with, or employed by, nor of the American Bar Association or the Imprint unless adopted pursuant to the bylaws of the Association.

Nothing contained in this book is to be considered as the rendering of legal advice for specific cases, and readers are responsible for obtaining such advice from their own legal counsel. This book is intended for educational and informational purposes only.

Printed in the United States of America.

18 17 16 15   5 4 3 2 1

ISBN: 978-1-63425-036-8
e-ISBN: 978-1-63425-037-5

Library of Congress Cataloging-in-Publication Data
Howell, Ally Windsor, author.
  Transgender persons and the law / Ally Windsor Howell. -- 2nd edition.
      pages cm
  Includes bibliographical references and index.
  ISBN 978-1-63425-036-8 (alk. paper)
  1. Transgender people--Legal status, laws, etc.--United States. I. Title.
  KF4754.5.H69 2015
  342.7308'7--dc23

                    2015011098

Discounts are available for books ordered in bulk. Special consideration is given to state bars, CLE programs, and other barrelated organizations. Inquire at Book Publishing, ABA Publishing, American Bar Association, 321 N. Clark Street, Chicago, Illinois 60654-7598.

www.ShopABA.org

Contents

ACKNOWLEDGMENTS

I wish to thank a transgender lawyer who has been an inspiration and encouragement to me since I first came out—Phyllis Randolph Frye. Phyllis has been an encouragement to so many in the transgender community and has been a pioneering agitator and fighter for rights of transgender persons.

I also wish to thank my wife, Donna; my son, Jeremiah; and my sister, Dot for their support of me and encouragement to me.

I also wish to thank the many transgender, lesbian, and gay friends I have made since transitioning for their encouragement, acceptance and support and the many straight allies for their support and encouragement.

For any glory that comes of this labor, may it be to God.

Ally Windsor Howell
2015

FOREWORD

As I read the text of *Transgender Persons and the Law*, I felt gratified at how far transgender (TG) legal gains have come—as expressed in this book by Ally Howell—since 1992 when I created the first international TG legal conference in Houston. (Editor's Note: Any scholar wishing to study the "roots" of TG legal activism can find all five volumes of the proceedings from the five international TG legal conferences at no cost at www.liberatinglaw.com. Select Phyllis Frye from the Our Lawyers pull-down menu, and then click on Phyllis's bio.)

Actually, my gratification goes further back, as I recall being fired as an engineer in 1976 and being told in 1978 by the Equal Employment Opportunity Commission after their investigation of my complaint that although my firing was discriminatory, it was not illegal in light of the 1977 federal appeals case *Holloway v. Arthur Anderson, 566 F.2d 659 (9th Cir. 1977)*. This was the time in my life that I used my benefits through the G.I. Bill to go to law school. (In 1972, I was honorably discharged, but no less forced out of the U.S. Army as a First Lieutenant, Regular Army, when they learned that I cross-dressed in private.)

Transgender Persons and the Law is a very comprehensive text. All lawyers and lay activists dealing with this area of the law either in the courts or in legislative lobbying should read it. Ms. Howell covers the following areas of the law: (1) what is transgendered, (2) identification documents, (3) public facilities, (4) housing issues, (5) military and veterans issues, (6) family law, (7) school issues, (8) health care, (9) personal safety concerns, (10) keeping a job and getting a job, (11) immigration issues, and (12) criminal imprisonment issues. The appendices are extensive and thorough.

Obviously, there is much more work to be done in the area of TG legal gains. Much of that work is currently being done by or through such organizations as the National LGBT Bar Association, the National Center for

Transgendered Equality, Lambda Legal, the National Center for Lesbian Rights, Gay and Lesbian Advocates and Defenders, the Human Rights Campaign and the American Bar Association. I have close friends in all of these organizations, and I salute their efforts and gains.

In closing, thank you, Ms. Howell, for your encompassing snapshot of all of our legal gains a mere two decades after the roots were planted.

Phyllis Randolph Frye, J.D.
First out-of-the-closet transgender judge in the U.S. and
"Grandmother of the National TG Legal and Political Movement"
prfrye@aol.com

CHAPTER 1

Who or What Is a Transgender Person and Why Should Anyone Care?

To paraphrase American playwright, performer, feminist, and activist Eve Ensler, transgender persons are immigrants into the world (read culture) of women and men. And immigrants are always hated, mistreated, and not appreciated when they first arrive.

Like other societies, the United States uses a binary system of gender in which being either male or female has great consequences. This binary system and its corollary system in which a "normal" society is made up of only couples comprising one man and one woman are the subject of much study and disputation. The most noticeable example of this is the rancorous public debate over same-sex marriages. Some say transgener persons, gays, and lesbians are not "normal." But to quote my favorite twentieth-century philosopher Erma Bombeck, "'Normal' is just a setting on a clothes dryer."

But there is also another debate about sex and gender, one that is not getting the same television and print media attention as the same-sex marriage debate. It centers on the issue of whether transgender persons are male or female for various legal purposes.

Most jurisdictions take the essentialist position that sex is fixed at birth—[that is,] by anatomy—and cannot be changed; only a small number of courts have recognized the complexity of the question and look to a person's gender identity as a "primary determinant of legal sex," and recognize a person who has transitioned into a different sex as having established [him- or] herself in that new condition. Thus, today a person's legal sex could change by simply crossing from one state into another, and an incoherent collection of statutes and legal rulings determines "one of the most intimate and defining aspects of our lives—gender identity . . . our sense of ourselves as male or female." Each judge may think he [or she] "knows" what sex is; the result is a system that, quite aside from the horrendous personal losses imposed on transgender people, is contrary to our conceptions of individual autonomy. "Can the law make something as central to our notion of selfhood as our sex depend on . . . where we reside . . . or [our] ability to afford surgery?" Such attitudes are related to an essentially historical view that there exist only two very fixed sexes. Though the long history of hermaphroditism and the laws dealing with it attest otherwise, twentieth-century courts and statutes all tend to reflect this view.

Even when courts have "recognized" a person's new condition, far too often their obsession with anatomy leads them to require that in every case, extensive [and] invasive surgical interventions must have been undergone. For many, this project of achieving a perfect and acceptable appearance of the "other sex" is an ordeal that not only takes years and is prohibitively expensive but may involve "procedures that for some individuals are not only unnecessary but may cause permanent physical damage." Relying on one's gender identity rather than one's sex would avoid this. The way to that goal, envisioned by more and more people today, is explored here.[1]

We are not all born male or female as is commonly thought. If one asks experts at medical centers how often a child is born so noticeably atypical

---

1. Samuel E. Bartos, *Letting "Privates" Be Private: Toward a Right of Gender Self-Determination*, 15 Cardozo J. L. & Gender 67, 68–69 (2008).

in terms of genitalia that a specialist in sex differentiation is called in, the number comes out to about 1 in 1,500 to 1 in 2,000 births. But a lot more people than that are born with more subtle forms of sex anatomy variations, some of which won't show up until later in life. Below we provide a summary of statistics drawn from an article by Brown University researchers.[2] The basis for that article was an extensive review of the medical literature from 1955 to 1998 aimed at producing numeric estimates for the frequency of sex variations. One should note that the frequency of some of these conditions, such as congenital adrenal hyperplasia, differs for different populations.

Condition	Frequency*
Not XX and not XY	1 in 1,666 births
Klinefelter Syndrome (XXY)1	1 in 1,000 births
Androgen Insensitivity Syndrome2	1 in 13,000 births
Partial Androgen Insensitivity Syndrome	1 in 130,000 births
Classical Congenital Adrenal Hyperplasia3	1 in 13,000 births
Late Onset Adrenal Hyperplasia	1 in 66 individuals
Vaginal Agenesis4	1 in 6,000 births
Ovotestes5	1 in 83,000 births
Complete Gonadal Dysgenesis6	1 in 150,000 births
Hypospadias (urethral opening in perineum or along penile shaft)	1 in 2,000 births
Hypospadias (urethral opening between corona and tip of glans penis)	1 in 770 births
Total number of people whose bodies are different from standard male or female	1 in 100 births

2. Melanie Blackless, Anthony Charuvastra, Amanda Derryck, Anne Fausto-Sterling, Karl Lauzanne & Ellen Lee, How sexually dimorphic are we? Review and synthesis, 12 AM. J. OF HUM. BIOLOGY 151–166 (2000). See also Alice Domurat Dreger, Ambiguous Sex—or Ambivalent Medicine? Ethical Issues in the Treatment of Intersexuality, 3 Hastings Center Report 28, 24–35 (1998).

Condition	Frequency*
* All statistics are from: Melanie Blackless, Anthony Charuvastra, Amanda Derryck, Anne Fausto-Sterling, Karl Lauzanne, and Ellen Lee, *How sexually dimorphic are we? Review and synthesis,* 12 American Journal of Human Biology 151–166. (2000).	

1. A genetic disorder that affects males and occurs when a boy is born with one or more extra X chromosomes. Having extra X chromosomes can cause a male to have some physical traits unusual for males. WebMD® http://men.webmd.com/tc/klinefelter-syndrome-topic-overview (last visited July 31, 2011).

2. An inability of the body to respond properly to male sex hormones (androgens) produced during pregnancy. WebMD® http://www.webmd.com/sexual-conditions/andro-gen-insensitivity-syndrome-partial (last visited July 31, 2011). The development of what are superficially external female characteristics by a male. THOMAS L. STEDMAN, STEDMANS MEDICAL DICTIONARY (27th ed. 2000).

3. A series of inherited inborn errors of metabolism with hyperplasia of the adrenal cortex and overproduction of virilizing hormones. THOMAS L. STEDMAN, STEDMANS MEDICAL DICTIONARY (27th ed. 2000).

4. A primary amenorrhea due to müllerian duct ageneis, resulting in absence of the vagina, or presence of a short vaginal pouch, and absence of the uterus with normal karyotype and ovaries. THOMAS L. STEDMAN, STEDMANS MEDICAL DICTIONARY (27th ed. 2000).

5. A very rare disorder in which an infant is born with the internal reproductive organs (gonads) of both sexes (female ovaries and male testes). The gonads can be any combination of ovary, testes or combined ovary and testes. The external genitalia are usually ambiguous but can range from normal male to normal female. WebMD® http://www.webmd.com/sexual-conditions/hermaphroditism-true (last visited July 31, 2011).

6. A defective gonadal development, which is true hermaphroditism. THOMAS L. STEDMAN, STEDMANS MEDICAL DICTIONARY (27th ed. 2000).

The term *gender* is a misunderstood one. It is often used as a synonym for *sex*, even though the two terms are different.

> We are meaning-making animals. And among the meanings we create are the meanings of what breasts or vaginas mean, what penises mean, what broken wrists and uplifted pinkies mean, and what body hair or long blond hair mean. In effect, gender is a language, a symbolic language. Put another way, gender is a system of symbols and meanings, and the rules for access to these meanings, for strength and weakness, power and vulnerability, "masculinity" and "femininity." . . . Gender, is then, more than a bit like standing a few inches from the Empire State Building—it is at once so close, so familiar, and yet so

overwhelming that it is difficult to conceptualize all at once or think about it clearly.[3]

To understand this identity issue, it is necessary to recognize that transsexualism is not a choice. It is now thought to be genetic in origin.[4] Research increasingly shows that one's gender identity has very little to do with one's sex organs or genitalia.[5]

Gender variance is not new. It has been described throughout history and in many different cultures. Child development specialists used to believe that gender-typical and gender-variant behaviors were the result of the ways in which children were raised. Today, experts believe that the presence or absence of these behaviors is partly the result of the biological or genetic diversity among individuals. In other words, the genetic propensity for these behaviors is hard-wired in the brain before or soon after birth. Of course, the specific content of male and female roles has to be learned by all children, even though some children seem to be biologically predisposed toward manifesting some of the gender-role characteristics of the other sex. Some experts used to believe that gender variance represented abnormal development, but today many have come to believe that children with gender-variant behaviors are normal children with unique qualities—just as children who develop left-handedness are normal.

Although science has yet to pinpoint the causes, we know that gender-variant traits are not typically caused by parenting style or by childhood events, such as divorce, sexual abuse, or other traumatic experiences. Children do not choose to have gender-variant interests any more than other children choose gender-typical interests. Both

3. Nicole Ansonia, *Gender Non-Conformists Under Title VII: A Confusing Jurisprudence in Need of a Legislative Remedy*, 3 GEO. J. OF GENDER AND THE LAW 871, 875 (2003), quoting from an interview with Riki Wilchins, Executive Director of the Gender Public Advocacy Coalition.

4. "Genes behind transsexualism possibly found," *World Science*, http://www.world-science.net/exclusives/050511_transfrm.htm (last visited July 16, 2011).

5. John Gearhart, M.D., et al., *Sex Determination, Differentiation, and Identity*, 350 NEW ENG. J. OF MED. 2204 (2004).

types of interests represent what comes naturally to each child. Gender variance is not caused by an emotional disorder. However, because of societal prejudice, children with gender-variant traits may experience ongoing rejection, criticism, and bullying, causing adjustment difficulties.[6]

Transgendered and *transgender* have become umbrella terms. Whether to call persons "transgendered" or "transgender" is a matter of dispute among some in the community of transgender persons. For this work, the term "transgender" was chosen as it seems to have the widest use. Even when gender terms are being employed correctly, other terms elaborating on the concept are still widely misunderstood. For example, the terms include transsexuals; cross-dressers (also called transvestites); intersexed persons (also called hermaphrodites); drag queens (gay men who predominantly cross-dress for theatrical purposes); drag kings (lesbians who predominantly cross-dress for theatrical purposes); and an emerging group known as gender-variant persons, or gender queers or gender benders (persons who are either very androgynous in their appearance or who look like effeminate men or masculine women).[7] Contrary to popular misconception, "the bottom line is that sexual orientation, being lesbian or gay, has nothing to do with gender identity, and they're really parallel lines."[8]

The Diagnostic and Statistical Manual IV (DSM-IV), of the American Psychiatric Association (APA) contained a classification entitled "Gender Identity Disorder," previously called "Gender Dysphoria." This recognition by the APA made gender identity disorder a recognized medical condition and, thus, facilitates its recognition by the courts. Gender identity disorder has several diagnostic criteria:

---

6. Catherine Tuerk, Edgardo Menvielle & James de Jesus, *If you are concerned about your child's gender behaviors* (The Children's National Medical Center, Children's Hospital, Washington, D.C., undated). Copy in author's files and available online at http://www.childrensnational.org/files/PDF/DepartmentsandPrograms/Neuroscience/Psychiatry/Gender-VariantOutreachProgram/GVParentBrochure.pdf (last visited July 16, 2011).

7. See the Glossary of Transgendered Terms in Appendix 1 for definitions of these various terms.

8. Kaiser Family Foundation, *Transcript of 17th National HIV/AIDS Update Conference: Vulnerable Communities Track: Forging New Ground: Transgendered Issues and Corrections Medicine*, p. 8 (April 12, 2005).

A. A strong persistent cross-gender identification (not merely a desire for any perceived cultural advantages of being the other sex)
B. Persistent discomfort with his or her sex or sense of inappropriateness in the gender role of that sex
C. The disturbance is not concurrent with physical intersex condition.
D. The disturbance causes clinically significant distress or impairment in social, occupational, or other important areas of functioning[9]

In effect, the APA characterized transgenderedism or gender identity disorder as both a medical and a mental disorder. Many in the transgender community contested this classification and argue that transgenderedism should not be classified as a pathology.[10] They note the parallel between this classification as a disorder and the prior listing in the DSM-I (1952), the DSM-II (1968), and the DSM-III (1980) in which homosexuality was listed as a mental disorder. It was removed in the DSM-III-R (1987), the DSM-IV (1994), the DSM-IV TR (2000), and the DSM-V (2012) after scientific developments challenging the previous paradigm of sexual orientation as a disorder were considered. Then, in 2012, the APA announced that the DSM-V which will be released in May of 2013 will delete the diagnosis of gender identity disorder. Instead, the DSM-V will again include a listing for "gender dysphoria" which is described as emotional distress from "a marked incongruence between one's experienced/expressed gender and assigned gender." This will allow for affirmative treatment and transition care without the stigma of disorder.[11] In 2012, the APA also released new health guidelines for transgender patients[12], as well as a position statement

---

9. DIAGNOSTIC AND STATISTICAL MANUAL IV (DSM-IV), "Diagnostic Criteria for Gender Identity Disorder" (American Psychiatric Association 4th ed. 2000).

10. *See, e.g.,* Justin Cascio, *Bias in writings on Gender Identity Disorder*, Trans-Health. com, at http://www.trans-health.com/displayarticle.php?aid=49 (last visited July 16, 2011); and Katherine K. Wilson, *Gender as Illness: Issues of Psychiatric Classification* (1997, Gender Identity Center of Colorado, Inc.) copy in author's files and retrieved from http://www. gendercare.com/library/GENDERASILLNESS.html (last visited July 16, 2011).

11. Beredjick, C. (July 23, 2012). *DSM-V To Rename Gender Identity Disorder 'Gender Dysphoria'*, THE ADVOCATE (retrieved on March 9, 2013 from http://www.advocate.com/ politics/transgender/2012/07/23/dsm-replaces-gender-identity-disorder-gender-dysphoria).

12. Byne, W., *et al.* (2012). *Report of the American Psychiatric Association Task Force on Treatment of Gender Identity Disorder*, 41 ARCHIVES OF SEXUAL BEHAVIOR 759–796.

affirming transgender care and civil rights. Both documents align with a new standard for respecting transgender people in the medical community.[13]

Some have contended that gender identity disorder is a disability. Most in the transgender community do not want to be labeled as "disabled," but others wish they could because of the difficulty keeping and/or obtaining employment once one comes out as transgender. The federal courts have rejected classifying gender identity disorder as a qualifying condition under the Americans with Disabilities Act.[14] However, the Supreme Court for New York County, New York held that an MtF transgender minor in the custody of the state at a foster care facility was entitled to wear skirts at the facility because her gender identity disorder was a "disability" under the N.Y. Human Rights Law.[15]

The foregoing criteria from the DSM for a diagnosis of gender identity disorder are all subjective in nature and are basically matters that are self-reported by the patient, as opposed to observed behavior in a clinical setting or results from a medical test. As a noted expert in the field of transgender medical care so eloquently put it:

> [M]edicine has just gotten so high-tech, and there is so much science to it. . . . We want to know what's the latest study. Well, there aren't very many studies. There's no way to do a test. We can't draw blood, do an x-ray, do a PET scan, and prove that someone is transgendered. You just have to accept it. You have to accept the patient directing their own care, and that is often hard, and it's probably the most challenging part, is to kind of get over ourselves and kind of let them be in the driver's seat. So, don't look for any test; there is nothing probably on the cover of *Time Magazine* about any part of the brain that's going to give a good answer. Basically, we have to trust Popeye, and Popeye

---

13. Beredjick, C., *supra* note 11.

14. *See, e.g.,* Myers v. Cuyahoga County, 182 Fed.Appx. 510, 2006 WL 1479081 (6th Cir. 2006)

15. Doe v. Bell, 194 Misc.2d 774, 754 N.Y.S.2d 846 (N.Y. Sup. Ct. N.Y. County 2003), and N.Y. Executive Law § 296, sub. 18(2).

says, "I am what I am," and that's just about as far as you can go in terms of making an accurate diagnosis, okay?[16]

Notwithstanding this disclaimer, there are recognized treatment standards of care,[17] which bring transgender persons into the worlds of the mental health professionals and medical professionals. These standards provide that a person diagnosed with gender identity disorder should be under the care of a psychologist, psychiatrist, or both for evaluation and psychotherapy. Upon the recommendation of the psychologist or psychiatrist the person should begin hormone therapy under the supervision and care of a physician.[18] For male-to-female (MtF) transgender persons, this would also be the time to begin facial and body hair removal by either laser treatments or electrolysis. Then the transgender person would begin cross-living in the opposite gender role full time. If the cross-living is successful for at least a year, transgendered upon the recommendation of the person's psychologist or psychiatrist, the transgender person can seek gender reassignment surgery (also called sex reassignment surgery, GRS, or SRS). Many male-to-female transgender persons also seek and obtain plastic surgery to reduce the size of the Adam's apple, feminize the face, and enlarge the breasts. The standards of care are advisory and provided as "clinical guidance" and specifically devised to be flexible, not a fixed step by step procedure and they should not be presented as any type of binding or fixed process. There are also other protocols, for example, the informed consent model, and some doctors use those protocols.

Sometimes, the terms *transgender* and *transsexual* can be confusing. However, for the purposes of this book, the word *transgender* will be used

---

16. Kaiser Family Foundation, Transcript of 17th National HIV/AIDS Update Conference: Vulnerable Communities Track: Forging New Ground: Transgendered Issues and Corrections Medicine, p. 7 (April 12, 2005).

17. World Professional Association for Transgendered Health (formerly the Harry Benjamin International Gender Dysphoria Association), *The Standards of Care for Gender Identity Disorders Sixth Version*, http://www.wpath.org/documents2/socv6.pdf (last visited July 16, 2011).

18. For male-to-female (MtF) transgendered persons, this involves taking estrogen and sometimes involves taking a testosterone suppressant. For female-to-male transgendered persons, this involves taking testosterone and an estrogen suppressant. Some MtFs have an orchiectomy (removal of the testes) and this obviates the need to take a testosterone suppressant.

exclusively to refer to *transsexuals* (defined in Appendix 1, "Glossary of Transgender Terms"). This choice is not designed to minimize, denigrate, or marginalize others under the transgender umbrella who are also denied equal civil rights. However, within the criminal justice system, it is only the transsexuals (preoperative, postoperative, and nonoperative) who seem to encounter significant problems related to their gender. Interestingly, in 2011, India and Nepal announced that they had decided to add a third gender to their upcoming censuses—for transgender persons. The announcement by Nepal's Central Bureau of Statistics was in response to a landmark decision of the Nepalese Supreme Court on December 21, 2007, that directed the government to guarantee the rights of transgender, gay, lesbian and bisexual people.[19]

Why Be Concerned about Transgender Persons?

Despite popular belief that transgender persons are a small and insignificant group who choose to be the way they are, science suggests otherwise. Professor Lynn Conway of the University of Michigan estimates that 1 in 250 to 500 men are male-to-female transsexuals and that 1 in 2,500 people designated as male at birth have gender reassignment surgery.[20] From an epidemiological point of view,[21] the number of transsexual persons is statistically significant. Thus, transgenderedism, for lack of a better term, is

---

19. *India & Nepal introduce transgendered census category*, Tongzhi Community Joint Meeting at http://tcjm.org/2011/01/13/nepal-india-transgendered-census-category/ (last visited September 12, 2011). *See also Nepal court rules on gay rights*, BBC News (21 December 2007) at http://news.bbc.co.uk/2/hi/south_asia/7156577.stm (last visited September 12, 2011), and Kelly Bourdet, *Transgendered now an official sex in Nepal*, Nerve.com, Inc. (January 9, 2011) at http://www.nerve.com/news/politics/transgendered-now-an-official-sex-in-nepal (last visited September 12, 2011).

20. Lynn Conway, *How Frequently Does Transsexualism Occur?*, copy in author's files and retrieved from http://ai.eecs.umich.edu/people/conway/TS/TSprevalence.html (last visited July 16, 2011).

21. "Statistically significant" is defined as "a mathematical measure of difference between groups. The difference is said to be statistically significant if it is greater than what might be expected to happen by chance alone." *Glossary of Statistical Terms,* THE NATIONAL CANCER INSTITUTE, http://www.cancer.gov/statistics/glossary#S (last visited July 16, 2011). *See also* John Gay, *Clinical Epidemiology & Evidence-Based Medicine Glossary: Experimental Design and Statistics Terminology*, Washington State University (2006), http://www.vetmed.wsu.edu/courses-jmgay/GlossExpDesign.htm (last visited July 16, 2011).

more common than the following conditions or diseases, which are better known and have large research budgets devoted to their study:

- Multiple sclerosis has an incidence of 91.7 per 100,000 people = **less than 1 per 1,000**[22]
- Duchenne and Becker's muscular dystrophy affects about one in every 3,500 to 5,000 newborn males = **less than 1 per 1,000**[23]
- Amyotrophic lateral sclerosis (ALS or Lou Gehrig's disease) has an incidence of 1 per 100,000 persons = **less than 1 per 1,000**[24]

Societal attitudes towards transgender persons, however, means that there are no telethons or foundations that exist to fund research to find better ways to assist transgender persons to live in the sex or gender that conforms to their inner gender identity.

Society does not understand what it is to be transgender. Remarkably, most transgender persons, especially those who are over thirty, also do not understand initially who and what they are. Dr. Lori Kohler, a transgender medical expert, has observed:

So, in the past, being transgendered—it's not like any of us grow up and say "Oh, I understand what that is." It's not even like someone who is transgendered grows up understanding what it means, and naturally having a language, and naturally being able to articulate their experience. But I think that the more we talk about it, the easier it becomes for younger people to realize what they're feeling, and actually for their parents to be there and to be supportive of that, and to work with them.[25]

---

22. Multiple Sclerosis Information Trust, *All About Multiple Sclerosis*, http://www.mult-sclerosis.org/prev_tab.html (last visited July 16, 2011).

23. Sherri Garcia, *Duchenne Muscular Dystrophy*, CENTERS FOR DISEASE CONTROL (2005), http://www.cdc.gov/excite/ScienceAmbassador/ambassador_pgm/lessonplans/Garcia%20MD.ppt (last visited July 16, 2011).

24. *Lou Gehrig's Disease (ALS)—Fear, Symptoms, and Statistics*, NEUROLOGY24.COM, http://www.neurology24.com/lou-gehrigs-disease.htm (last visited July 16, 2011).

25. Kaiser Family Foundation, Transcript of 17th National HIV/AIDS Update Conference: Vulnerable Communities Track: Forging New Ground: Transgendered Issues and Corrections Medicine, pp. 10–11 (April 12, 2005).

Dr. Kohler's observation appears to be accurate based on my own experiences and observations as well as the life stories of transgender persons from two support groups which I have facilitated in Rochester, New York, and Montgomery, Alabama. However, because the main rule of those groups is that "what is said in the group stays in the group," I am unable to discuss particulars and identities.

Dr. Kohler's observation that it is easier for younger people now to come to terms with their true gender identity is equally astute. An encouraging example of what can happen when one comes out early in life is best demonstrated by the first-person account *Mom, I Need to be a Girl*,[26] the story of a single mother whose son successfully transitions into her daughter with the help of her mother and her siblings.

Even though it is now easier for younger people to acknowledge and deal with their true gender identity, there are still major societal hurdles, if not roadblocks, to overcome. These include health care and mental health services, which are too often inadequate or nonexistent due to medical and mental health providers who share societal biases and medical and mental health providers who are unwilling to learn the proper treatment modalities for transgender persons. However, the major problem is that society values men more than women and places the societal rank of men above that of women.[27]

Professor Katherine Franke cogently analyzes the myths of sex, sexuality, and gender and their effects on society's views:

---

26. EVELYN D. LINDENMUTH, MOM, I NEED TO BE A GIRL (Water Trook Pub., 1998). This book was originally published in soft cover format. But now, in a selfless gesture to share it with the world, it can be found on the web and downloaded for free. *See* http://ai.eecs.umich.edu/people/conway/TS/Evelyn/Mom_I_need_to_be_a_girl.pdf (last visited July 16, 2011). A copy is also in the author's files.

27. This is generally based on the Christian Bible's statement by St. Paul to the church at Ephesus when he said "Wives, submit to your husbands as to the Lord. For the husband is the head of the wife as Christ is the head of the church, his body, of which he is the Savior. Now as the church submits to Christ, so also wives should submit to their husbands in everything." Ephesians 5:22–24. *See also* Becky L. Jacobs, *PMS HAHAcronym: Perpetuating Male Superiority*, 14 TEX. J. WOMEN & L. 1 (2004), and Christine M. Venter, *Community Culture And Tradition: Maintaining Male Dominance In Conservative Institutions*, 12 J.L. & RELIGION 61.

In the end, bodies end up meaning less in the fight for equality than the roles, clothing, myths, and stereotypes that transform a vagina into a she. "Analyzing the social processes that construct the categories we call 'female and male,' 'women and men,' 'homosexual and heterosexual' uncovers the ideology and power differentials congealed in these categories." . . .

[T]he law assumes a natural and biological foundation of sexual difference, thereby distinguishing sexual differentiation from sexual discrimination. Upon examination, however, this assumption is revealed to be a fiction: gender norms, not precultural biological facts, make up the difference that sexual difference makes. . . .

[I]n those circumstances in which people present a challenge to the intrapersonal unity of biological sex, core gender identity, and gender role identity, they find themselves legal outsiders, either suffering judicial punishment or being refused the rights and benefits afforded as a matter of course to people who conform to contemporary gender norms.[28]

Gender norms devalue qualities that are deemed feminine *vis-à-vis* those that are deemed masculine.[29] Transgender persons discover a truth as they transition: in our society, women are valued less than men. Professor Mary Ann Case accurately describes this:

The man who exhibits feminine qualities is double despised, for manifesting the disfavored qualities and for descending from his masculine gender privilege to do so. The masculine woman is understandable; it can be a step up for a woman, and the qualities associated with masculinity are also associated with success. . . . So long as stereotypically feminine behavior, from wearing dresses and jewelry to speaking

---

28. Katherine M. Franke, *The Central Mistake of Sex Discrimination Law: The Disaggregation of Sex from Gender*, 144 U. PA. L. REV. 1, at 39–41 (1995).

29. Nicole Anzuoni, *Gender Non-Conformists Under Title VII: A Confusing Jurisprudence in Need of a Legislative Remedy*, 3 GEO. J. OF GENDER AND THE LAW 871, 875–76 (2003).

softly or in a high-pitched voice, to nurturing children, is forced into a female ghetto, it may be continued to be devalued. [30]

And, as one study noted:

> Transgender and transsexual people face a lifetime of inequalities and discrimination, despite often being amongst the most well educated members of society. As children, they can be bullied and abused for being gender different. As adults their families, friends and [neighbors] can reject them once their trans status is known, and they are very likely to experience assault and abuse at home, in the workplace and out on the streets. . . .
>
> When they are seeking treatment to transition, they will start a medical process which reduces every aspect of their life and, in particular, their health down to the most minimal of issues, their trans mental health. Practitioners, at every level of medicine, ignore the trans person's abilities to cope with ongoing crises that would destroy other people, their educational standing and the nature of the actual illness they are presenting with. The fact that some qualified nursing staff will insist on calling a person who has been transitioned for over 30 years in their former gender, is indicative of the level of ignorance that exists within our health services. [31]

Americans who identify as Lesbian, Gay, Bisexual, or Transgender (LGBT) report lower well-being than do non-LGBT Americans. Importantly, these differences hold true even after taking into account the effects of gender, age, race and ethnicity, educational attainment, state of residence, and population density. The disadvantage in overall well-being is more acute for LGBT women than for LGBT men. These findings are as part of the Gallup-Healthways Well-Being Index survey. Across all five elements of

---

30. Mary Ann Case, *Disaggregating Gender from Sex and Sexual Orientation: The Effeminate Man in the Law and Feminist Jurisprudence*, 105 YALE L. J. 1, 3–4 (1995).

31. Stephen Whittle, Lewis Turner, and Maryam Al-Alami, *Engendered Penalties: Transgendered and Transsexual People's Experiences of Inequality and Discrimination*, EQUALITIES REVIEW, 77 (Manchester Metropolitan University, September 30, 2006).

well-being, LGBT Americans—particularly LGBT women—trail their non-LGBT counterparts, even after taking into account possible differences in the demographic and geographic characteristics of LGBT and non-LGBT adults. These findings are consistent with research from UCLA's Williams Institute, which shows that the LGBT population is at a disproportionate risk for poverty and food insecurity.[32]

Rates of food insecurity are higher for LGBT adults when compared with non-LGBT adults across several national surveys, and across gender, age, racial/ethnic, and education-level groups. After taking these factors into account, LGBT adults are 1.7 times more likely than non-LGBT adults to not have had enough money to feed themselves or their family in the past year. Certain sub populations within the LGBT community are particularly vulnerable to food insecurity or report relatively high rates of participation in SNAP. These include bisexuals, women, and people of color. More than a third (34 percent) of LGBT-identified women did not have money for food in the last year compared with 20 percent of non-LGBT women and 24 percent of LGBT men. And, while nearly 1 in 4 White LGBT adults (23 percent) experienced food insecurity at some point last year, the figure was more than 1 in 3 for African American LGBT adults (37 percent), more than 1 in 2 for LGBT Native Americans (55 percent), and more than three in four for Native Hawaiians (78 percent).[33]

32. Gary J. Gates (August 25, 2014), *LGBT Americans Report Lower Well-Being: Significant differences seen in financial and physical well-being elements*, Gallup, Inc., http://www.gallup.com/poll/175418/lgbt-americans-report-lower.aspx (last visited August 28, 2014).

33. Gary J. Gates (February 2014). *Food Insecurity and SNAP (Food Stamps) Participation in LGBT Communities*, Williams Institute, UCLA School of Law, http://williamsinstitute.law.ucla.edu/wp-content/uploads/Food-Insecurity-in-LGBT-Communities.pdf (last visited August 28, 2014).

CHAPTER 2

Identification Documents

There are several limitations to this chapter. First, it does not address youth-specific issues in name or gender marker changes. That is because parental consent, often the consent of both parents, is required. Thus, this chapter is devoted to the issues involving adults.[1]

In determining whether one can change his or her name or birth certificate without parental involvement, one needs to know the age of majority in one's state of residence. The age of majority is 18 in all but four states, Alabama[2] and Nebraska[3] where it is 19 and Mississippi[4] and Pennsylvania[5] where it is 21. Of course, if the person seeking a name change is a minor who had been judicially relieved of the disabilities of non-age, such person's age would not matter. Some people in the United States still do not have and have never had a birth certificate. Their birth, birth date, and therefore, citizenship can be proven by alternative means. An alternative to a birth certificate is an entry in a family Bible, or a baptismal record

---

1. *See also* Alyson Dodi Meiselman, Katrina C. Rose & Phyllis Randolph Frye, *Cause of Action for Legal Change of Gender*, 24 CAUSES OF ACTION 2d 135 (2004).
2. ALA. CODE § 26-1-1.
3. NEB. REV. STAT. § 43-2101.
4. MISS. CODE ANN. § 1-3-21.
5. 1 PA. CONS. STAT. § 1991.

under common law exceptions to the hearsay rule. Also, a hospital record of the birth would be admissible as a business record. The following agencies accept such records:

- U.S. Department of Health and Human Services, Social Security Administration[6]
- U.S. Railroad Retirement Board[7]
- U.S. Department of Homeland Security[8]
- U.S. State Department[9]
- U.S. Department of Veterans Affairs[10]

The federal courts[11] and state courts[12] generally accept such records as evidence.

Changing one's name and getting identification documents to match that new name and one's newly acknowledged gender are of vital importance to transgender persons. Why? Because to obtain employment, one must usually produce proof that he or she is legally in the United States, which requires a certified copy of one's birth certificate from one of the fifty states, the District of Columbia, or the U.S. State Department; a U.S. passport; a Certificate of U.S. Naturalization (Department of Homeland Security Form N-550 or N-570); or a Permanent Resident Card, commonly known as a green card (Department of Homeland Security Form I-551). And if the sex or gender designation on the proof of legal residence does not match one's presented gender, then he or she has been outed as being transgender and is subject to legal denial of employment on the basis of being transgendered in two-thirds of the states (see Chapter 10, "Employment"). Then one must produce his or her Social Security card, and the name on it needs

---

6. *See* 20 C.F.R. § 416.804, 20 C.F.R. § 416.803, 20 C.F.R. § 416.1610, and 20 C.F.R. § 404.716.

7. *See* 20 C.F.R. § 219.21.

8. *See* 8 C.F.R. § 245a.2, 8 C.F.R. § 245a.4, 8 C.F.R. § 210.3, and 8 C.F.R. § 204.1.

9. *See* 22 C.F.R. § 50.5.

10. *See* 38 C.F.R. § 3.209, and 38 C.F.R. § 3.210.

11. *See* FED. R. EVID. 803(11) (12) and 19.

12. *See* 29 AM. JUR. 2d *Evidence* § 1248, 29 AM. JUR. 2d *Evidence* § 694, and 29 AM. JUR. 2d *Evidence* § 690.

to match the proof of citizenship document. Then the person seeking a job usually has to produce a photo identification card, a valid driver's license or a non-driver's identification card issued by one of the fifty states or the District of Columbia or a military identification card. Once again, if the sex or gender designation on the picture identification card does not match one's presented gender, then he or she has been outed as being transgender and is subject to legal denial of employment in two-thirds of the states on the basis of being transgender.

§2.1 Official Name Changes

Changing a name might seem like a minor matter for those who are changing their gender identities or facing challenges such as finding knowledgeable doctors, trying hormones, and experimenting with painful hair-removal procedures. But many who have gone through the switch say a name change sends an important message to the world, a message solidified and made official with a court's approval.[13]

Whether and under what conditions one can change his or her name depends on the law of the state where he or she resides or was born. See Appendix 2, "State Laws Relating to Changing One's Name," for a table that cites the applicable laws of each state and any limitations. Most states allow for a common law name change, which is simply adopting a new name and using it.[14] But few states will accept that as a basis for changing identification documents.

Every state by statute or common law denies one the privilege of changing his or her name if there is an intent to deceive or defraud another. If the person seeking a name change has a felony conviction, he or she may encounter problems changing his or her name. Some states require that the

---

13. William Glaberson, For Transgendered People, Name Is a Message, *New York Times*, January 24, 2010, at A12.

14. *See, e.g., Application of Halligan*, 46 A.D.2d 170, 171–172, 361 N.Y.S.2d 458, 459–460 (N.Y. App. Div. 4th Dept. 1974) (Under the common law, change of name is accomplished by usage or habit. A person may change his or her name at will so long as there is no fraud, misrepresentation, or interference with the rights of others.) and State v. Hansford, 219 Wis.2d 226, 245, 580 N.W.2d 171 (1998), which recognizes "a common law right to change one's name through consistent and continuous use, as long as the change is not effected for a fraudulent purpose."

district attorney who prosecuted the case be notified. And if the felony is a sex related offense, the change will be either denied or made very difficult because of the requirement that sex offenders be registered.

The First Department of the Appellate Division of the New York Supreme Court became the first appellate court to go on record and hold that Paulo Cesar, a Costa Rican–born immigrant who is a transgender person and who wanted to change his name to Raquel Ramirez, was entitled to do so. The New York Civil Court had denied the name change. The Appellate Division reversed and ordered the Civil Court to grant the name change. The court stated:

> That the Costa Rican born petitioner was unable to provide the court with proof of citizenship or lawful immigration status was not fatal to the otherwise meritorious name change application. Civil Rights Law § 61 requires verification of a name-change applicant's "residence," not legal residence, and considerations of citizenship and immigration status should not be lightly imported by implication into the statutory scheme where to do so would ignore the plain meaning of the statute as written. Clearly, the term "residence" as used in the name change statute is "neither synonymous [with] nor interdependent [of]" [citation omitted] the legal residency construct fashioned by Civil Court in denying petitioner relief under the statute. To be distinguished is *Matter of Beals*, 40 Misc.3d 61 (2013), in which we recognized the court's authority to require a name change applicant to produce evidence tending to confirm "the accuracy of ... *pertinent* background and pedigree information required to be disclosed" under the name change statute (at 62)(emphasis added)
>
> Any risk of "fraud and confusion" potentially created by a change in name of an undocumented immigrant—a concern expressed by the court in denying petitioner's application—is adequately addressed by requiring petitioner through counsel to promptly notify federal immigration authorities of the name change, a requirement consented to by counsel at oral argument of the appeal [citation omitted].[15]

---

15. In re Cesar,___ A.D.2d ___, ___ N.Y.S.2d ___, 2014 WL 5334031, 2014 N.Y. Slip Op. 24313 (N.Y.Sup.App.Div. 1st Dept. 2014)

§2.2 Birth Certificate Changes—
Name and Sex Identifier

Whether and under what conditions one can change his or her birth certificate as to his or her name or sex identifier depends on the law of the state where he or she was born. And even in states that allow changes, some only issue amended birth certificates (with the word *amended* prominently printed or typed on the document) as opposed to a new or replacement birth certificate. Most states will change the name on birth certificates with a certified copy of the court order changing one's name. Most states will change the sex designator on birth certificates with an affidavit or other documentation from the surgeon who performed the sex-change surgery. Some states require a court order to change birth certificates, which increases the cost and complexity of the process.

See Appendix 3, "State Laws Relating to Changing Birth Certificates," for a table that cites the applicable laws of each state and has the contact information for the appropriate state agency. Check a specific state's website for the current fees for such changes.

For U.S. citizens born overseas, such as children of military personnel, a different process is required. The Certificate of Report of Birth (State Department Form DS-1350) is no longer issued. On January 3, 2011, the State Department began issuing a new Consular Report of Birth Abroad (State Department Form FS-240). All previously issued FS-240 and DS-1350 documents are still valid for proof of identity, citizenship, and other legal purposes. To amend either form, one must follow the following procedure:

1. Provide a notarized written (or typed) request detailing the amendment or correction needed.
2. Provide a certified copy of the court order changing one's name.
3. Provide the original DS-1350 or FS-240, a replacement FS-240 or DS-1350, or a notarized affidavit stating the whereabouts of the original FS-240 or DS-1350.
4. Provide a copy of the requester's valid identification.
5. Provide a $50.00 check or money order payable to "Department of State."

6. Mail complete packet to: Department of State, Passport Services, Vital Records Section, Room 510, 1111 9th Street, N.W., Washington, D.C. 20036[16]

For persons born in the states on the following list, name or sex changes can be made to birth certificates by using the PDF forms indicated. These forms can be found on the CD version of this book or by searching the Internet or state department's website for the specific form using the name of the state department listed in Appendix 3 and the name or number of the form. For states not listed, no specific forms could be found, and the applicant should contact the state's department listed in Appendix 3.

1. Alabama
   - ADPH-HS-33 Amendment Package for Alabama Birth and Death Certificates (A Petition to Circuit Court to Recognize Sex Change will also be required, and a sample petition is available in the CD version of this book.)
2. California
   - Obtaining a New Birth Certificate after Gender Reassignment Instructional package
   - VS-24 Affidavit to Amend a Birth Record
3. Colorado
   - Procedure to Change a Colorado Birth Certificate as a Result of a Gender Change via Surgical Procedure
   - Form to Correct or Change a Colorado Birth Certificate
4. Florida
   - DH Form 660 Instructions for Amending a Certificate of Live Birth
   - DH Form 429 Application for Amendment to Florida Birth Record
   - DH Form 430 Affidavit of Amendment of Certificate of Live Birth
   - DH Form 427 Report of Legal Change of Name

---

16. *Replace or Amend a Consular Report of Birth Abroad (CRBA)*, USA.gov, http://travel. state.gov/passport/get/first/first_825.html (last visited November 14, 2011).

5. Illinois
   - IOCI 12–402 State of Illinois Gender Reassignment Application Instructions
6. Kansas
   - VS241 Affidavit of Applicant Re Changes to Birth Certificate
7. Maine
   - Gender Designation Form. There is not an instruction form or any published section of the Bureau of Motor Vehicles (BMV) manual or a rule available online about this form that I am aware of, but it is part of the internal BMV policy manual.[17]
8. Michigan
   - DCH-0847 Application to Correct or Change a Michigan Birth Record
9. Minnesota
   - Requirements Checklist for Amending a Birth Record with a Court Order
   - Minnesota Birth Record Amendment Application
10. Nebraska
    - HHS-81 Application for Amendment [of Birth Certificate]
11. New Hampshire
    - [Instructions for] Correcting a Vital Record
12. New York
    - DOH-4380 (12/05) Mail-in Application for Copy of Birth Certificate
    - DCH-297 (1/2002) Application for Correction of Certificate of Birth
        The application *must* be submitted with copies of either A *or* B:
        a. One (1) of the following forms of valid photo-ID:
           - Driver license
           - State issued non driver photo-ID card
           - Passport
           - U.S. Military issued photo-ID

---

17. The form can be found at http://www.maine.gov/sos/bmv/licenses/GENDER%20 DESIGNATION%20FORM.pdf.

  b. Two (2) of the following showing the applicant's name and
      address:
      • Utility or telephone bills
      • Letter from a government agency dated within the last
        six (6) months

13. New York City amended the Administrative Code of N.Y. City by add-
    ing a new § **17-167.1 Sex designation on birth records.**[18] The forms had
    not been designated at the time the manuscript for this second edition
    was submitted. The new law provides as follows:

> **§ 17-167.1 Sex designation on birth records.** a. The depart-
> ment shall make a new birth record when an applicant submits
> an application and supporting documentation pursuant to this
> subdivision and subdivision b of this section requesting the cor-
> rection of sex designation to the applicant's birth record. Such
> application shall be made in a form or manner to be provided
> or approved by the department. If the department requests
> information, documentation, or a copy of an acceptable cur-
> rent signed photographic identification, the department may not
> take into account the sex designation listed on such identifica-
> tion in reviewing such application.
>
> b. An application made pursuant to subdivision a of this section
> shall be accompanied by supporting documentation that is an
> affirmation from a physician licensed to practice medicine in
> the United States, or an affidavit from a professional licensed to
> practice in the United States who is a: doctoral-level psycholo-
> gist (PhD or PsyD) in clinical or counseling psychology, clinical
> social worker, master social worker, physician assistant, nurse
> practitioner, marriage and family therapist, mental health coun-
> selor, or midwife. Such affirmation or affidavit shall include a
> declaration affirming or attesting under penalty of perjury that:

---

18. File # Int 0491-2014, A Local Law to amend the administrative code of the city of
New York, in relation to amending sex designation on birth records (12/8/2014). (Act number
not yet assigned because it is awaiting the Mayor's expected signature.)

1. the professional is licensed and in good standing in the jurisdiction in the United States in which such professional is licensed; and

2. in keeping with contemporary expert standards regarding gender identity, the applicant's requested correction of sex designation of male or female more accurately reflects the applicant's sex or gender identity.

14. North Carolina
  - Request to Amend a Record
15. Oregon
  - 45–13A Oregon Birth Record Order Form
  - Request to Change Birth Certificate Based on Court Order of Name Change
16. Texas
  - VS-170 Application to Amend Certificate of Birth

§2.3 Social Security Card and Records

The U.S. Department of Health and Human Services, Social Security Administration will allow a person to change his or her name on his or her Social Security account and will issue a new Social Security card in the new name. An application must be submitted to the Social Security Administration along with a certified copy of the name change court order.

To correct or change one's gender on Social Security's records, one must have in one's possession:

1. full-validity, ten-year U.S. passport with the new sex (Social Security Administration will not accept passports with less than ten years of validity);
2. State-issued amended birth certificate (BC) with the new sex;
3. court order directing legal recognition of change of sex;
4. medical certification of appropriate clinical treatment for gender transition in the form of an original signed statement from a licensed physician (i.e., a Doctor of Medicine (MD) or Doctor of Osteopathy (DO)). The statement must include the following:

a. physician's full name;

b. medical license or certificate number;

c. issuing state, country, or other jurisdiction of medical license or certificate;

d. address and telephone number of the physician;

e. language stating that the individual has had appropriate clinical treatment for gender transition to the new gender (male or female);

f. language stating the physician has either treated the individual in relation to the individual's change in gender or has reviewed and evaluated the medical history of the individual in relation to the individual's change in gender and that the physician has a doctor–patient relationship with the individual;

g. language stating "I declare under penalty of perjury under the laws of the United States that the forgoing is true and correct."[19]

All documents must be either originals or copies certified by the issuing agency. The Social Security Administration will not accept photocopies or notarized copies of documents.[20]

§2.4 Driver's Licenses, Non-Driver ID Cards, and Passport Changes—Name and Sex Identifier

States have differing requirements for obtaining a driver's license or non driver's identity card. And the requirements for getting such an identity card modified or changed to reflect a new name, and especially a new sex, vary even more. Generally, a copy of a court order changing one's name is sufficient to have one's name changed on such an identity card. But to have one's sex marker identifier changed is another matter. Many states allow such changes and have statutes or regulations regarding such. But other states have neither a law nor a regulation on the topic of changing a

---

19. U.S. Department of Health & Human Services, Social Security Administration, *Program Operations Manual System*, Part 1, Chapter 102, Subchapter 12, "Legal Names and Name Changes for an SSN," RM 10212.200 (Effective Date: September 30, 2013).

20. *Changing gender on Social Security records*, U.S. Social Security Administration, http://ssa-custhelp.ssa.gov/app/answers/detail/a_id/1667/~/correct-or-change-gender-on-your-social-security-record (last visited August 4, 2011).

sex marker but allow it on an "unofficial" basis through policies or practices not embodied in any regulation or statute. Some of these practices or policies can be found by looking on the state agency's website, but a few exist (according to accounts from other lawyers) if the lawyer knows which state agency employee or official to contact and how to approach such employee or official.

The REAL ID Act of 2005[21] was enacted May 11, 2005 and Title II of the act modified federal law pertaining to security, authentication, and issuance procedure standards for state driver's licenses and non driver identification cards, among other things. Title II of the act sets forth certain requirements for state driver's licenses and ID cards to be accepted by the federal government for "official purposes," as defined by the Secretary of Homeland Security (DHS). The DHS has currently defined official purposes as presenting state driver's licenses and identification cards for boarding commercially operated airline flights and entering federal buildings and nuclear power plants.

In January 2008, the DHS issued a final rule[22] to establish minimum standards for state-issued driver's licenses and identification cards in accordance with the REAL ID Act of 2005. Pursuant to the regulation, states were to be in full compliance with the act by May 11, 2011. A final rule issued March 7, 2011, changed that date to December 1, 2014.[23] This change gives states the time necessary to ensure that driver's licenses and identification cards issued by states meet the security requirements of the REAL ID Act. After December 1, 2017, "a Federal agency may not accept, for any official purpose, a driver's license or identification card issued by a state to any person unless the state is meeting the requirements" specified in the REAL ID Act.[24] People born on or after December 1, 1964, will have to obtain a REAL ID by December 1, 2014. Those born before December 1, 1964, will have until December 1, 2017 to obtain their REAL ID.

This poses a problem for transgender individuals because it will make it more difficult to obtain identification documents needed to not just travel

---

21. Pub. L. 109–13, 119 Stat. 302 (2005).
22. 6 C.F.R. § 37.1, *et seq.*
23. 6 C.F.R. § 37.5.
24. *Id.*

but to obtain employment, or to prove their citizenship in the face of the draconian state anti-immigration laws in states such as Alabama[25] and Arizona.[26] The act makes it harder for all persons, including transgender persons, to get a driver's license or non driver identification card because a birth certificate is required to prove citizenship. Some people do not have a birth certificate, and the DHS has no regulation allowing the alternative proof of birth and parentage allowed in common law and by the Federal Rules of Evidence, which are also accepted by other federal agencies. Also, even where one has a birth certificate, many states do not allow a change of the sex marker, which creates a situation where the transgender person will be outed and may not be able to get the license or identification card with the desired sex marker.

Whether and under what conditions one can change his or her driver's license or non driver's state identification card as to his or her name or sex identifier depends on the law of the state where the license was issued. See Appendix 4, "State Laws Relating to Changing Driver's Licenses and Non-Driver Identification Cards," for a table that cites the applicable laws of each state and has the contact information for the appropriate state agency. Currently name changes are commonly available on driver's licenses, but the availability of changes of sex identifiers is rarely available. One should check a particular state's website for the current fees for such changes. Further evidence of the biases that transgender persons confront on a more or less continual basis is demonstrated by the actions of West Virginia DMV personnel who refused to allow two transitioning transgender women to wear makeup or women's jewelry when having their photographs taken for updated driver's licenses after getting legal name changes. They were also called "it" by those same personnel.[27] And, the Transgender Legal Defense & Education Fund filed a federal lawsuit against the South Carolina Department of

---

25. *See* ALA. CODE 1975 § 31-13-1, *et seq.*

26. *See* ARIZ. REV. STAT. ANN. §§ 11-1051,13-2929, 15-1803, 15-1825, and 46-140.01.

27. See: Whitney Burdette, *Transgender women "humiliated" at W.Va. DMV offices*, Charleston Daily Mail (7/19/2014) at http://www.charlestondailymail.com/article/20140709/DM0104/140709334 (last visited July 17, 2014); and Michael Walsh, *DMV forces gender non-conforming South Carolina teen to remove makeup for license photo: activists*, New York Daily News (June 18, 2014) at http://www.nydailynews.com/news/national/dmv-forces-transgender-teen-remove-makeup-article-1.1833392 (last visited July 17, 2014).

Motor Vehicles (D.M.V.) on behalf of Chase Culpepper, a sixteen-year-old gender-nonconforming teen, who was targeted for discrimination in March 2014. When Chase attempted to get his first driver's license, he was told by the D.M.V. that he could not have his license photo taken unless he removed the makeup that he wears on a regular basis.[28]

The U.S. State Department will change a person's name on a passport or issue a passport in a name other than the name on a certified birth certificate with a certified copy of the name change order.[29] If the passport was issued one year or less before the name change, one should use State Department Form DS-5504. If the passport was issued more than one year before the name change, one should use State Department Form DS-82.[30] There is no regulatory authority about changing one's sex or gender on one's passport, but the State Department has announced a policy.[31] The applicant will have to present a "certification from an attending medical physician that the applicant has undergone appropriate clinical treatment for gender transition." The following requirements apply to the physician's statement:

1. It must be the signed original.
2. It must be on the doctor's letterhead.
3. The physician must be a medical doctor (MD) or doctor of osteopathy (DO). Statements from persons who are not licensed physicians, such as psychologists, nurse practitioners, health practitioners, or chiropractors, are not acceptable.
4. The statement **must** include the following information:
   a. physician's full name;
   b. medical license or certificate number;

---

28. Weiss, D. C. (September 3, 2014) Suit claims male has constitutional right to wear makeup in driver's license photo, *ABA Journal*, retrieved on 9/3/2014 from http://www.abajournal.com/news/article/suit_claims_male_has_constitutional_right_to_wear_makeup_in_drivers_license/?utm_source=internal&utm_medium=navigation&utm_campaign=most_read

29. 22 C.F.R. § 51.25.

30. *Change or Correct Passport*, U.S. Department of State, http://travel.state.gov/passport/correcting/correcting_2654.html (last visited July 25, 2011).

31. New Policy on Gender Change in Passports Announced, U.S. Department of State, PRN: 2010/766 of June 9, 2010 at http://www.state.gov/r/pa/prs/ps/2010/06/142922.htm (last visited July 25, 2011).

    c.   issuing state, country, or other jurisdiction of medical license/ certificate;

    d.   Drug Enforcement Administration (DEA) registration number assigned to the doctor or comparable foreign registration number, if applicable;

       i.   If the U.S.-based licensed physician does not provide a DEA number, you must request that this be provided in a new statement. If the statement with the DEA number is not provided after an appropriate period of time (generally 90 days), the application must be denied.

       ii.   Licensed physicians in foreign countries might not have a DEA number, but might have a comparable foreign registration number. Domestic passport agencies/centers must scan copies of the application and attach all submitted documents to the Adjudication Policy Division (CA/PPT/A/AP) at CA-PPT-AdjQ@state.gov. CA/PPT/A/AP will work with the Directorate of Overseas Citizens Services' Office of Policy Review and Inter Agency Liaison (CA/OCS/PRI) to verify the bona fides of the foreign physician with the applicable post abroad.

       iii.   Posts must verify their own foreign-based licensed physicians or, if the statement is from a physician in another country, contact the post that covers that country for verification.

    e.   address and telephone number of the physician;

    f.   language stating that he or she has treated the applicant or has reviewed and evaluated the medical history of the applicant and that he or she has a doctor–patient relationship with the applicant;

    g.   language stating the applicant has had appropriate clinical treatment for gender transition to the new gender of either male or female; and

    h.   language stating "I declare under penalty of perjury under the laws of the United States that the forgoing is true and correct."[32]

---

32. U.S. Department of State Foreign Affairs Manual (7 FAM 1300) Appendix M, pp. 3–4.

The State Department has a recommended template for the letter, although it is not the only form the statement from the physician may take. The recommended template is as follows:

Licensed Physician's Letterhead
(Physician's Address and Telephone Number)

I, (physician's full name), (physician's medical license or certificate number), (issuing U.S. State/Foreign Country of medical license/certificate), (DEA Registration number or comparable foreign designation), am the physician of (name of patient), with whom I have a doctor–patient relationship and whom I have treated (or with whom I have a doctor–patient relationship and whose medical history I have reviewed and evaluated).

(Name of patient) has had appropriate clinical treatment for gender transition to the new gender (specify new gender male or female).

OR

(Name of patient) is in the process of gender transition to the new gender (specify new gender male or female).

I declare under penalty of perjury under the laws of the United States that the forgoing is true and correct.

Signature of Physician

Typed Name of Physician

Date[33]

For any change or amendment to the passport, the current passport will have to be sent in with the application to change the passport. The website of the State Department's Bureau of Consular Affairs will need to be checked to determine the current fees.

---

33. U.S. Department of State Foreign Affairs Manual (7 FAM 1300) Appendix M, Exhibit B.

§2.5 Immigration Documents

A certificate of U.S. naturalization (Department of Homeland Security Form N-550 or N-570) or a permanent resident card, commonly known as a green card (Department of Homeland Security Form I-551), are the primary immigration identification documents. A legal transgender immigrant who wishes to change his or her name or gender on his or her certificate of U.S. naturalization or permanent resident card has the ability to do so.

§2.5(a) Permanent Residence Card

For a name change, the following information must be submitted in person, at the local district or suboffice of the U.S. Citizenship and Immigration Services of the U.S. Department of Homeland Security:[34]

1. Form I-90, Application to Replace Permanent Residence Card[35]
2. A certified copy of the court order legally changing your name
3. Original immigration documents
4. Two photographs of you that are less than six months old

For a gender change, the following information must be submitted in person at the local district or suboffice of the U.S. Citizenship and Immigration Services of the U.S. Department of Homeland Security:[36]

1. Form I-90, Application to Replace Permanent Residence Card[37]
2. Letter from doctor, surgeon, or hospital verifying that you have had gender reassignment surgery
3. Original immigration documents
4. Two photographs of you that are less than six months old

---

34. Locations can be found at http://uscis.gov/graphics/fieldoffices/distsub_offices/index.htm.

35. This form can be found at http://www.uscis.gov/portal/site/uscis/menuitem.eb1d4c2a3e-5b9ac89243c6a7543f6d1a/?vgnextoid=db029c7755cb9010VgnVCM10000045f3d6a1RCRD&vgnextchannel=db029c7755cb9010VgnVCM10000045f3d6a1RCRD.

36. Locations can be found at http://uscis.gov/graphics/fieldoffices/distsub_offices/index.htm.

37. This form can be found at http://www.uscis.gov/portal/site/uscis/menuitem.eb1d4c2a3e-5b9ac89243c6a7543f6d1a/?vgnextoid=db029c7755cb9010VgnVCM10000045f3d6a1RCRD&vgnextchannel=db029c7755cb9010VgnVCM10000045f3d6a1RCRD.

§2.5(b) Naturalization Papers

For a name change, the following information must be submitted in person, at the local district or suboffice of the U.S. Citizenship and Immigration Services of the U.S. Department of Homeland Security:[38]

1. Form N-565, Application for Replacement Naturalization/Citizenship Document[39]
2. A certified copy of the court order legally changing your name
3. Original immigration documents
4. Two photographs of you that are less than six months old

For a gender change, the following information must be submitted in person at the local district or suboffice of the U.S. Citizenship and Immigration Services of the U.S. Department of Homeland Security.[40]

1. Form N-565, Application for Replacement Naturalization/Citizenship Document.[41]
2. Letter from doctor, surgeon, or hospital verifying that you have had gender reassignment surgery
3. Original immigration documents
4. Two photographs of you that are less than six months old

It is important to note that all applications for a change of name or gender must be submitted *in person* at the local district or suboffice of the U.S. Citizenship and Immigration Services of the U.S. Department of Homeland Security. Once the transgender person gets medical treatment in the form

---

38. Locations can be found at http://uscis.gov/graphics/fieldoffices/distsub_offices/index.htm.
39. This form can be found at http://www.uscis.gov/portal/site/uscis/menuitem.eb1d4c2a3e-5b9ac89243c6a7543f6d1a/?vgnextoid=db029c7755cb9010VgnVCM10000045f3d6a1RCRD&vgnextchannel=db029c7755cb9010VgnVCM10000045f3d6a1RCRD.
40. Locations can be found at http://uscis.gov/graphics/fieldoffices/distsub_offices/index.htm.
41. This form can be found at http://www.uscis.gov/portal/site/uscis/menuitem.eb1d4c2a3e-5b9ac89243c6a7543f6d1a/?vgnextoid=db029c7755cb9010VgnVCM10000045f3d6a1RCRD&vgnextchannel=db029c7755cb9010VgnVCM10000045f3d6a1RCRD.

of hormones and sex change surgery, he or she has the problem of having his or her "new" sex recognized.

> [O]nce surgical intervention has taken place, whereby his anatomical sex is made to conform with his psychological sex, is not his position identical to that of the pseudo-hermaphrodite who has been surgically repaired? Should not society afford some measure of recognition to the altered situation and afford this individual the same relief as it does the pseudo-hermaphrodite?"
>
> [T]he application of a simple formula . . . should be the test of gender, and that formula is as follows: Where there is disharmony between the psychological sex and the anatomical sex, the social sex or gender of the individual will be determined by the anatomical sex. Where, however, with or without medical intervention, the psychological sex and the anatomical sex are harmonized, then the social sex or gender of the individual should be made to conform to the harmonized status of the individual and, if such conformity requires changes of a statistical nature, then such changes should be made. Of course, such changes should be made only in those cases where physiological orientation is complete.[42]

This failure to recognize a transgender person's transformation includes being disrespectful and disparaging in referring to the transgender person. There are numerous stories from transgender persons about the treatment that they have received in the courts when they are not parties. Parties to a civil suit or a criminal case often refer to the gender identity of a transgender witness in a derogatory manner to try to prejudice the jury against the witness and/or the party calling the transgender person as a witness. Unfortunately, those stories have no citations and even the transgender persons who were treated unfairly do not want to have their names published as the source of any story out of fear of being outed or fear of retribution.

---

42. Samuel E. Bartos, *Letting "Privates" Be Private: Toward a Right of Gender Self-Determination*, 15 Cardozo J. L. & Gender 67, 81–82 (2008).

In *People v. Sandra M. Arena,* the defendant contended "that her constitutional right to confrontation was violated when a prosecution witness testified in disguise." The witness was a male-to-female transgender person who had not changed her name and whose status was fully disclosed to the court and the jury. The defendant's contention was rejected by the New York Supreme Court Appellate Division's Fourth Department.[43]

In *Graham v. State,* the Indiana Court of Appeals held that the State was properly allowed to question a defense witness in a rape case with respect to the witness' status as a preoperative transsexual in order to verify the witness' identity. The witness stated that he was the rape victim's biological father and at the same time held a valid driver's license on which he listed himself as female.[44]

In *Alim v. Smith,* a case predating the use of the term *transgender* or even *transsexual,* the U.S. District Court for the Western District of New York granted a writ of habeas corpus. The court held that the state court prosecutor's deliberate appeal to juror prejudice through a poisonous and vituperative attack on the codefendant, who was the sole defense witness, and whose testimony formed the basis for the entire defense strategy, concerning fact that codefendant was a transvestite prostitute deprived the defendant of a fair trial.[45]

In the days of the segregated South, blacks could only be called by their first name in courts. They could not be called "Mister" or "Miss" or "Mrs." Nevertheless, my friend Fred D. Grey, Sr. did get permission to call a client "Sergeant" since his client was a Sergeant in the U.S. Air Force.[46] Black lawyers were referred to as "Lawyer" and their last name. There was no statute about this. It was an ingrained custom to keep whites above blacks. In court, it was acceptable to call blacks the "n" word.

Transgender persons have experienced similar humiliation and lack of respect in courts in which they are disrespected by judges and attorneys. This disrespect comes by intentional use of the wrong pronoun when referring to

---

43. People v. Sandra M. Arena, 107 A.D.3d 1440, 967 N.Y.S.2d 301 (N.Y. App. Div. 2013).
44. Graham v. State, 736 N.E.2d 822 (Ind. App. 2000).
45. Alim v. Smith, 474 F.Supp. 54 (W.D. N.Y. 1979).
46. Fred D. Gray, Bus Ride to Justice: The Life and Works of Fred Gray (New South 2002).

the transgender person and refusing to recognize the transgender person's new name. Only New Mexico has specifically addressed this by providing in its Code of Judicial Conduct that:

> A judge shall require lawyers in proceedings before the court to refrain from manifesting bias or prejudice, or engaging in harassment, based upon attributes including, but not limited to, race, religion, color, national origin, ethnicity, ancestry, **sex, sexual orientation, gender iden-tity,** marital status, spousal affiliation, socioeconomic status, political affiliation, age, physical or mental handicap or serious medical condi-tion, against parties, witnesses, lawyers, or others.[47] [emphasis added]

The courts and legislatures of two states have extended similar protec-tions only as to "Sex."[48] Thirteen other states have similar rules as to "Sex and Sexual Orientation."[49] Three states, the U.S. District Court for the District of Idaho, and the Superior Court for San Francisco have similar wording covering "Gender and Sexual Orientation."[50] Twenty-one states and the U.S. District Court for the District of Utah have similar provisions

---

47. N.M. CODE OF JUD. CONDUCT, Rule 21-203.C.

48. S.C. CODE OF JUD. CONDUCT, Canon 3.B(6) and S.D. CODE OF JUD. CONDUCT, App., Ch. 16-2 Canon 3.B(6).

49. ALASKA CODE OF JUD. CONDUCT, Canon 3.B(6), FLA. CODE OF JUD. CONDUCT, Canon 3.B(6), ILL. CODE OF JUD. CONDUCT Rule 63.A(10), KY. RULES OF THE SUP. CT., Canon 3.B(5), ME. CODE OF JUDICIAL CONDUCT, Canon 3.B, MASS. SUP. JUD. CT., Rule 3:09, CODE OF JUD. CONDUCT, Canon 3.B6), N.J. CODE OF JUD. CONDUCT, Canon 3.A(5), N.Y. CODE OF JUD. CONDUCT., Canon 3(B)(5) and N.Y. CT. RULES, § 100.3, R.I. SUP. CT. RULES, Art. VI, CODE OF JUD. CONDUCT, Canon 3.B.7.

Tex. Code of Jud. Conduct, Tit. 2, Subt. G, App. B, Jud. Conduct, Canon 3.B(7), Vt. Sup. Ct. Admin. Order No. 10(6), Va. Canons of Jud. Canon 3.B(6), and W.V. Code of Jud. Con-duct, Canon 3(6).

50. CAL. STDS. OF JUD. ADMIN., Standard 10.20(a)(2) and CAL. CODE OF JUD. ETHICS, Canon 3.B(6), UNIFORM LOCAL RULES OF COURT FOR THE SAN FRANCISCO (CAL.) SUPERIOR COURT, Rule 2.5.A, U.S. DISTRICT COURT FOR DISTRICT OF IDAHO LOCAL CIVIL Rule 83.8, MISS. CODE OF JUD. CONDUCT, Canon 3.B(6), and WIS. CODE OF JUD. CONDUCT, Rule 60.04(1)(f).

as to "Sex, Gender and Sexual Orientation."[51] And, the Superior Court for Mono County, California has a local rule as to only "Gender."[52] Similarly, only nine state bar associations have rules of professional conduct that prohibit attorneys in those states from discriminating on the basis of "gender identity"[53] However, even without a statute or custom, life is slowly getting better in the courts for transgender persons. And, use of the correct pronouns (he and she), adjectives (his and her), and correct name is improving.

---

51. 17A Ariz. Rev. Stat. Sup. Ct. Rules, Rule 81, Ariz. Code of Jud. Conduct, Rule 2.3(C), Col. Code of Jud. Conduct, Rule 2.3(C), Conn. Code of Jud. Conduct, Rule 2.3(c) and Conn. Code of Probate .Jud. Conduct, Canon 3, §B(6), D.C. Rules of Jud. Conduct Rule 2.3(c), Hawai'i Code of Jud. Conduct, Rule 2.3(c), Ind. Code of Jud. Conduct, Canon 2, Rule2.3(C), Iowa Code of Judicial Conduct, Rule 51:2.3(C), Kan. Sup. Ct. Rule 601B and Kan. Code of Jud. Conduct, Canon 2, Rule 2.3(C), 52 Minn. Stat. Ann., Code of Jud. Conduct, Rule 2.3(C), Mo. Sup. Ct. Rule 2-2.3(C), Mont. R. Code of Jud. Conduct Rule 2.3(C), Neb. Code of Judicial Conduct § 5-302.3(C), Nev. Code of Jud. Conduct, Canon 2, **Rule 2.3(C)**, N.H. Sup. Ct. Rules, Rule 38, N.H. Code of Jud. Conduct, R. Canon 2, Rule 2.3(C), N.D. Code Jud. Conduct, Rule 2.3.C, Ohio Code of Jud. Conduct Rule 2.3(C), it. 5, Ch. 1, Ok. Stat. Ann., App. 4, Canon 2, Rule 2.3(C), 42 Pa. Cons. Stat. Ann., Pa. Code of Jud. Conduct, Rule 2.3(C).

Tenn. Code of Jud. Conduct, Rule 2.3(C), Utah Code of Jud. Admin., Canon 2, Rule 2.3(C), U.S. District Court for District of Utah Local Civil Rule 83.8, and Wy. Code of Jud. Conduct, Rule 2.3(C)

52. Mono County, Superior Court of California, Local Rules, Rule 2.4.b.

53. California, Colorado (June 2005) District of Columbia, Illinois, New Jersey, Oklahoma, Puerto Rico, Texas, and Virginia. See: Ally Windsor Howell (2006) Leading or Following? An Evaluation of the Bar's Non-Discrimination Policies (LL.M. Independent Study at the State University of New York at Buffalo, School of Law).

CHAPTER 3

Use of Public Facilities

We live in a binary society; one must be either female or male. Without getting into a long drawn-out explanation of hermaphroditism and inter-sexuality, one must say that not everyone fits into a neat little male or female box. This binary world naturally extends into the arena of public restrooms.

There are statutes mandating separate restrooms for women and men in public buildings and facilities, stadiums and arenas,[1] factories and mills,[2] mines,[3] migrant and farm worker camps,[4] railroad cars,[5] almshouses,[6] and

---

1. *See, e.g.,* CAL. BUS. & PROF. CODE § 13651, Del. Code Ann. tit. 16 § 7933, Fla. Code Ann. § 553.86, 60 Ill. Comp. Stat. 1/155-10, 65 Ill. Comp. Stat. 5/11-21-2, 410 Ill. Comp. Stat. 35/15, Ky. Rev. Stat. Ann. § 58.200, 8 ME. REV. STAT. ANN. § 161, MD. CODE ANN. HEALTH-GEN. § 24-211, WIS. CODE ANN. § 101.128, WASH. REV. CODE § 70.54.160, TEX. ALCO. BEV. CODE § 61.43, TEX. HEALTH & SAFETY CODE § 341.068, TENN. CODE ANN. § 68-120-503, TENN. CODE ANN. § 4-24-301, TENN. CODE ANN. § 4-24-303, N.Y. LABOR LAW § 381, N.J. STAT. ANN. § 26:4B-1, N.J. STAT. ANN. § 34:6-119.2, NEV. REV. STAT. § 618.720, MO. ANN. STAT. § 701.450, CAL. CODE OF CIV. PROC. § 216, CAL. HEALTH & SAFETY CODE § 114276, R.I. GEN. LAWS § 11-24-3.1, ARK. CODE ANN. § 17-20-408, TEX. OCC. CODE § 1602.303, TEX. LABOR CODE § 92.024, R.I. GEN. LAWS § 32-7-11, and R.I. GEN. LAWS § 16-38-1.1.
2. *See, e.g.,* ARK. CODE ANN. § 11-5-112, S.D. CODIFIED LAWS § 60-12-7, 43 PA. CON. STAT. § 1, 43 PA. CON. STAT. § 109 and N.Y. LABOR LAW § 295.
3. OKLA. STAT. tit. 45 § 426.
4. *See, e.g.,* N.Y. LABOR LAW § 212-d and MICH. COMP. LAWS § 286.642.
5. S.C. CODE ANN. § 58-15-720.
6. N.J. STAT. ANN. § 44:1-69.

public assemblages and mass gatherings (e.g., Farm Aid, Woodstock).[7] There are even laws mandating baby changing stations in men's and women's restrooms.[8] Many cities and towns have ordinances making it a crime for a male to use a female-designated restroom, and in places where it is not a crime in and of itself, it has been prosecuted as a breach of the peace or as disorderly conduct.[9] There are also ordinances making cross-dressing in public illegal.[10]

Over a hundred cities, towns, and counties have nondiscrimination ordinances regarding public accommodations that include gender identity. A list can be found in Appendix 9, "Cities and Counties with Public Accommodations Nondiscrimination Ordinances and Laws That Include Gender Identity or Expression." Most of these do not address the use of restrooms, bathrooms, locker rooms, or showers. A few provide that establishments covered by the ordinances cannot deny access to facilities, including dressing, shower, and bathroom facilities, consistent with the person's gender identity. A few others provide that the transgender person's access to such areas can be subject to proof that he or she is transgender as evidenced by a letter from a doctor, or an identity document that has the sex identifier for the particular bathroom, shower room, locker room, and so on.

This binary thinking about restrooms has led to problems for transgender persons, especially male-to-female transgender persons. Most cases of a male-to-female transgender person being denied access to women's restrooms are only reported anecdotally in the media, if at all. Here are some examples of these cases:

---

7. *See, e.g.,* Colo. Rev. Stat. § 19a-437, Ind. Code § 16-41-22-10, and Wyo. Stat. Ann. § 35-15-107, and Tenn. Code Ann. § 68-112-104.

8. *See, e.g.,* Utah Code Ann. § 15A-3-304, Utah Code Ann. § 15A-3-112, and Mich. Comp. Laws § 125.1508a.

9. *See, e.g.,* State v. Williams, 203 Neb. 649, 279 N.W.2d 847 (1979) (affirmed conviction for loitering for being present in women's restroom) and Commonwealth v. Young, 370 Pa.Super. 42, 535 A.2d 1141 (Pa. Sup. Ct. 1978) (affirmed disorderly conduct conviction for entering women's restroom in dormitory).

10. Doe v. McConn, 489 F. Supp. 76 (S.D. Tex. 1980) (declaring Houston ordinance unconstitutional which made it unlawful for any person to appear in public dressed with designed intent to disguise his or her true sex as that of the opposite sex).

The Cosmopolitan Resort in Las Vegas has come under fire from the LGBT community and its allies after a report surfaced that a transgendered guest was banned for life from the hotel and casino — for using an empty women's restroom. The guest, identified as a preoperative transgendered named Stephanie, said upon leaving the women's room, she was escorted from the resort by security guards and told she was trespassing and that she would be arrested if she didn't leave. She said she was photographed and told she was banned from ever returning to the hotel. Since the blog was posted, commenters have flooded the Cosmopolitan's Facebook page with complaints on the reported incident. In a statement, Cosmopolitan officials said they regretted the incident and would "welcome her back to the resort anytime." But Stephanie said that had it been their original response, it would have seemed more sincere. "The simple fact is that the Cosmopolitan chose not to issue any sort of meaningful reply until such time as there was a huge upswell of anti-Cosmopolitan commentary across the entire social media landscape, until there was almost universal vilification of their behavior, until they received a call from GLAAD, and until they received a call from Community Marketing to revoke their TAG[11] Approval rating, and calls from who knows how many media organizations requesting comment."[12]

Tyjanae Moore was arrested last week for using the women's restroom at the public library in downtown Houston because police said she was still officially a man. Moore, 26, pleaded guilty even though she was in compliance with an executive order by Mayor Annise Parker that extends the city's nondiscrimination ordinance to allow transgendered people to use the city restroom of their choice. The Houston Area Pastor Council, which opposes the change, has asked the Texas attorney general to determine whether the executive order contradicts state law. In the past, Moore had used the men's restroom,

---

11. TAG is "Travel Alternatives Group." TAG Approved® is a registered certification mark owned by Community Marketing, Inc. designating a gay or lesbian friendly hotel.

12. Randy Slovacek, *Las Vegas hotel ejects, bans transgendered guest; now says it regrets the incident*, LGBTQ NATION http://www.lgbtqnation.com/2011/04/las-vegas-hotel-ejects-bans-transgendered-guest-now-says-it-regrets-the-incident/ (last visited August 4, 2011).

but she told Fox News that made her feel unsafe. She is in the process of transitioning. "I went to the males' restroom, and the man followed me into the restroom, so I figured that was not good," she said. "It wasn't safe, and I started going to female restrooms, and that's where I'm comfortable with."[13]

Helena Stone is upset that she's been arrested for using the women's restroom at Grand Central Terminal. The 70-year-old transgendered phone repair worker said she's been arrested three times by transit police in the last six months. She's filed a complaint with the city Commission on Human Rights and with the Metropolitan Transportation Authority police, claiming an MTA officer called her "a freak, a weirdo and the ugliest woman in the world." City guidelines said that restrooms must be available to transgendered people. After Stone held a rally and news conference, an MTA spokesman said the charges would be dropped.[14]

In one unusual case, three preoperative transsexual patrons at a Toys "R" Us store sued the company, alleging discrimination in public accommodation in violation of a local law. The jury only awarded nominal damages to the plaintiffs, but the U.S. District Court awarded $193,551 in attorneys' fees to patrons. Answering certified questions from the U.S. Court of Appeals for the Second Circuit, the New York Court of Appeals held that the plaintiffs' case had served significant public purpose deserving of attorneys' fees.[15]

Such discrimination can also interfere with the ability of nonprofit organizations to provide services to transgender employees. In New York City, a nonprofit organization was not allowed to renew its lease because of tenant complaints about its male-to-female transgender clients' use of the public women's restrooms. An appellate court, while not explicitly sanctioning the landlord's actions held that the organization failed to state a cause of

---

13. *Trans Woman Speaks About Restroom Arrest*, THE ADVOCATE.COM, http://www.advocate.com/News/Daily_News/2010/11/24/Trans_Woman_Speaks_About_Restroom_Arrest/ (last visited August 4, 2011).

14. Transgendered Woman Arrested For Using Women's Room, NBC30.com, http://www.nbc30.com/news/7556566/detail.html (last visited August 4, 2011).

15. McGrath v. Toys "R" Us, Inc., 3 N.Y.3d 421, 821 N.E.2d 519, 788 N.Y.S.2d 281 (2004).

action for gender discrimination based on the landlord's refusal to renew its lease because of its transgender clients' use of common areas in the building violated N.Y. state and city human rights laws.[16]

The Supreme Judicial Court of Maine held that a school violated the Maine Human Rights Act[17] (MHRA) and discriminated against a transgender student on the basis of the student's gender identity when it prohibited the student from using the girls' communal bathroom and required her to use the unisex staff bathroom.[18] The same result was reached by the Colorado Division of Civil Rights in another case involving a transgender girl student.[19]

Perhaps most important, the inability to use women's restrooms affects the employment of male-to-female transgender persons and transsexuals who are transitioning on the job. A bit of explanation is needed here. A transgender person who wishes to obtain sexual reassignment surgery must cross-live, or go through "real-life experience" as the opposite gender, before he or she can obtain surgery from a reputable surgeon because of the Standards of Care for Gender Identity Disorders, which are followed by many reputable surgeons who perform sexual reassignment surgery. However, the Standards of Care are advisory and provided as "clinical guidance" and are specifically devised to be flexible, not fixed step by step procedures. They should not be presented as any type of binding or fixed process. There are also other protocols—for example, the Informed Consent model—that some doctors use. The Standards of Care provide:

Parameters of the Real-Life Experience. When clinicians assess the quality of a person's real-life experience in the desired gender, the following abilities are reviewed:

a. To maintain full or part-time employment
b. To function as a student

---

16. Hispanic Aids Forum v. Estate of Bruno, 16 A.D.3d 294, 792 N.Y.S.2d 43 (N.Y. App. Div. 1st Dept. 2005), *rev'g* Hispanic Aids Forum v. Estate of Bruno, 195 Misc.2d 366, 759 N.Y.S.2d 291 (N.Y. Sup. Ct. N.Y. County 2003).

17. 5 Maine Rev. Stat. Ann. § 4602.

18. Doe v. Regional School Unit 26, 86 A.3d 60 (Maine 2014).

19. Coy Mathis v. Fountain-Fort Carson School District 8, Col. Div. of Civil Rights Determination, Charge No. P20130034X (June 17, 2013), http://www.transgenderlegal.org/media/uploads/doc_529.pdf (last visited July 21, 2014).

c. To function in community-based volunteer activity

d. To undertake some combination of items a through c

e. To acquire a (legal) gender-identity-appropriate first name

f. To provide documentation that persons other than the therapist know that the patient functions in the desired gender role[20]

Thus, the transgender person who is not independently rich or being supported by someone else must gain his or her real-life experience while earning a living. Frequently, it is other female employees whose imagings about what is going on in the stall next to them who cause the problem.[21] Furthermore, it has been most often held to provide a rational, legitimate, or nondiscriminatory basis for discharging a transitioning transgender employee.[22]

Of course, after the transgender person gets his or her identification documents changed, the real challenge begins to get the "real world" to recognize his or her new sex. (See Chapter 5, "Military Service and Veterans Benefits"; Chapter 6, "Family Law"; Chapter 7, "Education and Students"; Chapter 8, "Health Care"; Chapter 10, "Employment"; Chapter 11, "Immigration"; and Chapter 12, "Criminal Justice and Corrections.")

---

20. World Professional Association for Transgendered Health (formerly the Harry Benjamin International Gender Dysphoria Association), *The Standards of Care for Gender Identity Disorders*, IX. The Real-Life Experience, pp. 17–18, http://www.wpath.org/documents2/socv6. pdf (last visited July 27, 2011).

21. *See* Cruzan v. Special School Dist, # 1, 294 F.3d 981 (8th Cir. 2002) (school's policy of allowing transgendered male to use women's faculty restroom did not create hostile work environment) and Goins v. West Group, 635 N.W.2d 717 (Minn. 2001) (transgendered former employee failed to establish factual basis for claim, where employer's policy of designating restroom use based on biological gender was not based on sexual orientation).

22. *See, e.g.*, Glenn v. Brumby, 724 F. Supp. 2d 1284 (N.D. Ga. 2010), *aff'd* 663 F.3d 1312 (11th Cir. 2011) (supervisor's concern over avoiding lawsuits from employee's use of multi person women's restrooms within Capitol Building was rational basis for terminating her); Kastl v. Maricopa County Community College Dist., 325 Fed. Appx. 492 (9th Cir. 2009), *rev'g* Kastl v. Maricopa County Community College Dist., 2004 WL 2008954 (D. Ariz. 2004) (alleged safety of other female employees was legitimate, nondiscriminatory justification under Title VII for the ban on transgendered employee's use of women's restroom); Etsitty v. Utah Transit Authority, 502 F.3d 1215 (10th Cir. 2007) (transsexuals were not members of a protected class under 14th Amendment's Equal Protection Clause and use of women's public restrooms by biological male driver could result in liability for employer was legitimate and nondiscriminatory reason for termination); and Johnson v. Fresh Mark, Inc., 98 Fed. Appx. 461 (6th Cir. 2004), *aff'g* Johnson v. Fresh Mark, Inc., 337 F.Supp.2d 996 (N.D. Ohio 2003) (pre surgical transsexual woman's dismissal for refusing to use men's restroom was not violative of Title VII).

CHAPTER 4

Housing

A recent survey of more than 6,000 transgender persons conducted by the National Center for Transgender Equality and the National Gay and Lesbian Task Force indicated significant levels of housing instability for transgender people. Twenty-six percent of respondents reported having to find different places to sleep for short periods of time due to bias. Eleven percent of respondents reported having been evicted due to bias, and 19 percent reported becoming homeless due to bias.[1]

As with violence against transgender persons, housing discrimination against transgender persons is pervasive. A study conducted between 1996 and 1997 found that 37 percent of transgender individuals surveyed had experienced employment discrimination.[2] In 2009, a National Transgendered Discrimination Survey found:

- **High rates of poverty:** Fifteen percent (15%) of transgender people in the sample lived on $10,000 per year or less—double the rate of the general population.

---

1. The rule referenced effect 3/15/12. *See* 77 Fed. Reg. 5662 (February 3, 2012).

2. Emilia L. Lombardi, Riki Anne Wilchins, Dana Priesing, and Diana Malouf, *Gender Violence: Transgendered Experiences with Violence and Discrimination,* 42 J. OF HOMO-SEXUALITY 89 (2001).

- **Significant housing instability:** Nineteen percent (19%) of the sample have been or are homeless, 11% have faced eviction, and 26% were forced to seek temporary space.[3]

§4.1 Federal Law—Fair Housing Act

Federal law lends no protection. The Fair Housing Act (Title VIII of the Civil Rights Act of 1968)[4] prohibits discrimination in the sale, rental, financing of, or other housing-related transactions based on race, color, national origin, religion, sex, family status, or disability. But it does not protect people against discrimination based on sexual orientation or gender identity.

However, the U.S. Department of Housing and Urban Development (HUD) is proposing to prohibit inquiries regarding sexual orientation or gender identity to further ensure equal access to its housing and housing-related service programs. This prohibition would preclude owners and operators of HUD-assisted housing or housing whose financing is insured by HUD from inquiring about the sexual orientation or gender identity of an applicant for or occupant of the dwelling, regardless of whether the dwelling is renter or owner occupied. While the rule would prohibit inquiries regarding sexual orientation or gender identity, nothing in the rule would prohibit any individual from voluntarily self-identifying his or her sexual orientation or gender identity. Additionally, this rule would not be intended to prohibit otherwise lawful inquiries of an applicant or occupant's sex where the housing provided or to be provided to the individual involves the sharing of sleeping areas or bathrooms. The rule would define gender identity, consistent with the definition in the Matthew Shepard and James Byrd Jr. Hate Crimes Prevention Act,[5] as "actual or perceived gender-related characteristics."[6]

The first known discrimination case under the Fair Housing Act involving a transgender person was filed in the U.S. District Court for the Eastern District of Texas against a recreational vehicle trailer park and its owner by the Attorney General of the United States on behalf of the U.S. Department

---

3. National Center for Transgendered Equality and the National Gay and Lesbian Task Force, *National Transgendered Discrimination Survey* (November 2009) at http://transequality.org/Resources/NCTE_prelim_survey_econ.pdf (last visited July 31, 2011).

4. 42 U.S.C. § 3601, *et seq.*

5. 18 U.S.C. § 249(c)(4).

6. 24 C.F.R. § 5.105, § 200.300, and § 570.3.

of Housing and Urban Development (H.U.D.) and two tenants of the park.[7] This came after H.U.D. had filed an administrative Charge of Discrimination.[8]

§4.2 State and Local Laws

Sixteen states and the District of Columbia ban discrimination in housing on the basis of gender identity or gender expression:

1. California[9]
2. Colorado[10]
3. District of Columbia[11]
4. Hawaii[12]
5. Illinois[13]
6. Iowa[14]
7. Maine[15]
8. Massachusetts[16]
9. Minnesota[17]
10. New Hampshire[18]

---

7. Carol Christian, *U.S. government sues Texas RV park for alleged discrimination against transgender woman*, HOUSTON CHRONICLE (October 8, 2013), http://www.chron.com/news/houston-texas/houston/article/U-S-government-sues-Texas-RV-park-for-alleged-4879379.php (last visited July 21, 2014). The complaint can be viewed at http://www.justice.gov/crt/about/hce/documents/toonecomp.pdf.

8. A copy of the charge can be viewed at http://portal.hud.gov/hudportal/documents/huddoc?id=13HUDVTOONE.PDF.

9. CAL. GOV. CODE § 12926 and §12949.

10. COLO. REV. STAT. § 24-34-501, § 24-34-301.

11. D.C. CODE §2-1402.21.

12. HAW. REV. STAT. §§ 368-1, 489-2, 489-3.

13. 775 ILL. COMP. STAT. 5/1-102 and 5/1-103.

14. IOWA CODE §§216.2 and 216.8.

15. ME. REV. STAT. ANN. tit. 5 §4553 and §4581.

16. MASS. GEN. LAWS ANN. ch. 151B, §§ 1 and 4. While gender identity is not explicitly included in the state's anti-discrimination law, several courts and the state Commission Against Discrimination have ruled that transgendered individuals can pursue an anti-discrimination claim under the category of sex or disability discrimination. Jette v. Honey Farms Mini Market, 2001 Mass. Comm. Discrim. LEXIS 50 (Mass. Comm. Against Discrimination 2001).

17. MINN. STAT. §363A.01 to §363A.41.

18. N.H. REV. STAT. ANN. § 354-A:1 (2002). While gender identity is not explicitly included in the state's anti-discrimination law, the New Hampshire Superior Court ruled that transgendered individuals can pursue an anti-discrimination claim under the law's disability discrimination category. Jane Doe v. Electro-Craft Corp, 1988 WL 1091932 (N.H. Super. Ct. 1988).

11. New Jersey[19]
12. New Mexico[20]
13. Oregon[21]
14. Rhode Island[22]
15. Vermont[23]
16. Washington[24]

Courts and administrative agencies in several additional states (Florida, Massachusetts, and New York) have interpreted either their sex or disability discrimination statutes to prohibit certain forms of discrimination against transgender people.[25]

In New York, a homeless transgender woman sued a residential drug treatment facility and the director of its induction unit, alleging various claims arising from her stay and ultimate departure from facility. Defendant moved to dismiss due to lack of standing and for failure to state a claim. The Supreme Court of Kings County held that the woman's participation in the drug treatment program constituted a "housing accommodation" and that the woman stated claims alleging discrimination in violation of New York State and City Human Rights Laws.[26]

The Human Rights Campaign reports that more than 240 local jurisdictions prohibit discrimination based on sexual orientation in employment and, in most cases, housing and public accommodations. About 112 of these also prohibit discrimination based on gender identity or expression.[27] Those cities and counties with verified laws are listed in Appendix 6, "Cities and Counties with Employment Nondiscrimination Ordinances and Laws That Include Gender Identity or Expression," with citations to their laws.

---

19. N.J. Stat. Ann. § 10:5-1-49.
20. N.M. Stat. Ann. §§ 28-1-2, 7, 9.
21. Ore. Rev. Stat. Ann. § 659A.004.
22. R.I. Gen. Laws § 34-37-1, *et seq.*
23. Vt. Stat. Ann. tit. 9 § 4503.
24. Wash. Rev. Code §§ 49.60.030 and 49.60.040.
25. Discrimination in Housing, Human Rights Campaign website at http://www.hrc.org/issues/5499.htm (last visited August 5, 2011).
26. Wilson v. Phoenix House, 978 N.Y.S.2d 748 (N.Y.SupCt. Kings Co. 2013).
27. *Id.*

CHAPTER 5

Military Service and Veterans Benefits

§5.1 Military Service

Transgender people are denied the ability to join the armed forces as a result of various discriminatory policies. Not only is this unjust to individual transgender people who wish to serve their country through military service, it weakens our national defense by barring qualified people from duty.

For all of the progress President Obama has made in protecting the rights of LGBT persons in every area controlled by the federal government, there has been no progress in the way the uniformed military services treat transgender persons. Anecdotal evidence from former service members has shown that transgender persons are being forced out of the military if they come out while in the military, very often with a less than honorable discharge. No recent reported cases of courts martial of transgender persons have been found. In the past, officers and enlisted men have been subjected to courts martial for "prohibiting conduct which is prejudicial to good order and discipline in the armed forces or is of nature to bring discredit upon the armed forces,"[1] "cross-dressing in the presence of others,"[2] and "eight specifications of conduct unbecoming an officer and gentleman" by cross-dressing.[3]

The Department of Defense has declared that anyone with a "current or history of psychosexual conditions, including but not limited to transsexualism, exhibitionism, transvestism, voyeurism, and other paraphilias" is unfit for appointment, enlistment, or induction in the military services of the United States.[4]

Members of the military services of the United States who are transgender and who come out while in the service of the United States can be prosecuted under the Uniform Code of Military Justice's catchall of "all disorders and neglects to the prejudice of good order and discipline in the armed forces, all conduct of a nature to bring discredit upon the armed forces."[5] Or if the service member is an officer, he or she can be prosecuted under the other catchall of "conduct unbecoming an officer and a gentleman,"[6] which, at least to the author, raises the question, how does a female officer conduct herself as an "officer *and a gentleman*"? A general, special, or summary court martial can result in a dishonorable discharge, a bad-conduct discharge, or confinement.[7]

---

1. U.S. v. Guerrero, 31 M.J. 692 (Navy Marine Corps Ct. Mil. Rev. 1990), aff'd 33 M.J. 295 (Ct. Mil. App. 1991) (Navy Storekeeper First Class (E–6) convicted of "two specifications of dressing in women's clothing in public view in violation of article prohibiting conduct which is prejudicial to good order and discipline in the armed forces or is of nature to bring discredit upon the armed forces"); and U.S. v. Davis, 26 M.J. 445 (Ct. Mil. App. 1988) (Navy Electrician's Mate Second Class convicted of "at a particular place on a military base, dressed in women's clothing to the prejudice of good order and discipline and in a manner to bring discredit upon the armed forces").

2. U.S. v. Gunkle, not Reported in M.J., 1999 WL 35021320 (Army Ct. Crim. App. 1999), aff'd 55 M.J. 26 (Ct. Mil. App. 2001) (Staff Sergeant convicted of "cross-dressing in the presence of others").

3. U.S. v. Modesto, 39 M.J. 1055 (Army Ct. Crim. App. 1994), aff'd 43 M.J. 315 (Ct. App. for Armed Forces 1995) (Colonel convicted of "eight specifications of conduct unbecoming an officer and gentleman" by cross-dressing) (failure to disclose that court member had dressed as woman at Halloween party did not warrant reversal of conviction).

4. Department of Defense Directive 6130.3, "Medical Standards for Appointment, Enlistment, and Induction," (April 28, 2010), Enclosure 4, ¶ 28.r.

5. 10 U.S.C. § 934.

6. 10 U.S.C. § 933.

7. 10 U.S.C. §§ 818–820.

While being court-martialed is the extreme end of what the military can and will do to a transgender member, the more common result, according to anecdotal evidence, is to be given what are known as administrative separations or discharges. There are three types of administrative discharges, which are determinations "reflecting a member's military behavior and performance of duty during a specific period of service."

1. **Honorable**—a separation from the naval service with honor. The issuance of an honorable discharge is contingent upon proper military behavior and performance of duty.

2. **Under honorable conditions** (also termed general discharge)—a separation from the naval service under honorable conditions. The issuance of a discharge under honorable conditions is contingent upon military behavior and performance of duty, which is not sufficiently meritorious to warrant an honorable discharge.

3. **Under other than honorable conditions** (formerly termed undesirable discharge)—a separation from the naval service under conditions other than honorable. It is issued to terminate the service of a member of the naval service for one or more of the reasons/basis listed in the Naval Military Personnel Manual, Marine Corps Separation and Retirement Manual, and their predecessor publications.[8]

The same or very similar definitions are also found in Air Force[9] and Army[10] regulations.

---

8. 32 C.F.R. § 724.109.

9. *See* AIR FORCE REGULATIONS 35–41, Vol. III, Separation Procedures for USAFR Members (October 30, 1975), 36-2, Officer Personnel, Administrative Discharge Procedures (August 2, 1976), 36-3, Officer Personnel, Administrative Discharge Procedures(August 2, 1976), 36-12, Officer Personnel, Administrative Separation of Commissioned Officers and Warrant Officers (July 15, 1977), and 39-10, Separation Upon Expiration of Term of Service, for Convenience of Government, Minority, Dependency and Hardship (January 3, 1977); AIR FORCE MANUAL 39-12, Separation for Unsuitability, Misconduct, Resignation, or Request for Discharge for the Good of the Service and Procedures for the Rehabilitation Program (September 1, 1966); AIR NATIONAL GUARD REGULATION 39-10, Enlisted Personnel-Separation (December 30, 1971); and AIR FORCE INSTRUCTIONS 36-3208, Section 1.18, Administrative Separation of Airmen (July 9, 2004) and 36-3209, Separation and Retirement Procedures for Air National Guard and Air Force Reserve Members (April 14, 2005).

10. ARMY REGULATIONS 135–178, ¶ 2-9, Characterization of service (March 13, 2007) and 635–200, ¶ 3-7, Types of administrative discharges/character of service (September 9, 2011).

§5.2 Veterans Benefits

The type of discharge one receives is important because it determines the veteran's eligibility for medical benefits and disability pensions through the Department of Veterans Affairs (VA, formerly the Veterans Administration). A discharge or release from service under one of the conditions listed below is a bar to the payment of benefits unless it is found that the person was insane at the time of committing the offense causing such discharge or release or unless otherwise specifically provided:

1. As a conscientious objector who refused to perform military duty, wear the uniform, or comply with lawful order of competent military authorities
2. By reason of the sentence of a general court-martial
3. Resignation by an officer for the good of the service
4. As a deserter
5. As an alien during a period of hostilities, where it is affirmatively shown that the former service member requested his or her release
6. By reason of a discharge under other than honorable conditions issued as a result of an absence without official leave (AWOL) for a continuous period of at least 180 days[11]

A discharge or release because of one of the following offenses is considered to have been issued under dishonorable conditions:

1. Acceptance of an undesirable discharge to escape trial by general court-martial
2. Mutiny or spying
3. *An offense involving moral turpitude*
4. *Willful and persistent misconduct*
5. *Homosexual acts involving aggravating circumstances or other factors affecting the performance of duty*[12] [emphasis added]

---

11. 38 C.F.R. § 3.12 and 38 U.S.C. § 5303.
12. *Id.*

The reasons shown in italics are reasons open to manipulation and inter-pretation in ways that can be used against transgender persons—especially those who want to begin transitioning. They certainly could fit under the Uniform Code of Military Justice's catchall of "all disorders and neglects to the prejudice of good order and discipline in the armed forces"[13] or, if the member is an officer, the other catchall of "conduct unbecoming an officer and a gentleman."[14] In fact, convictions for conduct "neglect[ing] to the prejudice of good order and discipline in the armed forces" for cross-dressing have been affirmed by military appellate courts.[15] Furthermore, the repeal[16] of "Don't ask, don't tell"[17] will not benefit transgender service members even though many people who do not understand transgender people and gender identity disorder mistakenly assume that transgender people, especially male-to-female transgender people, are gay.

The Transgendered American Veterans Association (TAVA)[18] is a 501(c) (3) nonprofit, tax-exempt organization. TAVA "was formed to address the growing concerns of fair and equal treatment of transgender veterans and active duty service members. As the population of gender-different people increases, so does the population of veterans and active-duty service mem-bers who identify as such. TAVA serves as an educational organization that will help the Veterans Administration and the Department of Defense to better understand the individuals they encounter who identify as being gender-different. As veterans, [TAVA members] have also served proudly, and will continue to do so. TAVA is here to help where [they] can." Help for transgender veterans can also be had from the Servicemembers Legal Defense Network, which was originally founded to assist gay and lesbian service members, but like so many other organizations,[19] has also embraced the cause of equal rights for transgender persons.

---

13. 10 U.S.C. § 934.

14. 10 U.S.C. § 933.

15. *See* United States v. Davis, 26 M.J. 445 (C.M.A. 1988) and United States v. Guerrero, 33 M.J. 295 (C.M.A. 1991), *cert. den.* 502 U.S. 1096, 112 S.Ct. 1173, 117 L.Ed. 2d 418 (1992).

16. Don't Ask, Don't Tell Repeal Act of 2010, Pub. L. No. 111–321, 124 Stat. 3515 (2010) and Statement by the President on Certification of Don't Ask, Don't Tell Repeal Act, 2011 WL 2940967 (White House, July 22, 2011).

17. 10 U.S.C. § 65.

18. TAVA's website is at http://www.tavausa.org/.

19. Those other organizations include (in alphabetical order): Gay, Lesbian and Straight

§5.3 Health Benefits for Transgender Veterans

For many years, there was a problem with transgender veterans receiving appropriate health care from VA health care facilities. That has improved. The VA, through Robert A. Petzel, M.D., Under Secretary for Health, adopted a policy directive on June 9, 2011, regarding the provision of care to transgender and intersexed veterans. Unfortunately, it expired November 30, 2012. That directive provides:

Providing Health Care for Transgendered and Intersex Veterans

1. **PURPOSE:** This Veterans Health Administration (VHA) Directive establishes policy regarding the respectful delivery of health care to transgendered and intersex Veterans who are enrolled in the Department of Veterans Affairs (VA) health care system or are otherwise eligible for VA care.

2. **BACKGROUND:** In accordance with the medical benefits package (title 38 Code of Federal Regulations (CFR) Section 17.38), VA provides care and treatment to Veterans that is compatible with generally accepted standards of medical practice and determined by appropriate health care professionals to promote, preserve, or restore the health of the individual.

   a. VA provides health care for transgendered patients, including those who present at various points on their transition from one gender to the next. This applies to all Veterans who are enrolled in VA's health care system or who are otherwise eligible for VA care, including: those who have had sex reassignment surgery outside of VHA, those who might be considering such surgical intervention, and those who do not wish to undergo sex reassignment surgery, but self-identify as transgendered. Intersex individuals may or may not have interest in changing gender or in acting in ways that are discordant with their assigned gender.

Education Network (GLSEN), Human Rights Campaign (HRC), Lambda Legal, National Center for Lesbian Rights (NCLR), National Gay and Lesbian Task Force (NGLTF), National Lesbian and Gay Law Association (NLGLA), and Parents, Families & Friends of Lesbians and Gays (PFLAG).

b. VA does not provide sex reassignment surgery or plastic reconstructive surgery for strictly cosmetic purposes.

c. Definitions

(1) **Sex.** Sex refers to the classification of individuals as female or male on the basis of their reproductive organs and functions.

(2) **Gender.** Gender refers to the behavioral, cultural, or psychological traits that a society associates with male and female sex.

(3) **Transgendered.** Transgendered is a term used to describe people whose gender identity (sense of themselves as male or female) or gender expression differs from that usually associated with their sex assigned at birth.

(a) Transsexual (Male-to-Female). Male-to-female (MTF) transsexuals are individuals who are male sex at birth, but self-identify as female and often take steps to socially or medically transition to female, including feminizing hormone therapy, electrolysis, and surgeries (e.g., vaginoplasty, breast augmentation).

(b) Transsexual (Female-to-Male). Female-to-male (FTM) transsexuals are individuals who are female sex at birth, but self-identify as male and often take steps to socially or medically transition to male, including masculinizing hormone therapy and surgeries (e.g., phalloplasty, mastectomy).

(4) **Sex Reassignment Surgery.** Sex reassignment surgery includes any of a variety of surgical procedures (including vaginoplasty and breast augmentation in MTF transsexuals and mastectomy and phalloplasty in FTM transsexuals) done simultaneously or sequentially with the explicit goal of transitioning from one gender to another. This term includes surgical revision of a previous sex reassignment surgery for cosmetic purposes. *NOTE: This term does not apply to nonsurgical therapy (e.g., hormone therapy, mental health care) or Intersex Veterans in need of surgery to correct inborn conditions related to reproductive or sexual anatomy or to correct a functional defect.*

(5) **Gender Identity Disorder (GID).** GID is a conflict between a person's physical sex and the gender with which the person identifies.

(6) **Intersex.** Intersex individuals are born with reproductive or sexual anatomy and/or chromosome pattern that doesn't seem to fit typical definitions of male or female. People with intersex conditions are often assigned male or female gender by others at birth (e.g., parents), although the individual may or may not later identify with the assigned gender.

3. **POLICY:** It is VHA policy that medically necessary care is provided to enrolled or otherwise eligible intersex and transgendered Veterans, including hormonal therapy, mental health care, preoperative evaluation, and medically necessary postoperative and long-term care following sex reassignment surgery. Sex reassignment surgery cannot be performed or funded by VHA or VA.

4. **ACTION**

   a. **Veterans Integrated Service Network (VISN) Director.** Each VISN Director must ensure that necessary and appropriate health care is provided to all enrolled or otherwise eligible Veterans based on the Veteran's self-identified gender, regardless of sex or sex reassignment status.

   b. **Medical Center Director and Chief of Staff.** The Medical Center Director and Chief of Staff are responsible for ensuring that:

      (1) Transgendered patients and intersex individuals are provided all care included in VA's medical benefits package, including, but not limited to: hormonal therapy, mental health care, preoperative evaluation, and medically necessary postoperative and long-term care following sex reassignment surgery to the extent that the appropriate health care professional determines that the care is needed to promote, preserve, or restore the health of the individual and is in accord with generally accepted standards of medical practice:

         (a) Patients will be addressed and referred to on the basis of their self-identified gender.

(b) Room assignments and access to any facilities for which gender is normally a consideration (e.g., restrooms) will give preference to the self-identified gender, irrespective of appearance and/or surgical history, in a manner that respects the privacy needs of transgendered and non-transgendered patients alike. Where there are questions or concerns related to room assignments, an ethics consultation may be requested.

(c) The documented sex in the Computerized Patient Record System (CPRS) should be consistent with the patient's self-identified gender. In order to modify administrative data (e.g., name and sex) in CPRS, patients must provide official documentation as per current VHA policies on Identity Authentication for Health Care Services and Data Quality Requirements for Identity Management and Master Patient Index Functions.

(2) **Sex reassignment surgery, as defined in subparagraph 2b(4), will not be provided or funded.** [emphasis added]

(3) **Nonsurgical, supportive care for complications of sex reassignment surgery will be provided.** [emphasis added]

(4) While care is delivered to the Veteran on the basis of that Veteran's self-identified gender, there may be health issues associated with some transgendered patients that necessitate appropriate sex-specific screenings and/or treatments. For example, an MTF transsexual patient over the age of 50 may require breast cancer and prostate cancer screening. An FTM transsexual patient may require screening for breast and cervical cancer. A diagnosis of GID, or other gender dysphoria diagnoses, is not a precondition for receiving care consistent with the Veteran's self-identified gender.

All other health services are provided to transgendered Veterans without discrimination in a manner consistent with care and management of all Veteran patients.

All staff, including medical and administrative staff, are required to treat as confidential any information about a patient's transgendered status or any treatment related to a patient's gender transition, unless the patient has given permission to share this information.

Mandated diversity awareness is maintained and a zero-tolerance standard for harassment of any kind.[20]

§5.4 The Documented Story of One Heroic Veteran[21]

The injustice of this policy is exemplified by the case of Diane Schroer, a male-to-female transsexual. Although born male, Schroer has a female gender identity, an internal, psychological sense of herself as a woman. In August 2004, before she changed her legal name or began presenting herself as a woman, Schroer applied for the position of specialist in terrorism and international crime with the Congressional Research Service (CRS) at the Library of Congress. The terrorism specialist provides expert policy analysis to congressional committees, members of Congress, and their staffs. The position requires a security clearance.

Schroer was well qualified for the job. She is a graduate of both the National War College and the Army Command and General Staff College, and she holds Master's degrees in history and international relations. During Schroer's twenty-five years of service in the U.S. Armed Forces, she held important command and staff positions in the Armored Calvary, Airborne, Special Forces and Special Operations Units, and combat operations in Haiti and Rwanda. Before her retirement from the military in January 2004, Schroer was a Colonel assigned to the U.S. Special Operations Command, serving as the director of a 120-person classified organization that tracked and targeted high-threat international terrorist organizations. In this position, Colonel Schroer analyzed sensitive intelligence reports, planned a range of classified and conventional operations, and regularly briefed senior military and government officials, including the vice president, the secretary of defense, and the chairman of the Joint Chiefs of Staff. At the time of her military retirement, Schroer held a Top Secret Sensitive Compartmented

---

20. Department of Veterans Affairs, VHA Directive 2011-024 (June 9, 2011).

21. Based on the Findings of Fact and Conclusions of Law by U.S. District Judge James Robertson in the case of Schroer v. Billington, 577 F. Supp. 2d 293, 295–300 (D. D.C. 2008).

Information security clearance and had done so on a continuous basis since 1987. After her retirement, Schroer joined a private consulting firm, Benchmark International. When she applied for the CRS position, she was working as a program manager on an infrastructure security project for the National Guard.

When Schroer applied for the terrorism specialist position, she had been diagnosed with gender identity disorder and was working with a licensed clinical social worker, Martha Harris, to develop a medically appropriate plan for transitioning from male to female. The transitioning process was guided by a set of treatment protocols formulated by the leading organization for the study and treatment of gender identity disorders, the Harry Benjamin International Gender Dysphoria Association. Because she had not yet begun presenting herself as a woman on a full-time basis, however, she applied for the position as David J. Schroer, her legal name at the time. In October 2004, two months after submitting her application, Schroer was invited to interview with three members of the CRS staff: Charlotte Preece, Steve Bowman, and Francis Miko. Preece, the assistant director for foreign affairs, defense and trade, was the selecting official for the position. Schroer attended the interview dressed in traditionally masculine attire, a sport coat and slacks with a shirt and tie.

Schroer received the highest interview score of all eighteen candidates. In early December, Preece called Schroer, told her that she was on the shortlist of applicants still in the running, and asked for several writing samples and an updated list of references. After receiving these updated materials, the members of the selection committee unanimously recommended that Schroer be offered the job. In mid-December, Preece called Schroer, offered her the job, and asked whether Schroer would accept it, before Preece processed the administrative paper work. Schroer replied that she was very interested but needed to know whether she would be paid a salary comparable to the one she was currently receiving in the private sector. The next day, after Preece confirmed that the library would be able to offer comparable pay, Schroer accepted the offer, and Preece began to fill out the paperwork necessary to finalize the hire.

Before Preece had completed and submitted these documents, Schroer asked her to lunch on December 20, 2004. Schroer's intention was to tell Preece about her transsexuality. She was about to begin the phase of her gender transition during which she would be dressing in traditionally femi-nine clothing and presenting herself as a woman on a full-time basis. She believed that starting work at CRS as a woman would be less disruptive than if she started as a man and later began presenting as a woman.

When Schroer went to the Library of Congress for this lunch date, she was dressed in traditionally masculine attire. Before leaving to walk to a nearby restaurant, Preece introduced Schroer to other staff members as the new hire who would soon be coming aboard. Preece also gave Schroer a short tour of the office, explaining where her new colleagues' offices were and describing Schroer's job responsibilities. As they were sitting down to lunch, Preece stated that they were excited to have Schroer join CRS because she was "significantly better than the other candidates." Schroer asked why that was so, and Preece explained that her skills, her operational experience, her ability to creatively answer questions, and her contacts in the military and in defense industries made her application superior.

About a half hour into their lunch, Schroer told Preece that she needed to discuss a personal matter. She began by asking Preece if she knew what *transgendered* meant. Preece responded that she did, and Schroer went on to explain that she was transgendered, that she would be transitioning from male to female, and that she would be starting work as Diane. Preece's first reaction was to ask, "Why in the world would you want to do that?" Schroer explained that she did not see being transgendered as a choice and that it was something she had lived with her entire life. Preece then asked her a series of questions, starting with whether she needed to change Schroer's name on the hiring documentation. Schroer responded that she did not because her legal name, at that point, was still David. Schroer went on to explain the Harry Benjamin Standards of Care and her own medical process for transitioning. She told Preece that she planned to have facial feminization surgery in early January and assured her that recovery from this surgery was quick and would pose no problem for a mid-January start date. In the context of explaining the Benjamin Standards of Care, Schroer explained that she would be living full-time as a woman for at least a year before having sex reassignment surgery. Such surgery, Schroer explained, could normally be accomplished during a two-week vacation period and would not interfere with the requirements of the job.

Preece then raised the issue of Schroer's security clearance, asking what name ought to appear on hiring documents. Schroer responded that she had several transgendered friends who had retained their clearances while transitioning and said that she did not think it would be an issue in her case. Schroer also mentioned that her therapist would be available to answer any questions or provide additional background as needed. Because Schroer expected that there might be some concern about her appearance when presenting as a woman, she showed Preece three photographs of herself, wearing traditionally feminine professional attire. Although Preece did not say it to Schroer, her reaction on seeing these photos was that Schroer looked like "a man dressed in women's clothing." Preece did not ask Schroer whether she had told her references or anyone at Benchmark International of her transition.

Although Schroer initially thought that her conversation with Preece had gone well, she thought it "ominous" that Preece ended it by stating, "Well, you've given me a lot to think about. I'll be in touch."

Preece did not finish Schroer's hiring memorandum when she returned to the library after lunch. Instead, she went to speak with Cynthia Wilkins, the personnel security officer for the Library of Congress. Preece told Wilkins that she had just learned that the candidate she had planned to recommend for the terrorism specialist position would be transitioning from male to female and asked what impact that might have on the candidate's ability to get a security clearance. Wilkins did not know and said that she would have to look into the applicable regulations. Preece told Wilkins that the candidate was a twenty-five-year military veteran. She did not recall whether she mentioned that Schroer currently held a security clearance. Preece did not provide, and Wilkins did not ask for, the sort of information, such as Schroer's full name and Social Security number, that would have allowed Wilkins access to information on Schroer's clearance history. Had Preece requested her to do so, Wilkins had the ability to access Schroer's complete investigative file through a centralized federal database.

Preece testified that at this point, without waiting to hear more from Wilkins, she was leaning against hiring Schroer. She said that Schroer's transition raised five concerns for her. First, she was concerned about Schroer's ability to maintain her contacts within the military. Specifically, Preece

thought that some of Schroer's contacts would no longer want to associate with her because she is transgendered. At no point after learning of
Schroer's transition, however, did Preece discuss the continuing viability
of her contacts with Schroer nor did she raise this concern with any of
Schroer's references, all of whom in fact knew that she was transitioning.
Second, Preece was concerned with Schroer's credibility when testifying
before Congress. When CRS specialists testify before Congress, they typically provide members with brief biographical statements to give them
credibility. Preece was concerned "that everyone would know that Schroer
had transitioned from male to female because only a man could have her
military experiences." Preece thought that this would be an obstacle to
Schroer's effectiveness. Third, Preece testified that she was concerned with
Schroer's trustworthiness because she had not been up front about her transition from the beginning of the interview process. Preece did not, however,
raise this concern to Schroer during their lunch. Fourth, Preece thought
that Schroer's transition might distract her from her job. Although Preece
seems to have connected this concern to Schroer's surgeries, she did not
ask for additional information about them or otherwise discuss the issue
further with Schroer. Finally, Preece was concerned with Schroer's ability
to maintain her security clearance. In Preece's mind, David Schroer had a
security clearance, but Diane Schroer did not. Even before speaking with
Wilkins, Preece "strongly suspected" that David's clearance simply would
not apply to Diane. She had this concern, but she did not ask Schroer for
any information on the people she knew who had undergone gender transitions while retaining their clearances.

After her lunch with Schroer, Preece also relayed the details of her conversation to a number of other officials at CRS, including Daniel Mulholland,
the director of CRS, and Gary Pagliano, one of the defense section heads,
whose reaction was to ask Preece if she had a good second candidate for
the job. Later the same afternoon, Preece received an e-mail from one of
the Library's lawyers, setting up a meeting for the next morning to discuss
the terrorism specialist position. That evening, as Preece thought about
the issue, she was puzzled by the idea that "someone [could] go through
the experience of [s]pecial [f]orces [and] decide that he wants to become a

woman." Schroer's background in the [s]pecial [f]orces made it harder for Preece to think of Schroer as undergoing a gender transition.

The next morning, on December 21, 2004, at nine o'clock, Preece met with Kent Ronhovde, the director of the Library of Congress; Wilkins; and two other members of the CRS staff from workforce development. Preece described her lunch conversation with Schroer and stated that Schroer had been, but no longer was, her first choice for the position. As Preece recalls the meeting, Wilkins stated that she was unable to say one way or another whether Diane Schroer would be able to get a security clearance. Preece testified that Wilkins proposed that Schroer would have to have a "psychological fitness for duty examination," after which the library would have to decide whether to initiate a full background investigation. Wilkins testified that she was not familiar with such an "examination" and likely would not have used such a phrase, but she confirmed that she told those with whom she met that she would not approve a waiver for Schroer so that she could start working before the clearance process was complete. Wilkins made this decision without having viewed Schroer's application, her resume, or her clearance status and history. Preece understood the substance of Wilkins's comments to be that David's security clearance was not relevant to Diane, and that Diane would need a separate clearance. She assumed that that process could take up to a year.

At no point during the meeting did Preece express a continuing interest in hiring Schroer. She did not suggest that Wilkins pull and review David Schroer's security file to confirm her own assumption that the security clearance process would be a lengthy one. No one in the meeting asked whether the organization currently holding Schroer's clearance knew of her transition. There was no discussion of whether anyone else at the library had dealt with a similar situation.

By the end of the meeting, Preece had made up her mind that she no longer wanted to recommend Schroer for the terrorism specialist position. Preece testified that the security clearance was the critical, deciding factor because of "how long it would take." She also testified, however, that she would have leaned against hiring Schroer even if she had no concerns regarding the security clearance because her second candidate, John Rollins, presented "fewer complications." Unlike Schroer, he was not transitioning from male to female.

"In refusing to hire Diane Schroer because her appearance and background did not comport with the decision maker's sex stereotypes about how men and women should act and appear, and in response to Schroer's decision to transition, legally, culturally, and physically, from male to female, the Library of Congress violated Title VII's prohibition on sex discrimination."[22] The court ultimately awarded Schroer $491,190.80,[23] which is the largest known award to a transgendered person in a discrimination case. The case began under the administration of President George W. Bush but ended under the administration of President Barack H. Obama, whose Justice Department decided in 2009 not to appeal and to pay the award to Ms. Schroer.[24]

---

22. Schroer v. Billington, 577 F. Supp. 2d 293, 295–300 (D. D.C. 2008).

23. Schroer v. Billington, Not Reported in F.Supp.2d 2009 WL 1543686 (D. D.C. 2009).

24. Technical Answer Group, CCH Wolters Luwer Aspen Publishers , *DOJ will not appeal transgendered veteran's $491,190 award against the Library of Congress* (July 15, 2009), http://hr.cch.com/news/employment/071509a.asp (last visited November 26, 2011).

CHAPTER 6

Family Law

Family is one of the emotionally charged areas of human life. Humans love and are deeply protective of their children. They seek to protect their children from even perceived harm. They feel a deep sense of betrayal if their spouse betrays them or even if they perceive such a betrayal.

Emotion clouds judgment. When bias and prejudice are mixed with emotion and familial feelings and attachments, the combination can be explosive.

§6.1 Marriage

A transgender person in transition or even a transsexual after sexual reassignment surgery has a personal relationship dilemma: "Do I or don't I tell this person I love and care for about my past life as a male (or female)?" If one tells the other person, he or she may back out of the relationship, which will only deepen and magnify the sense of fear that comes with being "different." If one does not tell the other person, and he or she discovers one's past later, it's likely to cause a break up or domestic violence.

Transgender persons have been caught in the same-sex marriage issues that have been debated so vigorously during the last number of years. Why would that be? The answer is that even though a person has sex change surgery, the reported court decisions have taken the position that that person is considered legally for the purpose of marriage to be the sex assigned and designated on that person's birth certificate.

Section 3 of the Defense of Marriage Act, Pub. L. No. 104-199, 110 Stat. 2419, 2419 (1996), 1 U.S.C.A. § 7, is no longer an impediment to the recognition of lawful same-sex marriages and spouses under the Immigration and Nationality Act if the marriage is valid under the laws of the State where it was celebrated. It was declared to be unconstitutional by the U.S. Supreme Court in *United States v. Windsor*.[1] This solves the matter as to federal benefits. However, in the last half of 2014, federal courts declared as unconstitutional same sex bans in a number of states. See Appendix 5, which has been updated to recognize those court rulings. But for state law issues, marriages classified as same-sex marriages will still not be recognized. Thus, inheritance and other benefits of marriage under state law will remain lost to some transgender persons in such marriages by virtue of the fact that the transgender persons' sex changes are given no legal effect.

The view of the overwhelming majority of jurisdictions on this issue is represented by the *Littleton* case from Texas:

1. Medical science recognizes that there are individuals whose sexual self-identity is in conflict with their biological and anatomical sex. Such people are termed transsexuals.

2. A transsexual is not a homosexual in the traditional sense of the word, in that transsexuals believe and feel they are members of the opposite sex. Nor is a transsexual a transvestite. Transsexuals do not believe they are dressing in the opposite sex's clothes. They believe they are dressing in their own sex's clothes.

3. Christie Littleton is a transsexual.

4. Through surgery and hormones, a transsexual male can be made to look like a woman, including female genitalia and breasts. Transsexual medical treatment, however, does not create the internal sexual organs of a woman (except for the vaginal canal). There is no womb, cervix, or ovaries in the postoperative transsexual female.

---

1. United States v. Windsor, 570 U.S. ___, 133 S.Ct. 2675, 186 L.Ed.2d 808 (2013).

5. The male chromosomes do not change with either hormonal treatment or sex reassignment surgery. Biologically a postoperative female transsexual is still a male.

6. The evidence fully supports that Christie Littleton, born male, wants and believes herself to be a woman. She has made every conceivable effort to make herself a female, including a surgery that would make most males pale and perspire to contemplate.

7. Some physicians would consider Christie a female; other physicians would consider her still a male. Her female anatomy, however, is all man-made. The body that Christie inhabits is a male body in all aspects other than what the physicians have supplied.[2]

One cannot help wondering about the motivations behind such pronouncements—aside from a sheer hatred of transsexuals, which of course exists. Certainly they are reminiscent of fundamentalist, Biblical approaches to other policy questions, but also of the strange interplay between Puritan doctrine and turning a blind eye to reality that seems to operate when fundamentalist voting blocs fall in line behind "conservative" candidates whose adulteries and divorces have been well publicized. Yet it may be worth remembering that the Senator who compared homosexuality with bestiality has been voted out of office and that as much as jurists similar to those sitting on the Texas Supreme Court may try to keep government out of matters like sexual or gender identity, the Supreme Court, as we shall see below, has not always been quite as shy.[3]

Kansas, Florida, Illinois, Ohio, and New York courts have reached the same result.

§6.1(a) The Kansas Case—Gardiner

In the Kansas case, after his father died intestate, the son petitioned for letters of administration, naming himself as sole heir and claiming that

---

2. Littleton v. Prange, 9 S.W.3d 223, 230–231 (Tex.App. 1999), rev. den. (Tex. 2000), cert. den. 531 U.S. 872, 121 S.Ct. 174, 148 L.Ed. 2d 119 (2000).

3. Samuel E. Bartos, Letting "Privates" Be Private: Toward a Right of Gender Self-Determination, 15 CARDOZO J. L. & GENDER 67, 73–74 (2008).

marriage between his father and a postoperative male-to-female transsexual was void. The trial court granted summary judgment to the son and denied partial summary judgment to the transgender wife. The Kansas Court of Appeals reversed and remanded with directions. The court of appeals held that under the full faith and credit clause, the court could give little or no weight to a Wisconsin amended birth certificate designating the transsexual as female, but genuine issues of material fact existed as to whether the transsexual was a female at the time she obtained a marriage license and whether the transsexual fraudulently induced the father into marriage. The Kansas Supreme Court affirmed in part and reversed in part and held that a postoperative male-to-female transsexual is not a woman within the meaning of the Kansas statutes recognizing marriage and that a marriage between a postoperative male-to-female transsexual and a man is void as against public policy. The court noted that a traditional marriage is the legal relationship between a biological man and a biological woman for the discharge to each other and the community of the duties legally incumbent on those whose relationship is founded on the distinction of sex. The Supreme Court of Kansas stated: "'Male' is defined as 'designating or of the sex that fertilizes the ovum and begets offspring: opposed to female.' 'Female' is defined as 'designating or of the sex that produces ova and bears offspring: opposed to male.'" Of course a transsexual female cannot produce ova or bear offspring.[4]

What this court and others have failed to recognize is that there are many infertile genetic women in the world who produce no ova. For instance, there are genetic women who suffer from vaginal agenesis,[5] and there are people who have ovotestes[6] who are neither male nor female under the court's definition.

---

4. *In re* Estate of Gardiner, 273 Kan. 191, 212–213, 42 P.3d 120 (2002), *cert. den.* 537 U.S. 825 (2002).

5. A primary amenorrhea due to müllerian duct ageneis, resulting in absence of the vagina, or presence of a short vaginal pouch, and absence of the uterus with normal karyotype and ovaries. STEDMAN'S MEDICAL DICTIONARY (27th ed., 2000).

6. A very rare disorder in which an infant is born with the internal reproductive organs (gonads) of both sexes (female ovaries and male testes). The gonads can be any combination of ovary, testes or combined ovary and testes. The external genitalia are usually ambiguous but can range from normal male to normal female. WebMD® http://www.webmd.com/sexual-conditions/hermaphroditism-true (last visited July 31, 2011).

§6.1(b) The Florida Case—Kantaras

In the *Kantaras* case, the circuit court engaged in a very thorough and scholarly analysis and rendered a trial court opinion 809 pages in length in an obvious attempt to create a thorough record to support its conclusion that a marriage between an anatomical female and a female-to-male transsexual was valid. However, the Florida District Court of Appeal reversed and held, as matters of first impression, that Florida law does not provide for or allow a postoperative female-to-male transsexual person to marry a female; that a marriage between a wife and her husband who was a postoperative female-to-male transsexual person was void *ab initio*; and that any marriage that is not between persons of the opposite sex, as determined by their biological sex at birth, will be invalidated.[7]

§6.1(c) The Illinois Case—Simmons

A transsexual male, who was born female, and his wife sought marriage dissolution and custody of their minor child. The trial court declared the marriage invalid, awarded sole care and custody of the child to the wife, and terminated the transsexual male's parental rights. The Appellate Court of Illinois affirmed and held that a transsexual male's marriage to his wife was invalid as a same-sex marriage and did not become valid when he had his internal female organs removed and a transsexual male was not officially sexually reassigned when the state issued him a new birth certificate designating his sex as "male." The court also held that the Parentage Act, under which husbands of artificially inseminated wives were treated as the natural fathers of any children thereby conceived, did not include transsexual males; that the Parentage Act, under which a child born from artificial insemination to two married parents retained his right to parentage with both parents even if the marriage was subsequently held invalid, did not include transsexual males; and that a transsexual male, who was born female, could not be declared the *de facto* parent of a minor child

---

7. Kantaras v. Kantaras, 884 So. 2d 155 (Fla.App. 2nd Dist. 2004) , *rev. den.* 898 So. 2d 80 (Fla. 2005).

based upon his long, loving and close relationship with the minor child. The court stated:

> Were we to accept petitioner's argument that the mere issuance of the new birth certificate conclusively establishes that he is now a man who may legally marry a woman in this state, we would also be compelled to declare that the marriage is valid based upon the mere fact that the county clerk of Cook County issued the parties a marriage license in 1985. The issuance of marriage licenses and new birth certificates are ministerial acts that generally do not involve fact-finding. Here, there was no fact-finding whatsoever on the part of the State Registrar of Vital Records. While the State Registrar had the right to conduct an investigation and make inquiries upon receipt of the application for a new birth certificate, no such investigation was ever conducted. The courts, on the other hand, are fact-finding bodies, and in this particular instance the trial court found facts which the State Registrar did not find and ruled accordingly.[8]

§6.1(d) The Ohio Case—Nash

Two parties, one of whom was a postoperative female-to-male transsexual, applied for a marriage license. The Court of Common Pleas, Probate Division denied the motion because the application had failed to disclose the transsexual's prior marriage. The parties appealed. While the appeal was pending, the parties filed a second application disclosing the marriage and subsequent divorce. The Court of Common Pleas denied the application. The parties appealed, and the two appeals were consolidated. In so doing, the Ohio Court of Appeals affirmed and held that the probate court did not violate the parties' equal protection rights in inquiring into the sexual designation of the transsexual, that the amended out-of-state birth certificate designating the postoperative female-to-male transsexual as male was not conclusive proof of the fact of the marriage license applicant's gender, and that the public policy in Ohio prohibited the postoperative female-to-male transsexual from marrying a genetic female. Ohio law prohibited

---

8. *In re* Marriage of Simmons, 355 Ill. App. 3d 942, 949–950, 825 N.E.2d 303, 309–310, 292 Ill. Dec. 47 (Ill. App. 1st Dist. 2005), *app. den.* 216 Ill. 2d 734, 839 N.E.2d 1037 (2005).

marriage between members of same sex, and the transsexual retained the biological organs of a female. Changes to birth certificates were only permitted to allow corrections of errors or mistakes on original certificates, and any changes to public policy regarding transsexuals and marriage or expanding the definition of male and female had to come from the state legislature.[9]

§6.1(e) The New York Case—Anonymous

The plaintiff, a noncommissioned officer in the U.S. Army, sought a declaration as to his marital status with the defendant. The basis of the action was that the defendant was a male at the time of the alleged marriage. The plaintiff testified that in November 1968 he met the defendant, who appeared to be a female, on a street in Augusta, Georgia. He went with the defendant to a house of prostitution where they spent a short time together, but the plaintiff did not see the defendant unclothed or have any sexual relations. Thereafter, in early February 1969, the defendant followed the plaintiff to his new duty station at Fort Hood, Texas. On February 22, the parties took part in a marriage ceremony in Belton, Texas. They returned to the plaintiff's apartment. Being intoxicated, the plaintiff went to sleep. He awoke at two o'clock in the morning, reached for the defendant and upon touching the defendant discovered that the defendant had male sexual organs. He immediately left the bed, "got drunk some more," and went to the bus station. Finding no buses running, he returned to the apartment and slept on the couch. The next day, the defendant informed the plaintiff that he intended to undergo an operation to have his male organs removed. The parties never lived together and never had any type of sexual relationship. The plaintiff was sent overseas in March 1969 and returned in April 1970. In the interim, the defendant sent numerous letters to the plaintiff and medical bills for hospital and surgical expenses. The army also deducted an allotment for the defendant from the plaintiff's pay. After the plaintiff returned from overseas, he saw the defendant once in court in San Francisco, and he arranged the defendant's release from jail on a prostitution charge and later traveled with the defendant to New York City for the purpose

---

9. *In re* Marriage License for Nash, Not Reported in N.E.2d, 2003 WL 23097095 (Ohio App. 2003).

of arranging a legal divorce or separation. The defendant told him on this trip that surgery had been completed and that "she" was now a woman.

The Supreme Court of Queens County, New York found as a fact that the defendant was not a female at the time of the marriage ceremony. "It may be that since that time the defendant's sex has been changed to female by operative procedures, although it would appear from the medical articles and other information supplied by counsel, that mere removal of the male organs would not, in and of itself, change a person into a true female. What happened to the defendant after the marriage ceremony is irrelevant, since the parties never lived together. The law makes no provision for a 'marriage' between persons of the same sex. Marriage is and always has been a contract between a man and a woman."

> The instant case is different from one in which a person seeks an annulment of a marriage or to declare the nullity of a void marriage because of fraud or incapacity to enter into a marriage contract or some other statutory reason. Those cases presuppose the existence of the two basic requirements for a marriage contract, [that is], a man and a woman. Here, one of these basic requirements was missing. The marriage ceremony itself was a nullity. No legal relationship could be created by it. Since the action, then, is in actuality not one to annul a marriage or to declare the nullity of a void marriage, but to declare that no marriage could legally have taken place between the plaintiff and defendant.
>
> Accordingly, the court declares that the so-called marriage ceremony in which the plaintiff and defendant took part in Belton, Texas, on February 22, 1969, did not in fact or in law create a marriage contract and that the plaintiff and defendant are not and have not ever been "husband and wife" or parties to a valid marriage.[10]

This case is understandable. The marriage was founded upon a fraud, and the "wife" had not had sex change surgery at the time of the marriage.

---

10. Anonymous v. Anonymous, 67 Misc. 2d 982, 984–985, 325 N.Y.S.2d 499, 500–501 (N.Y. Sup. Ct. Queens Co. 1971).

However, the other cases are not understandable on the basis of anything other than ignorance and probable prejudice.

The only U.S. appellate court to take a contrary position is New Jersey, where the Superior Court, Appellate Division held that a postsurgical male-to-female transsexual's marriage was valid.[11]

So, until the courts decide that a person's sex or gender is not immutably fixed at birth, transgender persons will be subject to the problems experienced by gay and lesbian couples who wish to marry and have their relationships recognized by the law.

Same-sex marriage in the United States exists in nine states and the District of Columbia, but such marriages are not recognized by the federal government for federal benefits and other purposes. The lack of federal recognition was codified in 1996 by the Defense of Marriage Act,[12] which was enacted before Massachusetts became the first state to grant marriage licenses to same-sex couples in 2004. For a list of the state laws relating to marriage and which states by constitutional provision or statute deny recognition to same sex marriages, see Appendix 5, "State Laws Relating to Marriage."

The validity of marriages of transgender persons after transition also affects immigration cases of their spouses.[13]

§6.1(f) The Surprising Minnesota Case—Radtke

In 2012, the U.S. District Court for the District of Minnesota became the first court in the United States to recognize the validity of a marriage between a postoperative transsexual to a person of the opposite sex to the

---

11. M.T. v. J.T., 140 N.J. Super. 77, 355 A.2d 204.
(N.J. Sup. Ct. App. Div. 1976), *cert. den.* 71 N.J. 345, 364 A.2d 1076 (1976).
12. 28 U.S.C. § 1738C.
13. *See In re* Esperanza Martinez Widener, 2004 WL 2375065 (Bd. Immigration App. 2004) (remanding for reconsideration of marriage of male-to-female transsexual to a genetic male holding DOMA "does not preclude recognition of the marriage at issue in this case for purposes of federal law"), and *In re* Ady Oren, 2004 WL 1167318 (Bd. Immigration App. 2004) (Unpublished Decision, Not Intended For Citation As Precedent) (remanding petition to classify status of alien relative for issuance of immigrant visa for reconsideration of marriage of female-to-male transsexual to a genetic female). *But See In re* Luiza Alexandra Price, 2009 WL 3448162 (Bd. Immigration App. 2009) (denying petition to classify status of alien relative for issuance of immigrant visa due to invalidity of marriage of male-to-female transsexual to a genetic male).

sex which the transsexual transitioned.[14] Christine Alisen Radtke was born in Prairie du Chien, Wisconsin, in 1965. At birth, upon inspection of her anatomy, she was declared to be male and was named Richard William Barker. While in her early twenties, she was diagnosed with gender dysphoria. In 1986, the Hennepin County, Minnesota, District Court granted Richard Barker's request to change her name to Christine Alisen Jensen. In the mid-1980s, Radtke participated in the Transgendered Program at the Program in Human Sexuality through the Department of Family Practice and Community Health at the University of Minnesota Medical School. Radtke received gel breast implants. In 2003, Radtke underwent sex reassignment surgery in Colorado.

In 2005, Radtke filed a Petition for Modification of Birth Record and Issuance of Replacement Birth Certificate with the Goodhue County, Minnesota, District Court. The petition requested that the court direct the Wisconsin State Registrar to register a replacement birth record changing the name on the birth certificate and designating her sex as female as is allowed by Wisconsin law.[15] The Goodhue County court heard the petition and entered an order directing the Wisconsin State Registrar to register a replacement birth certificate for Radtke designating her name as Christine Alisen Jensen and designating her sex as female. On July 14, 2005, the Wisconsin State Registrar issued a birth certificate to the plaintiff stating her name as Christine Alisen Jensen and identifying her sex as female.

On July 12, 2005, Calvin Radtke and Christine Alisen Jensen applied for a marriage license. A marriage license was granted by Goodhue County, Minnesota, that same day. On August 10, 2005, they were married in a civil ceremony by an authorized official before two witnesses at the Goodhue County courthouse in Red Wing, Minnesota. Goodhue County recorded the marriage and issued a marriage certificate on August 10, 2005. As a result of the marriage, Christine Alisen Jensen's legal name was changed from Christine Alisen Jensen to Christine Alisen Radtke.

Mr. Radtke was a member of the Miscellaneous Drivers & Helpers Union Local # 638 and participated in its Health, Welfare, Eye & Dental Fund. The fund, after discovering that Mrs. Radtke was a transsexual, refused

---

14. Radtke v. Miscellaneous Drivers & Helpers Union Local No. 638 Health, Welfare, Eye & Dental Fund, 867 F.Supp.2d 1023 (D. Minn. 2012)

15. WIS. STAT. § 69.15(1).

to recognize her as Mr. Radtke's wife and as a dependent on his coverage under the plan. The fund used the Minnesota statutory definition of marriage as one of the tests for eligibility under the fund, which states that "[l] awful marriage may be contracted only between persons of the opposite sex."[16] The court soundly rejected this assertion, stating:

> The Court places little weight on Defendant's reliance upon four non-Minnesota cases refusing to recognize marriages between a transgender individual and an individual of the opposite sex. *See In re Estate of Gardiner*, 42 P.3d 120, 137 (Kan. 2002); *Kantaras v. Kantaras*, 884 So.2d 155, 161 (Fla. Ct. App. 2004); *Littleton v. Prange*, 9 S.W.3d 223, 231 (Tex. Ct. App. 1999); *In re Ladrach*, 513 N.E.2d 828, 832 (Ohio Prob. Ct. 1987). First, these are cases from only four jurisdictions. In jurisdictions that do allow transgender individuals to marry someone of the opposite sex, there is no need for anyone to litigate the issue. Therefore, the lack of cases from other jurisdictions affirmatively holding that a transgender individual can marry someone of the opposite sex does not signal that most other jurisdictions prohibit such marriages.[17]

§6.2 Child Custody and Rearing

Some courts view transsexuals and transgender persons along with lesbian and gay persons as evil or unnatural. This is the same view taken by many courts as to gays and lesbians. Their views are typically framed on so-called natural law and religion. The worst example is the concurring opinion of Chief Justice Roy Moore[18] of the Alabama Supreme Court, who stated, in part:

> I write specially to state that the homosexual conduct of a parent—conduct involving a sexual relationship between two persons of the

---

16. MINN. STAT. § 517.01.

17. Radtke v. Miscellaneous Drivers & Helpers Union Local No. 638 Health, Welfare, Eye & Dental Fund at 12 867 F.Supp.2d 1023 (D. Minn. 2012).

18. Moore was removed as chief justice for refusing to obey a valid order of a U.S. District Court requiring him to remove a monument engraved with the Ten Commandments which he had placed in the Alabama State Judicial Building. *See* Moore v. Judicial Inquiry Comm. of State of Alabama, 891 So. 2d 848 (Ala. 2004). Note: This did not seem to matter to Alabama voters who elected Roy Moore as Chief Justice again in November 2012 after he lost two bids to become Alabama's governor in 2006 and 2010.

same gender—creates a strong presumption of unfitness that alone is sufficient justification for denying that parent custody of his or her own children or prohibiting the adoption of the children of others.[19]

These same opinions permeate the treatment of transgender persons in family law matters concerning custody of and visitation with children of the marriage.

Most courts that have addressed the issue, nominally apply the "best interests" test when addressing whether to grant custody or visitation to a transgender parent. However, reading between the lines it is easy for one to discern a bias against the transgender person and his or her gender identity. A Nevada court even went so far as to affirm the termination of the father's parental rights because of his gender identity. The Missouri appellate court stated, *inter alia*:

> The trial court's order provided that father's visitation rights would not begin until twelve months after the entry of the decree. Thus, the trial court placed a restriction on father's visitation. . . . Here, although the trial court did not make an express finding of impairment, it is implicit from its finding of no immediate contact, that immediate contact between the children and father would impair the boys' emotional development.
>
> Further, the implicit finding is clearly supported by the evidence. All the experts agreed that father's immediate contact with the children would cause harm to them. . . .
>
> This is a unique situation and it is imperative that evaluations of the parents and children are made prior to the children's face-to-face reunification with father. . . . Based upon those findings the trial court should decide what remedial measures, if any, should be taken to insure the best interest of the children are served while working toward their reunification with father. Likewise, the trial court should structure a visitation schedule appropriate to the children's best interest.[20]

---

19. *Ex parte* H.H., 830 So. 2d 21, 26 (Ala. 2002).
20. J.L.S. v. D.K.S., 943 S.W.2d 766, 772–773 (Mo. App. 1997).

The Washington appellate court stated, *inter alia*:

> First, the trial court carefully considered each child's relationship with each parent before entering FF 2.21 X. The court did not interview the children, but relied upon specific evidence given by the parties and the GAL [guardian *ad litem*] when finding the impact of Robbie's surgery on the children was unknown. The court acted within its fact-finding discretion when drawing inferences from the given evidence of the children's present uncomfortable and nervous behavior to make the future impact finding. While Robbie points to evidence of the children's adjustment, we are in no position to find facts, reweigh the evidence, or decide witness credibility . . . .
>
> Indeed, the court found Robbie was "undergoing an authentic gender transformation," and "has a right to be happy in her chosen life ahead." . . . And, Robbie received substantial residential time with the children without limitation or restriction. . . .
>
> In sum, the need of each child, not Robbie's transgender status, was the court's focus in determining residential placement. The court focused on the children's need for "environmental and parental stability" in granting the majority of residential time to Tracy, a permissible statutory factor addressing the children's emotional needs. . . .[21]

The Kentucky appellate court stated, *inter alia*:

> The circuit court found that M.B. suffered emotional harm, that she "suffered an injury to her mental or psychological capacity or emotional stability as demonstrated by her ability to function within a normal range of performance and behavior." . . . Specifically, the court found that M.B. "suffered major depression, suicidal ideation, decline in school performance, physical symptoms of stomach pain and headaches and withdrawn behavior." The trial court further found that the appellant's behavior caused this injury. The appellant's actions,

---

21. Magnuson v. Magnuson, 141 Wash. App. 347, 351–352, 170 P.3d 65, 67 (Wash.App. Div. 3 2007), *rev. den.* 163 Wash. 2d 1050, 187 P.3d 750 (2008).

as found by the court, included exhibiting "physical changes in [the appellant's] appearance" when the children visited in Florida, such as long finger nails, "wearing tight shirts and short shorts (with shaved legs and arms) and breast augmentation," without any warning to prepare M.B. or the others for those changes; sending a letter to M.B.'s sister with a photograph of the appellant as a female and traveling to Kentucky from Florida dressed as a woman and demanding visitation with M.B., knowing that M.B. did not want to see the appellant.

This finding of emotional harm is clearly supported by substantial evidence. Dr. Charles K. Embry, a psychiatrist who treated M.B. after she discovered that her biological father underwent a gender reassignment, testified that M.B. became depressed over the appellant's sex change and that M.B.'s suicide ideation, decline in school performance, and associated physical symptoms were related to the emotional injury occasioned by the appellant's actions.

M.B. herself testified poignantly and persuasively concerning the emotional distress the appellant's behavior caused her. She stated that she felt "abandoned," and that the worst part was "knowing that I did not have a father, where you go to school and say, 'I don't have a father, he's a woman.'" M.B.'s brother and mother also testified at length about the detrimental effects on M.B. brought about by the appellant's actions.[22]

The Nevada Supreme Court in terminating a transsexual father's parental rights stated, *inter alia*:

Dispositional grounds are satisfied when it is found that the termination is in the child's best interests. At trial, it was undisputed that Mary's mother, Nan, is a very loving and conscientious mother who provides a desirable environment for her daughter. Nan always keeps Mary well fed and clothed and is absolutely dedicated to her child. At the present time, Mary is happy and well adjusted. Nevertheless, if visitation were permitted, there would be a risk of serious maladjustment,

---

22. M.B. v. D.W., 236 S.W.3d 31, 35–36 (Ky. App. 2007).

mental or emotional injury. Hence, recognizing Mary's present situation, her attitude and feelings, and the substantial risk of emotional or mental injury were she forced to visit with her father, it appears clear that termination of appellant's parental rights is in Mary's best interest.[footnote deleted]

It was shown that Mary is at the tender age when she is very much concerned about the impression of her peers and doesn't want to have any sort of uncomfortable fears. Mary would prefer to have her personal life remain a private event. By terminating Suzanne's parental rights, Mary will finally have the assurance and comfort of knowing the visitation matter is settled. Also, Mary's emotional state is preserved, thereby providing her the forum to mature and resolve the situation in her own way. There is nothing to prevent Mary from rekindling the relationship with her father in later years if she so desires, but that choice should be hers, made at a time when the risk of emotional or mental injury is eliminated. . . .

Our review of the record indicates that the district court's findings are fully supported therein. Suzanne's efforts to regain visitation rights are shown to be a continuing source of apprehension to the child. Suzanne's solution is to subject the child to psychiatric counseling in order to change her mental attitude concerning her father's condition. Inferentially, the child will be more likely to succumb to a process of mental conditioning if she realizes that she will be forced to endure periods of visitation with Suzanne. However, expert testimony at trial reflects substantial doubt as to the success of such counseling at best, and a serious risk of further emotional injury to the child at worst. Such considerations are further complicated by the apparent degree of Mary's revulsion over Suzanne and the irretrievable loss of Suzanne's former relationship with Mary as a parent-father. The future prospects for emotional family stability are also dimmed by Suzanne's indication that Mary should know lesbians, homosexuals and transsexuals and "be a part of their lives" if "they are my [Suzanne's] friends." Suzanne, who admitted that many of her friends are to be found among the aforementioned groups, has thus postured herself in a position of recurring conflict with the child's mother and the "traditional" upbringing enjoyed by Mary during her formative years. The resulting equation does not bode well for the emotional health and well-being of the child. This Court can perceive no basis for such disruption of Mary's life. Nor do we see the necessity for inflicting a continuing sense of instability and uneasiness on this child. As noted previously, when Mary reaches the age of majority she can decide whether to reinstate a relationship with Suzanne. In the meantime, given the circumstances concerning Mary's view of Suzanne and the extent of her opposition to further ties with a vestigial parent, it can be said that Suzanne, in a very real sense, has terminated her own parental rights as a father. It was strictly Tim Daly's choice to discard his fatherhood and assume the role of a female who could never be either mother or sister to his daughter.[23]

The remarks by these appellate courts are called into question by expert opinions of others, such as psychologist Gianna E. Israel:

Fortunately most children are relatively accepting of a parent's cross-dressing or gender transition. This is especially so for those who have grasped the concept of self-parenting. Self-parenting means to be one's own parent after one's biological parents are no longer active day-to-day protectors and participants. Generally, young adults and emotionally mature adults have grasped these concepts. When they do so, they also begin to understand that parents have the right to follow a path separate from their children. Those parents, who must transition during a child's formative years, are strongly encouraged to follow through with their parenting responsibilities. This includes insuring that adequate gender role model representation is available to the child so that the child understands that parenting and even mentoring may come from persons of different gender. Mentors, or role models, are those individuals people look up to during life's transitions.

Finally, the vast majority of children are relatively accepting of a parent's cross-dressing or transgender identity. As with any important

---

23. Daly v. Daly, 102 Nev. 66, 70–71, 715 P.2d 56, 58–59, 59 A.L.R.4th 1155 (1986).

relationship, children should be reminded that their acceptance is valued. However, in circumstances where a child does not accept the parent's behavior, given the situation and/or time. There is nothing wrong with a child calling a transgender woman "Father" or "Daddy," until the young person understands that this label does not match the parent's presentation. Children can be encouraged to use appearance-appropriate labels and pronouns once they can comprehend the distinction.[24] They should not be required to do what is most comfortable to the transgender or non transgender parent but should be allowed to do what is most comfortable to him or her. For example, my youngest son calls me "Ally" and only refers to me as "dad" in Father's Day cards—which is what he chose to do.

In an Illinois case, the appellate court held:

- Under the Illinois Parentage Act, under which husbands of artificially inseminated wives were treated as the natural fathers of any children thereby conceived, did not include a transsexual male;
- Under the Illinois Parentage Act, under which a child born from artificial insemination to two married parents retained his right to parentage with both parents even if the marriage was subsequently held invalid, did not include a transsexual male; and
- A transsexual male, who was born female, could not be declared the *de facto* parent of minor child based upon his long, loving and close relationship with the minor child.[25]

In the Florida case of *Kantaras v. Kantaras,*[26] the trial court had granted joint custody to the parties in a case in which the father of the adopted children was a female-to-male transsexual. The appeals court did not address that issue but directed the trial court on remand to revisit the issue in light

---

24. Gianna E. Israel, *Impact on Children,* Gianna Israel Gender Library (1997), http://www.firelily.com/gender/gianna/impact.children.html (last visited August 6, 2011).

25. *In re* Marriage of Simmons, 355 Ill. App. 3d 942, 825 N.E.2d 303, 292 Ill. Dec. 47 (Ill. App. 1st Dist. 2005), *app. den.* 216 Ill. 2d 734, 839 N.E.2d 1037 (2005).

26. Kantaras v. Kantaras, 884 So. 2d 155 (Fla. App. 2nd Dist. 2004).

of the court of appeals holding that the marriage was void *ab initio* as a same-sex marriage.

The only case to not negatively address the issue was, interestingly, one that involved a transgender mother who was going through a transsexual change from female to male and had changed her name, and married a woman. The mother was allowed to retain custody.[27]

At the trial court level, few jurisdictions publish their trial court decisions. One reported case involving a transsexual and custody in New York from Kings County was very well reasoned and balanced. In that case, the court held that a transgender man who was the nonbiological father of the child and planned to undergo gender reassignment surgery in the future had formed a strong emotional and psychological bond with the child, thus establishing the extraordinary circumstances required to confer standing upon him to petition for custody. The child was conceived by artificial insemination during an eight-year "marriage," which was later voided, between him and the child's biological mother. The petitioner was the only father that the child had known, and the mother had entered into marriage knowing that the petitioner was transgender. The couple lived as husband and wife during the course of the marriage, completed an artificial insemination consent form with the petitioner, filed a birth certificate identifying the petitioner as the father of the child, and encouraged the child to address and consider the petitioner as his father for more than six years. That is similar to the result reached by the Florida appellate court in the *Kantaras* case.[28]

---

27. Christian v. Randall, 33 Colo. App. 129, 516 P.2d 132 (1973).
28. K.B. v. J.R., 26 Misc. 3d 465, 887 N.Y.S.2d 516 (Sup. Ct. Kings Co., NY 2009).

CHAPTER 7

Education and Students

As stated early on, this book deals with adults who are transgender. However, this chapter deals with minors as well as adults.

The U.S. Department of Justice under Attorney General Eric Holder and the U.S. Department of Education under Secretary Arne Duncan and President Barack Obama have interpreted Title IV of the Civil Rights Act of 1964(1) and Title IX of the Education Amendments of 1972[1] to cover transgender students. In doing so, they have pursued cases involving the harassment of and discrimination against transgender students and made remarkable progress. The following are a sampling of the cases that they have pursued and achieved settlements that helped ensure equal rights for transgender students and eliminate the harassment of transgender students.

- A consent decree was reached with the Anoka-Hennepin School District in Minnesota resolving complaints of sex-based harassment of middle and high school students in the school district. In November 2010, the Department of Justice received a complaint alleging that students in the school district were being harassed by other students because they didn't dress or act in ways that conform to gender stereotypes. The

---

1. 20 U.S.C.A. § 1681.

Departments of Justice and Education conducted an extensive investigation into sex-based harassment in the district's middle and high schools. Many students reported that the unsafe and unwelcoming school climate inhibited their ability to learn. The parties worked collaboratively to draft a consent decree addressing and resolving the allegations in the complaints. The consent decree ensures that the school district

1. Retains an expert consultant in the area of sex-based harassment to review the district's policies and procedures concerning harassment;
2. Develops and implements a comprehensive plan for preventing and addressing student-on-student sex-based harassment at the middle and high schools;
3. Enhances and improves its training of faculty, staff, and students on sex-based harassment;
4. Hires or appoints a Title IX coordinator to ensure proper implementation of the district's sex-based harassment policies and procedures and district compliance with Title IX;
5. Retains an expert consultant in the area of mental health to address the needs of students who are victims of harassment;
6. Provides for other opportunities for student involvement and input into the district's ongoing anti-harassment efforts;
7. Improves its system for maintaining records of investigations and responding to allegations of harassment;
8. Conducts ongoing monitoring and evaluations of its anti-harassment efforts; and
9. Submits annual compliance reports to the departments.[2]

- The Tehachapi Unified School District in Tehachapi, California agreed to resolve an investigation into the harassment of a middle school student based on his nonconformity with gender stereotypes. Title IV of the Civil Rights Act of 1964[3] and Title IX of the Education Amendments of 1972[4]

---

2. U.S. Dept. of Justice (March 5, 2012) Departments of Justice and Education Resolve Harassment Allegations in Anoka-Hennepin School District in Minnesota, http://www.justice.gov/opa/pr/2012/March/12-crt-286.html (last visited on June 24, 2014).

3. 42 U.S.C.A. § 2000c, *et seq.*

4. 20 U.S.C.A. § 1681.

each prohibit harassment based on sex, including harassment based on nonconformity with gender stereotypes and sexual harassment. In September 2010, Jacobsen Middle School student Seth Walsh committed suicide at the age of thirteen. In October 2010, the Department of Education received a complaint alleging that Walsh had been the victim of severe and persistent peer-on-peer sex-based harassment while he was a student at Jacobsen. After receiving the complaint, the Department of Education initiated an extensive investigation into the circumstances leading to Walsh's death and, together with the Department of Justice, worked collaboratively with the school district to resolve the violations. The investigation found that Walsh suffered sexual and gender-based harassment by his peers. The investigation also found that Walsh was targeted for harassment for more than two school years because of his nonconformity with gender stereotypes, including his predominantly female friendships and stereotypically feminine mannerisms, speech, and clothing. The departments determined that the harassment, which included ongoing and escalating verbal, physical, and sexual harassment by other students at school, was sufficiently severe, pervasive, and persistent to interfere with his educational opportunities. Despite having notice of the harassment, the district did not adequately investigate or otherwise respond to it. Based on the evidence gathered in the investigation, the departments concluded that the school district violated Title IX and Title IV. Under the terms of the resolution agreement, the district will take a variety of steps to prevent sexual and gender-based harassment at all of its schools, to respond appropriately to harassment that occurs, and to eliminate the hostile environment resulting from harassment. The district has agreed to revise its policies and regulations related to sexual and gender-based harassment and to retain a consultant to provide mandatory trainings on sexual and gender-based harassment for all students, administrators, teachers, counselors, and other staff who interact with students. In addition, the district will assess the presence of sexual and gender-based harassment in its schools through school climate surveys, adopt appropriate actions to address issues identified by those surveys, and form an advisory committee of administrators, students, and parents to advise the district on school climate issues related to sex-based harassment.[5]

• The Arcadia Unified School District in Arcadia, California, agreed to resolve an investigation into allegations of discrimination against a transgender student based on the student's sex. Under the agreement the school district will take a number of steps to ensure that the student, whose gender identity is male and who has consistently and uniformly presented as a boy at school and in all other aspects of his life for several years, will be treated like other male students while attending school in the district. The agreement, joined by the Department of Education's Office for Civil Rights, which participated in the investigation, resolves a complaint filed in October 2011 that the district had prohibited the student from accessing facilities consistent with his male gender identity, including restrooms and locker rooms at school, as well as sex-specific overnight accommodations at a school-sponsored trip, because he is transgender. The United States investigated this complaint under Title IV of the Civil Rights Act of 1964[6] and Title IX of the Education Amendments of 1972[7]. Under the settlement agreement, the district will

1. work with a consultant to support and assist the district in creating a safe, nondiscriminatory learning environment for students who are transgender or do not conform to gender stereotypes;

2. amend its policies and procedures to reflect that gender-based discrimination, including discrimination based on a student's gender identity, transgender status, and nonconformity with gender stereotypes, is a form of discrimination based on sex; and

3. train administrators and faculty on preventing gender-based discrimination and creating a nondiscriminatory school environment for transgender students.

   Additionally, the district will take a number of steps to treat the student like all other male students in the education programs and

5. U.S. Dept. of Justice (July 1, 2011), Departments of Justice and Education Reach Agreement with Tehachapi, California, Public Schools to Resolve Harassment Allegations, http://www.justice.gov/opa/pr/2011/July/11-crt-872.html (last visited on June 24, 2014).

6. 42 U.S.C.A. § 2000c, *et seq.*

7. 20 U.S.C.A. § 1681.

activities offered by the district. The district-wide provisions of the agreement will be in place until the end of the 2015–2016 school year. The student-specific provisions of the agreement will be in place as long as the student is enrolled in the district.[8]

- The Justice Department reached an out-of-court settlement in the matter of *J.L. v. Mohawk Central School District*, a lawsuit that the United States sought to join to address alleged violations of the Equal Protection Clause of the Fourteenth Amendment to the United States Constitution and Title IX of the Education Amendments of 1972, both of which prohibit discrimination based on sex, including discrimination based on gender stereotypes. On January 14, 2010, in the Northern District of New York, the United States sought to join a lawsuit filed by the New York Civil Liberties Union on behalf of a student, J.L., who was the alleged victim of severe and pervasive student-on-student harassment based on sex. According to the United States' motion, J.L. failed to conform to gender stereotypes in both behavior and appearance. He exhibited feminine mannerisms, dyed his hair, wore makeup and nail polish, and maintained predominantly female friendships. The United States alleged that the harassment against J.L. escalated from derogatory name-calling to physical threats and violence. The United States further alleged that the Mohawk Central School District had knowledge of the harassment, that the school district was deliberately indifferent in its failure to take timely, corrective action, and that the deliberate indifference restricted J.L.'s ability to fully enjoy the educational opportunities and benefits of his school. The district denied these allegations. The settlement among the United States, private plaintiff, and the district was approved by the U.S. District Court in the Northern District of New York and requires the Mohawk Central School District to, among other things, (1) retain an expert consultant in the area of harassment and discrimination based on sex, gender identity, gender expression, and sexual orientation to review the District's policies and

---

8. U.S. Dept. of Justice (July 24, 2013) United States Reaches Agreement with Arcadia, California, School District to Resolve Sex Discrimination Allegations, http://www.justice.gov/opa/pr/2013/July/13-crt-838.html (last visited June 24, 2014).

procedures; (2) develop and implement a comprehensive plan for disseminating the District's harassment and discrimination policies and procedures; (3) retain an expert consultant to conduct annual training for faculty and staff, and students as deemed appropriate by the expert, on discrimination and harassment based on sex, gender identity, gender expression, and sexual orientation; (4) maintain records of investigations and responses to allegations of harassment for five years; and (5) provide annual compliance reports to the United States and private plaintiffs. As part of this settlement, $50,000 will be paid to J.L. and $25,000 in attorneys' fees will be paid to the New York Civil Liberties Foundation.[9]

In addition to the work of the Justice and Education Departments, private litigants have scored some victories for transgender rights as well. In perhaps the most significant case, the Supreme Judicial Court of Maine held that a school had violated the Maine Human Rights Act[10] (MHRA) and discriminated against a student on the basis of the student's sexual orientation when it prohibited the student from using the girls' communal bathroom and required her to use the unisex staff bathroom. The public accommodations provision of the MHRA did not conflict with a provision of the Sanitary Facilities subchapter that related to education.[11] The MHRA made it a violation to discriminate in providing access to school bathrooms on the basis of sexual orientation, and the Sanitary Facilities subchapter required schools to provide children with "clean toilets" separated according to sex.[12]

In California, Governor Jerry Brown signed a transgender rights bill, the Sex Equity in Education Act[13], into law, which allows students "to participate in sex-segregated programs, activities and facilities" based on their self-perception rather than birth gender. It became effective on January 1, 2014. This was on top of a number of other statutes in

---

9. U.S. Dept. of Justice (March 30, 2010) Justice Department Settles with New York School District to Ensure Students Have Equal Opportunities, http://www.justice.gov/opa/pr/2010/March/10-crt-340.html (last visited June 24, 2014).

10. 5 Me. Rev. Stat. Ann. §§ 4553(8)(J), 4592(1), and 4602(4).

11. 20 Me. Rev. Stat. Ann. § 6501.

12. Doe v. Regional School Unit 26, 86 A.3d 600 (Me. 2014).

13. Cal. Education Code § 221.5.

California protecting transgender students and prohibiting discrimination against transgender students.[14]

Whether as a matter of perceived legal obligation, or simply of institutional policy, many colleges and universities should address the concerns of transgender students. Many colleges and universities have, and some have had for some time, antidiscrimination or nondiscrimination policies that prohibit discrimination on the basis of sexual orientation. The best practice, which many universities now follow, is to have gender identity and expression added as a category to those policies. Interestingly, 391 colleges and universities have nondiscrimination policies that include gender identity or expression according to the Transgendered Law and Policy Institute.[15]

The elephant in the room for colleges and universities in cases where sex is an issue is Title IX of the Education Amendments of 1972.[16] Logically, it would seem to apply to transgender students' complaints against colleges and universities. So far, there has been only one district-court level decision on the issue. In 1997, in *Miles v. New York University*, the U.S. District Court for the Southern District of New York held that a student who was admitted to New York University as female, but who was in fact a male-to-female transsexual who was in the process of becoming female at the time of a professor's alleged sexual harassment, was subject to discrimination based on sex, and, thus, was protected by Title IX and that her complaint alleged sufficient facts to support the Title IX claim.[17]

The Family Educational Rights and Privacy Act[18] (FERPA) (20 U.S.C. § 1232g; 34 C.F.R. Part 99) protects the privacy of student education records. The law applies to all schools that receive funds under an applicable program of the U.S. Department of Education. FERPA gives parents and students certain rights with respect to their education records. These rights transfer to the student when he or she reaches the age of 18 or attends a school beyond the high school level. Students to whom the rights have transferred are "eligible students."

---

14. See: Cal. Education Code §§ 220, 51007, 66010.2, 66027, 66270, 66271.2, and 66271.3.

15. Transgendered Law and Policy Institute, Colleges/Universities table, http://www.transgenderedlaw.org/college/index.htm#best (last visited July 28, 2011).

16. 20 U.S.C. § 1681.

17. Miles v. New York University, 979 F.Supp. 248, 122 Ed. Law Rep. 452 (S.D. N.Y. 1997).

18. 20 U.S.C. § 1232g. Implementing regulations are at 34 C.F.R. Part 99.

- Parents or eligible students have the right to inspect and review the student's education records maintained by the school. Schools are not required to provide copies of records unless, for reasons such as great distance, it is impossible for parents or eligible students to review the records. Schools may charge a fee for copies.
- Parents or eligible students have the right to request that a school correct records which they believe to be inaccurate or misleading. If the school decides not to amend the record, the parent or eligible student then has the right to a formal hearing. After the hearing, if the school still decides not to amend the record, the parent or eligible student has the right to place a statement with the record setting forth his or her view about the contested information.
- Generally, schools must have written permission from the parent or eligible student in order to release any information from a student's education record. However, FERPA allows schools to disclose those records, without consent, to the following parties or under the following conditions (34 C.F.R. § 99.31):
  - School officials with legitimate educational interest;
  - Other schools to which a student is transferring;
  - Specified officials for audit or evaluation purposes;
  - Appropriate parties in connection with financial aid to a student;
  - Organizations conducting certain studies for or on behalf of the school;
  - Accrediting organizations;
  - To comply with a judicial order or lawfully issued subpoena;
  - Appropriate officials in cases of health and safety emergencies; and
  - State and local authorities, within a juvenile justice system, pursuant to specific State law.

Schools may disclose, without consent, "directory" information such as a student's name, address, telephone number, date and place of birth, honors and awards, and dates of attendance. However, schools must tell parents and eligible students about directory information and allow parents and eligible students a reasonable amount of time to request that the school not disclose directory information about them. Schools must notify parents and eligible students annually of their rights under FERPA.

Thirty cities and counties have ordinances banning discrimination in educational institutions and programs that include gender identity. A list of those can be found in Appendix 10, "Cities and Counties with Education Nondiscrimination Ordinances and Laws That Include Gender Identity or Expression." Oddly, the list does not include many larger population centers that have ordinances banning discrimination in employment, housing, and public accommodations based on gender identity. In fact, the list of those banning such discrimination is over one hundred. See Appendix 9, "Cities and Counties with Public Accommodations Nondiscrimination Ordinances and Laws That Include Gender Identity or Expression." The cities and counties banning gender identity discrimination in employment (120) and housing (112) are also more numerous. See Appendix 6, "Cities and Counties with Housing Nondiscrimination Ordinances and Laws That Include Gender Identity or Expression" and Appendix 7, "Cities and Counties with Employment Nondiscrimination Ordinances and Laws that Include Gender Identity or Expression." It is unusual that many large university towns do not ban educational discrimination when they ban other forms of gender identity discrimination. The list includes Ann Arbor, the home of the University of Michigan; the borough of State College, the home of Pennsylvania State University; and the University of Texas, which has campuses at Dallas and Austin. The cities of Dallas and Austin have nondiscrimination ordinances as to public accommodations and housing but not in the area of education.

Colleges and universities should adopt a nondiscrimination policy that includes gender identity and expression. Copying what many public schools and districts have done, officials should start a safe-zone sticker campaign designating transgender-friendly teachers, administrators, and bathrooms. They should also initiate training for staff and faculty on gender identity and expression. Training can usually be given by people experienced in such training either for a fee or for only the cost of materials from LGBT advocacy groups, which exist in most large metropolitan areas.

§7.1 Recordkeeping

Students are asked on various forms to identity their sex or gender and most forms offer two and only two options from which to choose: male and female, which is the result of our binary world. An institution should consider asking students to self-identify their gender and leave a blank space after the question. In addition, transgender persons may adopt a name different from their birth names, and their current gender identity or expression may not correspond to a birth name. Universities, therefore, should consider under what conditions institutional records and documents will (and can legally) be changed to reflect an individual's (new) gender identity.

> When asking gender on forms and surveys, one should use the following format:
> Gender Identity (select all that apply):
> __ Woman
> __ Man
> __ Transgender
> __ Another identity (please specify_____)

If one must legally ask sex, female or male, one should also ask gender identity as stated above.[19]

§7.2 Student Health Insurance

Chapter 8, "Health Care," includes a more detailed discussion of the issues involving the delivery of health care generally. However, college and universities typically offer or even require students to buy a group policy offered by the institution unless the student produces proof that he or she is covered under a parent's policy[20] or a policy of his or her own. Colleges and universities should make sure policies that are offered to students cover, at a minimum, hormone replacement therapy and counseling for gender identity disorder and associated problems such as depression.

The following colleges and universities have student health plans that provide the minimum or better transgender-inclusive coverage, including at least some transition-related surgeries.

---

19. Genny Beemyn, Best Practices to Support Transgendered and Other Gender-Nonconforming Students, Transgendered Law and Policy Institute, http://www.transgenderedlaw .org/college/index.htm#best (last visited July 28, 2011). Note: This did not seem to matter to Alabama voters who elected Roy Moore as Chief Justice again in November 2012 after having lost two bids to become Alabama's governor in 2006 and 2010.

20. The Patient Protection and Affordable Care Act, Pub. L. No. 111–148, § 2714, 124 Stat. 119 (2010), 42 U.S.C. § 300gg-14 requires that health insurers allow children of policy-holders to continue on their policy through age 26.

- California Institute of Technology (Fall 2010)
- Cornell University (Fall 2011)
- Emerson College (Fall 2007)
- Emory University (Summer 2010)
- Harvard University (2010, 2012)
- New York University
- Portland State University (Fall 2008)
- Stanford University (Fall 2010)
- The University at Buffalo (SUNY Buffalo)
- University of California Berkeley
- University of California Davis
- University of California Irvine
- University of California Los Angeles
- University of California Riverside
- University of California San Diego
- University of California San Francisco
- University of California Santa Barbara
- University of California Santa Cruz
- University of Connecticut (Fall 2010)
- University of Michigan (Fall 2007 - all students; Jan. 2006 grad student employees)
- University of Pennsylvania (Fall 2010)
- University of Vermont
- University of Washington (Fall 2008; updated 2011)
- Washington University in St. Louis

Washington University in St. Louis covers surgical services only and not hormone therapy.[21] Harvard University covers surgical services only for chest reconstruction or breast augmentation.[22]

Coverage for sexual reassignment surgery should be offered if possible. But most insurers are likely to deny such coverage because they know so

---

21. Human Rights Campaign (December 21, 2010) Student Health Plans: transgender-inclusive coverage, http://www.hrc.org/resources/entry/transgender-inclusive-benefits-colleges-universities (last visited March 11, 2013).

22. *Transgendered-Inclusive Benefits: Colleges & Universities*, HUMAN RIGHTS CAMPAIGN, http://www.hrc.org/issues/transgendered/college-university-transgendered-benefits. htm (last visited August 5, 2011).

little about it. The institutions that have done so report that there is little or no additional cost.[23]

§7.3 Restrooms

This topic was previously discussed. See Chapter 3, "Use of Public Facilities." Transgender students may be subject to harassment or violence when using restrooms that conform to their gender identity or its expression but not to their biological state. Similarly, non transgender employees and students may experience discomfort sharing such facilities with transgender individuals. Institutions should adopt policies allowing students to use the restroom that is consistent with his or her gender presentation. Creating gender-neutral, unisex, or single occupancy restrooms is another option.

The University of Texas at Austin addressed the issue through its Office of Institutional Equity and Workforce Diversity. Officials there adopted a policy of providing gender-neutral, one-stall bathrooms in all campus buildings. Linda Millstone, the associate vice president for the Office of Institutional Equity and Workforce Diversity, related that the vice president for University Operations agreed to fund the installation of gender-neutral restrooms in all existing campus buildings. "Most buildings already have one or two single-stall restrooms, so it has been as easy as taking down the male or female sign and installing a lock on the door," Millstone said. She added that gender-neutral restrooms benefit a number of different people, including LGBT-identified persons; people with disabilities; and people with medical conditions, such as diabetes, who need a private place to administer medication. "If I am a woman in a wheelchair, and my attendant is a male, where am I supposed to go?" Millstone said. "I identified this problem, and immediately, several committee individuals were willing to help with the project."[24]

---

23. Genny Beemyn, *Best Practices to Support Transgendered and Other Gender-Nonconforming Students*, TRANSGENDERED LAW AND POLICY INSTITUTE, http://www.transgenderedlaw. org/college/index.htm#best (last visited July 28, 2011).

24. *Gender-neutral restrooms to be phased in to broader use on campus*, THE DAILY TEXAN, http://dailytexanonline.com/news/2011/07/24/gender-neutral-restrooms-be-phased-broader-use-campus (last visited August 4, 2011) (originally printed July 25, 2001 as: *Campus to offer gender-neutral toilets*).

§7.4 Residence Halls and Dormitories

When placing students in residence halls, in particular with roommates, almost all universities make assignments based, in part, on the student's biological sex. This approach may not be appropriate in situations involving transgender students. Institutions, therefore, may wish to address such issues, for example, by creating gender-neutral or all-gender residence halls or floors offering housing to persons of any gender. Institutions should consider creating designated residence hall floors involving transgender students that maintain gender-neutral bathrooms and mixed-gender rooms. Additionally, an institution should consider single-occupancy rooms to house transgender students. The following example is not unusual.

> At Southern Utah University, Kourt Osborn, a transgender student, was denied a dorm room because of his gender identity. Born as a female, Osborn, who identifies as a male, applied to live in the male dorms. The University determined that Osborn could live in the men's dormitory only with physician supervision of his hormone treatment, therapist acknowledgment of his Gender Identity Disorder, and official documentation of sexual reassignment surgery. Osborn was told that the failure to present these three items would result in a denial of male housing. Furthermore, Osborn was also denied the option of female housing. Osborn filed a formal grievance, to which Dean O'Driscoll, assistant to the University's President and the University's spokesman, responded that the school was not discriminating against transgender students but following a policy that aims to ensure that all students feel safe and comfortable in on-campus housing. O'Driscoll admitted that proof of gender is not required of all students; only transgender students must provide written medical proof. In response to the University's statement that they only offer male or female student housing, Osborn stated that it was "archaic to believe people of different genders can't live in an apartment together." Osborn felt "dehumanized, degraded, demoralized."[25]

---

25. Lara E. Pomerantz, *Winning the Housing Lottery: Changing University Housing Policies for Transgendered Students*, 12 U. Pa. J. Const. L. 1215–1216 (2010).

This example demonstrates the collision between the basic human dignity sought by transgender students (and persons in general) and probably well-meaning administrators and bureaucrats. The excuse or reason given in this example of "following a policy that aims to ensure that all students feel safe and comfortable" is an oft-used one and one that only reinforces bias and prejudice. There is no evidence that transgender persons pose a safety risk to others. In fact, the opposite is more likely true as is discussed in Chapter 9, "Personal Safety." As for worrying about students' being comfortable, that is but a thinly veiled restatement of the safety argument and one used for many years to justify segregating students by race and one thoroughly discredited. University life for transgender students should not be marred by frustration and alienation within their living space and larger social college environment.

§7.5 Locker Rooms

Locker rooms may present intimidating situations for transgender persons who fear being exposed as transgender when changing in front of others. As with male and female bathrooms, public locker and shower rooms can be uncomfortable, intimidating, and even dangerous places for transgender students, who may subsequently be outed as transgender if they have to undress in front of others. Partly in response to this issue, a growing number of campuses, including The Ohio State University, the University of Maryland, and the University of Oregon, have created private changing rooms when they have renovated or built new recreation centers. These facilities not only serve the needs of transgender students but also parents with children of a different gender than themselves, people with disabilities who require the assistance of an attendant of a different gender, and anyone desiring greater privacy.[26]

Institutions should create private, unisex, or "family" locker rooms or sections of locker room areas, including private showering facilities, to address such issues. This issue arises not only with male-to-female student

---

26. Genny Beemyn, *Best Practices to Support Transgendered and Other Gender-Nonconforming Students*, Transgendered Law and Policy Institute, http://www.transgenderedlaw.org/college/index.htm#best (last visited July 28, 2011).

athletes but also with female-to-male student athletes. In contrast to the examples of male-to-female transsexual athletes, fewer well-known athletes have transitioned from female to male.

Two examples, both from college sports, illustrate the varied experiences among transsexual athletes that stem from the various forms that a transition can take. Alyn Libman's transition from female to male while in high school included a physical transition induced by testosterone. He went on to compete as a male on the University of California-Berkeley club figure skating team and under the auspices of U.S. Figure Skating. Keelin Godsey, an All-American thrower on the Bates College women's track and field team, transitioned from female to male before his senior year in 2005. To remain eligible for women's events sanctioned by the NCAA and USA Track and Field (in which Godsey still competes, seeking a position on the U.S. Olympic team), Godsey's transition did not include surgery or hormones. Identified as a male competing in women's sports, Godsey received the formal support of his school and conference but still faced challenges ranging from finding appropriate locker room space (Bates College provided him with a separate closet) to dealing with awkwardness and discomfort among some competitors.[27]

In 2010, the Maine Human Rights Commission (MHRC) became the first government entity to initiate public policy regarding transgender student athletes when it published a draft guidance document that would allow transgender athletes to compete in the sex category that matches their gender identity and use locker rooms and facilities consistent with their gender identity as well. The MHRC is a state agency charged with enforcing the Maine Human Rights Act,[28] which prohibits discrimination on the basis of sex, sexual orientation, and other categories in public accommodations, including all educational institutions in the state.[29] It has since withdrawn the draft but has indicated that it will reinitiate policymaking on this issue in the near

---

27. Erin E. Buzuvis, *Transgendered Student-Athletes and Sex-Segregated Sport: Developing Policies of Inclusion for Intercollegiate and Interscholastic Athletics*, 21 SETON HALL J. OF SPORTS & ENT. L. 1, 17–18 (2011).

28. ME. REV. STAT. ANN. § 4566.

29. *Id.* at § 4552 (listing protected categories).

future. Should the MHRC adopt a policy or guidance that requires schools and universities to honor an athlete's gender identity when determining their eligibility for athletics, such an interpretation would create a conflict for National Collegiate Athletic Association (NCAA) member-institutions in the state of Maine, whose women's teams would be ineligible for competition if they accepted athletes based on their gender identities in accordance with state policy, rather than their drivers' license classifications.[30]

---

30. Erin E. Buzuvis, *Transgendered Student-Athletes and Sex-Segregated Sport: Developing Policies of Inclusion for Intercollegiate and Interscholastic Athletics*, 21 SETON HALL J. OF SPORTS & ENT. L. 1, 27–28 (2011).

CHAPTER 8

Health Care

Transgender persons face several obstacles to getting proper health care, even when they can pay for it or are otherwise entitled to it. Health care professionals are like the general population; some of them are biased, uninformed, and so on too. This leads to a refusal to treat or a denial of care and, at its worst, leads to mistreatment and abuse.

It has been suggested by those who study such issues that better collection of data by including gender identity and sexual orientation information in electronic medical records would help reduce or maybe even eliminate bias and discrimination in the provision of health care to the Lesbian, Gay, Bisexual and Transgender (LGBT). "The Institute of Medicine's (IOM's) 2011 report on the health of LGBT people pointed out that there are limited health data on these populations and that we need more research. It also described what we do know about LGBT health disparities, including lower rates of cervical cancer screening among lesbians, and mental health issues related to minority stress. Patient disclosure of LGBT identity enables provider–patient conversations about risk factors and can help us reduce and better understand disparities. It is essential to the success of Healthy People 2020's goal of eliminating LGBT health disparities. This is why the IOM's report recommended data collection in clinical settings and on Electronic Health Records (EHRs). The Centers for Medicare and Medicaid

Services and the Office of the National Coordinator of Health Information Technology rejected including Sexual Orientation and Gender Identity (SOGI) questions in meaningful use guidelines for EHRs in 2012" but are reconsidering this issue again in 2014. "There is overwhelming community support for the routine collection of SOGI data in clinical settings, as evidenced by comments jointly submitted by 145 leading LGBT and HIV/AIDS organizations in January 2013. Gathering SOGI data in EHRs is supported by the 2011 IOM's report on LGBT health, Healthy People 2020, the Affordable Care Act, and the Joint Commission. Data collection has long been central to the quality assurance process. Preventive health care from providers knowledgeable of their patients' SOGI can lead to improved access, quality of care, and outcomes. Medical and nursing schools should expand their attention to LGBT health issues so that all clinicians can appropriately care for LGBT patients."[1] Unfortunately, these studies take time and current year data are only available as anecdotes.

§8.1 Bias and Prejudice in the Delivery of Health Care and Denial of Care

In responding to an inquiry from an LGBT advocacy organization, the Director of the Office for Civil Rights of the U.S. Department of Health & Human Services about Section 1557[2] of the Patient Protection and Affordable Care Act's nondiscrimination provisions stated, "We agree that Section 1557's sex discrimination prohibition extends to claims of discrimination based on gender identity or failure to conform to stereotypical notions of masculinity or femininity and will accept such complaints for investigation. Section 1557 also prohibits sexual harassment and discrimination regardless of the actual or perceived sexual orientation or gender identity of the individuals involved."[3]

1. Sean Cahill and Harvey Makadon (September, 2013) *Sexual Orientation and Gender Identity Data Collection in Clinical Settings and in Electronic Health Records: A Key to Ending LGBT Health Disparities*, LGBT HEALTH 1:1, http://online.liebertpub.com/doi/pdf/10.1089/lgbt.2013.0001 (last visited July 27, 2014).

2. 42 U.S.C.A. § 18116 (which incorporates the bans on discrimination in Title VI of the Civil Rights Act of 1964, 42 U.S.C.A. §§ 2000d, *et seq.*, Title IX of the Education Amendments of q972, 20 U.S.C.A. §§ 1681, *et seq.*, the Age Discrimination Act of 1975, 42 U.S.C.A. §§ 6101, *et seq.*, and Section 504 of the Rehabilitation Act of 1973, 29 U.S.C.A. §§ 794).

3. Letter from Leon Rodriguez, Dir. of Office for Civil Rights, Dept. of Health & Human Servs. to Maya Rupert, Fed. Pol'y Dir., Nat'l Ctr. for Lesbian Rights (July 12, 2012) (OCR Transaction No. 12-000800).

The Faces of Transgender People Denied Health Care—Tyra Hunter (1971–1995)

Among the most famous health care abuse stories is that of Tyra Hunter, a Washington, D.C., hit-and-run victim. On the morning of August 7, 1995, a car accident left 24-year-old passenger Tyra Hunter bleeding profusely. She had been on her way to work as a hairdresser, was pulled out of the car by bystanders before firefighters and emergency medical service workers arrived at the scene. Eyewitness Catherine Poole told investigators that Hunter was conscious and "starting to complain of pain" when the rescuers arrived.

"[T]he ambulance person that was treating [Hunter] said to her that 'Everything is going to be all right, honey,'" Poole continued. "At that point, she started to urinate on herself. The ambulance person started to cut the pants legs on the jeans. . . . [H]e started cutting up the leg and suddenly stopped and jumped back when he found out that she was a man and said, 'This bitch ain't no girl . . . it's a nigger; he's got a dick.'" Two other witnesses corroborated the slur and backed Poole's assertion that the emergency service workers and firefighters stopped treating Hunter for upwards of five minutes while "laughing and telling jokes" about her. People at the scene, frustrated with the firefighters' behavior, began shouting for them to help Tyra. Finally, some other firefighters went to work on treating her injuries.

Two hours later, Hunter died of blunt trauma at D.C. General Hospital—after also being denied treatment by a doctor. No firefighters or emergency or hospital personnel were disciplined, and the city refused to take responsibility for the death, saying that Hunter was too seriously injured to survive.

But when Hunter's mother sued the city, a jury found that Hunter's civil rights had been violated at the accident scene and that her death had likely been caused by medical negligence. Experts testified that with proper treatment, she had an 86% chance of surviving. On Friday, December 11, 1998, the jury in Margie Hunter's lawsuit against the city returned a verdict in favor of the plaintiff on about half a dozen counts, awarding her a total of $2,874,060. While $500,000 of the amount was awarded for damages attributable to the withdrawal of medical care at the accident scene, a further $1.5 million was for conscious pain and suffering endured by Hunter in the emergency room as the result of medical malpractice. After the jury verdict, the city further alienated its transgender residents by appealing the decision—ultimately agreeing to a $1.75 million settlement.[4]

Robert Eads (1945–1999)

Equally outrageous in its own way is the case of a Georgia man, Robert Eads. A "hillbilly" and "proud of it," he cuts a striking figure: sharp-tongued, bearded, tobacco pipe in hand. Robert passes so well as a male that the local Klu Klux Klan tried to recruit him to become a member.

He began his transition with a double mastectomy, which is common for female-to-male transgender persons. He was never able to afford the recommended hysterectomy and phalloplasty surgery.

In 1996, after a severe bout of abdominal pain and vaginal bleeding, he sought emergency medical treatment, and received a diagnosis of ovarian cancer. However, more than two dozen doctors subsequently refused to treat him on the grounds that taking him on as a patient might harm their practices. It was not until 1997 that he was finally accepted for treatment by the Medical College of Georgia hospital, where he underwent surgical, medical, and radiation therapy over the next year.

His plight was featured in the 2001 HBO documentary *Southern Comfort,* which was filmed in 1998. It won the Grand Jury Prize, Documentary Competition at the Sundance Film Festival in 2001. By the time of the HBO documentary, though, his cancer had metastasized to his uterus, cervix, and other abdominal organs, and his prognosis was poor. Despite aggressive treatment, he died at home in 1999 at the age of 53.[5]

---

4. The Tyra Hunter story is taken from the following sources: Susan Stryker and Stephen Whittle, eds., *The transgendered studies reader*, p. 712 (Routledge 2006); *Jury Gives $2.9 Million To Transvestite's Mother*, N.Y. TIMES (December 13, 1998), http://www.nytimes.com/1998/12/13/us/national-news-briefs-jury-gives-2.9-million-to-transvestite-s-mother.html (last visited July 29, 2011); District Settles Hunter Lawsuit for $1.75 Million, Joint press release by the D.C. Office of the Corporation Counsel and attorneys for Margie Hunter (August 10, 2000), http://www.glaa.org/archive/2000/tyrasettlement0810.shtml (last visited July 29, 2011); and *A Death Robbed of Dignity Mobilizes a Community*, WASHINGTON POST (December 10, 1995).

5. Information about Robert Eads came from viewing the HBO feature documentary *Southern Comfort*; Synopsys and Production Notes for Southern Comfort, http://www.nextwavefilms.com/southern/ (last visited July 29, 2011); Interview with Max from Southern Comfort, http://www.nextwavefilms.com/ulbp/max.html (last visited July 29, 2011); and Robert Eads, Wikipedia, http://en.wikipedia.org/wiki/Robert_Eads (last visited July 29, 2011).

These two sad stories demonstrate the problems of bias and prejudice that transgender persons face in the health care system. Fortunately, the American Medical Association has begun to try to improve that.

§8.2 The American Medical Association Response

In 2011, the American Medical Association finally acted to address transgender health issues for transgender patients, physicians, and medical students and adopted the following:

Transgendered individuals face complex medical, psychological, and social issues. Within the health care system issues of discrimination and unique access barriers to important medical and social support services can occur. These challenges are often beyond the control of the transgendered patient. As a result, transgendered individuals often view themselves and/or are perceived by others as the most marginalized sector of the GLBT community and are uniquely at risk for adverse health outcomes.

Transgendered physicians and medical students also may face difficulties as they progress through their medical education, post-graduate training, and subsequent professional career. The Advisory Committee has shared reports from transgendered physicians and medical students who have experienced discrimination in the residency application process or in their practice environment or hospital settings, as a result of openly declaring their transgendered status. These medical professionals have been unable to refer to AMA policy because of the absence of gender identity in existing policy.

RECOMMENDATIONS

In recent years, our AMA has strengthened policy, programming, and advocacy efforts to increase diversity in the profession and the AMA, eliminate racial and ethnic health disparities, and serve the varied interests of its constituents. The establishment of the Advisory Committee on GLBT Issues has advanced these efforts by demonstrating AMA responsiveness to GLBT physician issues, increasing member involvement, highlighting the health disparities experienced within the GLBT patient population, and recommending ways for the AMA to acknowledge and address those needs.

As an integral part of that process, the Board of Trustees recommends that the following be adopted and the remainder of the report be filed:

1. That our American Medical Association act on House of Delegates policies that are listed in Appendix 1 to this report in the manner indicated (Modify Current HOD Policy) and;

2. That our AMA forward the policies that are listed in Appendix 2 to this report to the Council on Ethical and Judicial Affairs requesting consideration of the modifications indicated. (Directive to Take Action)

Fiscal Note: Staff cost estimated at less than $500 to implement.[6]

§8.3 Hospital Visitation

The Department of Health and Human Services' Centers for Medicare & Medicaid Services as part of its Conditions of Participation for Hospitals has mandated that hospitals must protect and promote each patient's rights. Thus, a hospital must not "restrict, limit, or otherwise deny visitation privileges on the basis of race, color, national origin, religion, sex, gender identity, sexual orientation, or disability."[7]

§8.4 Denial of Coverage by Third-Party Payers

Another obstacle to transgendered people getting proper medical care and treatment is that health insurers and public health care plans, such as

---

6. *Recommendations to Modify AMA Policy to Ensure Inclusion for Transgendered Physicians, Medical Students and Patients,* AMERICAN MEDICAL ASSOCIATION BOARD OF TRUSTEES REPORT 11-A-07, www.ama-assn.org/ama1/pub/upload/mm/467/bot11a07.doc, (last visited July 29, 2011). *See also Modification of Ethics Policy to Ensure Inclusion for Transgendered Physicians, Medical Students, and Patients,* AMERICAN MEDICAL ASSOCIATION COUNCIL ON ETHICAL AND JUDICIAL AFFAIRS REPORT 2-I-07 (issued July 1986; updated June 1994) http://www.ama-assn.org/resources/doc/code-medical-ethics/912a.pdf, (last visited July, 29, 2011).

7. 42 C.F.R. §§ 482.13(h)(3) and 485.635(f)(3).

Medicare and Medicaid exclude not only sex change surgery, but hormone and other treatments from coverage. In the 1970s, the transgender community was winning court cases to have sex change surgery covered by health insurance and Medicaid. Then policy language was changed and regulations were adopted and statutes enacted which expressly excluded anything to do with sex changes or being transgendered or being a transsexual. The insurers and Medicaid argued that sex changes were either cosmetic surgery and thus not covered because of the cosmetic surgery exclusion or were not medically necessary and thus not covered.

§8.4(a) Medicaid

Early decisions under the Medicaid laws held that sex reassignment surgery was not cosmetic and was medically necessary.

- The California Court of Appeals in 1978 construed the Medicaid law and held that sex change surgery was not cosmetic.[8]
- The California Court of Appeals in 1978 construed the Medicaid law and held that sex change surgery was medically necessary.[9]
- The Superior Court in Suffolk County ordered the state of Massachusetts to pay for a surgical procedure it had denied to a transsexual woman, but would have provided to a non transsexual woman.[10]
- The Minnesota Supreme Court held (1) the total exclusion of transsexual surgery from eligibility for medical assistance payments was void; (2) standard of medical necessity requiring applicant for benefits to prove by conclusive evidence that requested medical treatment will eliminate disability and render applicant self-supporting was invalid; and (3) the Welfare Department's determination to deny medical assistance benefits to adult male transsexual was arbitrary and unreasonable.[11]
- The Eighth Circuit agreed in 1980.[12]

---

8. G.B. v. Lackner, 80 Cal. App. 3d 64, 145 Cal. Rptr. 555, 2 A.L.R.4th 752 (1978).

9. Doe v. Lackner, 80 Cal. App. 3d 90, 145 Cal. Rptr. 570 (1978).

10. Beger v. Division of Medical Assistance, 11 Mass.L.Rptr. 745, 2000 WL 576335 (Mass. Super.Ct. Suffolk County 2000).

11. Doe v. State, Dept. of Public Welfare, 257 N.W.2d 816 (Minn. 1977).

12. Pinneke v. Preisser, 623 F.2d 546 (8th Cir. 1980).

Then the Medicaid law and regulations were amended to expressly exclude sex changes.[13]

Medicaid still does not cover many transition-related procedures for transgender persons. That is because Medicaid (or Medi-Cal in California) is a joint state and federal program in which states provide up to half of the funding. Each state develops a State Plan for its Medicaid program, which has to be approved by the Department of Health and Human Services' Centers for Medicare & Medicaid Services and determines what is covered and to what extent, subject to federal guidelines. For example, Medicaid programs must cover physician's services, hospital services, prescription medications, dentist's services, and certain other "necessary" medical services.[14] However, a state may decide to cover only a certain number of prescriptions per month or a certain number of days in a hospital per year, etc. Thus, only Minnesota, California, and Massachusetts cover transition-related services for transgender persons and they only did so after court orders requiring it.[15]

On December 12, 2014, the State of New York issued a proposed change to its Medicaid regulations to provide coverage for gender reassignment surgery for persons over 18 years of age or over 21 if the surgery would result in sterilization.[16] The protocols to qualify for the surgery basically mirror the World Professional Association for Transgendered Health (WPATH) Standards of Care.[17]

§8.4(b) Medicare

Title XVIII of the Social Security Act, designated "Health Insurance for the Aged and Disabled," is commonly known as Medicare. As part of the

---

13. *See, e.g.,* Smith v. Rasmussen, 249 F.3d 755 (8th Cir. 2001) and DeMare v. Minnesota Dept. of Human Services, 2006 WL 2533922 (Minn. App. 2006).

14. 42 U.S.C.A. § 1396

15. Transgender Law Center (n.d.). A Quick and Easy Guide to Medicaid and Transition Related Procedures, http://www.hawaii.edu/hivandaids/A_Quick_and_Easy_Guide_to_Medicaid_and_Transition_Related_Procedures.pdf (last viewed July 27, 2014).

16. 36 N.Y. Reg. 1, HLT-50-14-00001-P (December 17, 2014)

17. World Professional Association for Transgendered Health (formerly the Harry Benjamin International Gender Dysphoria Association), *The Standards of Care for Gender Identity Disorders Sixth Version,* http://www.wpath.org/documents2/socv6.pdf (last visited July 16, 2011).

Social Security Amendments of 1965[18], the Medicare legislation established a health insurance program for aged persons to complement the retirement, survivors, and disability insurance benefits under Title II of the Social Security Act. Because it is wholly funded by Medicare payroll taxes paid by employees and their employers, what it covers and does not cover is wholly controlled by the federal government.

When first implemented in 1966, Medicare covered most persons aged 65 or older. Later, other groups were granted Medicare coverage. In 1973, the following groups also became eligible for Medicare benefits: persons entitled to Social Security or Railroad Retirement disability cash benefits for at least 24 months, most persons with end-stage renal disease (ESRD), and certain otherwise noncovered aged persons who elect to pay a premium for Medicare coverage. Beginning in July 2001, persons with Amyotrophic Lateral Sclerosis (Lou Gehrig's Disease) were allowed to waive the 24-month waiting period. Beginning March 30, 2010, individuals in the vicinity of Libby, Montana who are diagnosed with an asbestos-related condition are Medicare-eligible. Medicare eligibility could also apply to individuals in other areas who are diagnosed with a medical condition caused by exposure to a public health hazard for which a future public health emergency declaration is made under the Comprehensive Environmental Response, Compensation, and Liability Act of 1980[19]. As a separate issue, this history begs the question: "why can we not just extend Medicare to all persons with valid Social Security numbers so that everyone legally in the United States has health insurance coverage?"

Medicare originally consisted of two parts: Hospital Insurance (HI), also known as Part A, and Supplementary Medical Insurance (SMI), which in the past was also known simply as Part B. Part A helps pay for inpatient hospital, home health agency, skilled nursing facility, and hospice care. Part A is provided free of premiums to most eligible people; certain otherwise ineligible people may voluntarily pay a monthly premium for coverage. Part B helps pay for physician, outpatient hospital, home health agency,

---

18. PUBLIC LAW 89–97, 79 STAT. 286 (1965)
19. PUBLIC LAW 96–510, 94 STAT. 2767 (1980)

and other services. To be covered by Part B, all eligible people must pay a monthly premium (or have the premium paid on their behalf).

A third part of Medicare, sometimes known as Part C, is the Medicare Advantage program, which was established as the Medicare+Choice program by the Balanced Budget Act of 1997[20] and subsequently renamed and modified by the Medicare Prescription Drug, Improvement, and Modernization Act (MMA) of 2003.[21] The Medicare Advantage program expands beneficiaries' options for participation in private-sector health care plans.

The MMA also established a fourth part of Medicare, known as Part D, to help pay for prescription drugs not otherwise covered by Part A or Part B. Part D initially provided access to prescription drug discount cards, on a voluntary basis and at limited cost to all enrollees (except those entitled to Medicaid drug coverage) and, for low-income beneficiaries, transitional limited financial assistance for purchasing prescription drugs and a subsidized enrollment fee for the discount cards. This temporary plan began in mid-2004 and phased out during 2006. In 2006 and later, Part D provides subsidized access to prescription drug insurance coverage on a voluntary basis for all beneficiaries upon payment of a premium, with premium and cost-sharing subsidies for low-income enrollees.

In 1989, Medicare adopted a National Coverage Determination categorically excluding what it called "Transsexual Surgery" from Medicare coverage regardless of a person's individual medical conditions and needs. In May 2014, the U.S. Department of Health and Human Services (HHS) Departmental Appeals Board decided an appeal from a Medicare beneficiary and declared that the 1989 exclusion was based on outdated, incomplete, and biased science and did not reflect standards of care. Accordingly, the Medicare policy of categorically excluding coverage of transition-related surgery, regardless of medical need, was invalidated. This means that decisions about coverage for transition-related care will now be made on an individual basis like all other services under Medicare. The Board issued an interim ruling in January 2014 and, after giving the Center for Medicare and Medicaid Services (CMS) the opportunity to submit additional evidence,

---

20. PUBLIC LAW 105–33, 111 STAT. 251 (1997).
21. PUBLIC LAW 108–173, 117 STAT. 2066 (2003).

issued its final decision in May 2014. By law, CMS cannot appeal the decision. The decision simply eliminates the national rule that transition-related surgeries can never be covered regardless of medical need. This means that Medicare beneficiaries will no longer have claims for transition-related medical procedures automatically denied by Medicare. Individual coverage decisions will be made on the basis of medical necessity and accepted medical standards of care, just like other services under Medicare. Patients must be approved for any procedure by their medical provider(s), the provider(s) must accept Medicare coverage, and the patient must pay any applicable deductible or copay.

At present, many providers of transition-related procedures may not accept Medicare coverage. Because this care has always been categorically excluded from Medicare in the past, patients may encounter challenges at first in finding an appropriate provider who will accept Medicare coverage. It is hoped that, over time, the number of qualified providers accepting Medicare will grow. The Departmental Appeals Board ruling applies only to Medicare—the federal program for older adults and people with disabilities—it does not affect private plans or Medicaid.[22]

§8.4(c) Civilian Health and Medical Program of the Uniformed Services (CHAMPUS)

The Civilian Health and Medical Program of the Uniformed Services (CHAMPUS) excludes coverage for "[t]ranssexualism or such other conditions as gender dysphoria. All services and supplies directly or indirectly related to transsexualism or such other conditions as gender dysphoria are excluded under CHAMPUS. This exclusion includes, but is not limited to, psychotherapy, prescription drugs, and intersex surgery that may be provided in connection with transsexualism or such other conditions as gender dysphoria. There is only one very limited exception to this general exclusion, that is, notwithstanding the definition of congenital anomaly, CHAMPUS benefits may be extended for surgery and related medically necessary services

---

22. National Center for Transgender Equality (May 2014) Fact Sheet on Medicare Coverage of Transition-Related Care, http://transequality.org/PDFs/MedicareFactSheet.pdf (last visited July 28, 2014).

performed to correct sex gender confusion (that is, ambiguous genitalia), which has been documented to be present at birth."[23] CHAMPUS also excludes coverage for any "procedures related to transsexualism or such other conditions as gender dysphoria; . . . [p]enile implant procedure for psychological impotency, transsexualism, or such other conditions as gender dysphoria; . . . and [i]nsertion of prosthetic testicles for transsexualism, or such other conditions as gender dysphoria."[24] CHAMPUS will also not cover "repair of a prolapsed vagina in a biological male who had undergone transsexual surgery."[25]

§8.4(d) College and University Student Health Plans
The following are sixteen colleges and universities with student health plans that provide minimum or better transgender-inclusive coverage including at least some transition-related surgeries.

- Emerson College
- Emory University
- Portland State University
- Stanford University
- University of California Berkeley
- University of California Davis
- University of California Irvine
- University of California Los Angeles
- University of California Riverside
- University of California San Diego
- University of California San Francisco
- University of California Santa Barbara
- University of California Santa Cruz
- University of Michigan
- University of Pennsylvania
- University of Washington

---

23. 32 C.F.R. § 199.4(e)(7).
24. 32 C.F.R. § 199.4(e)(8)(ii)(P), (Q), AND (R).
25. 32 C.F.R. § 199.4(e)(9).

Washington University in St. Louis covers surgical services only and not hormone therapy. Harvard University covers surgical services only for chest reconstruction or breast augmentation.[26]

Coverage for sexual reassignment surgery should be offered if possible. But most insurers are likely to balk at such coverage because they know so little about it. The institutions that have done so report that there is little or no additional cost.[27]

§8.4(e) Health Care Insurers and Plans

Early on the courts supported the idea that sex reassignment surgery was not cosmetic, not experimental, and was medically necessary. For example, the Supreme Court for New York County rejected the proposition that sex change surgery was cosmetic in 1979.[28] Then the insurance companies began categorically excluded such treatments in order to avoid paying for them.

Now some insurers, such as Aetna[29] and CIGNA[30], are covering sexual reassignment surgery or even full treatment for transgender persons in group health insurance policies that they sell. In a groundbreaking, first-of-a-kind move, the New York State Department of Financial Services, New York's insurance regulator, on December 11, 2014, issued Insurance Circular Letter No. 7 (2014). Its opening paragraph states:

> The purpose of this circular letter is to provide guidance to issuers regarding health insurance coverage for the treatment of gender dysphoria. An issuer may not deny medically necessary treatment otherwise

---

26. *Transgendered-Inclusive Benefits: Colleges & Universities*, HUMAN RIGHTS CAMPAIGN, http://www.hrc.org/issues/transgendered/college-university-transgendered-benefits.htm (last visited August 5, 2011).

27. Genny Beemyn, *Best Practices to Support Transgendered and Other Gender-Nonconforming Students*, TRANSGENDERED LAW AND POLICY INSTITUTE, http://www.transgenderedlaw.org/college/index.htm#best (last visited July 28, 2011).

28. Davidson v. Aetna Life & Casualty Insurance Co., 101 Misc. 2d 1, 420 N.Y.S.2d 450 (Sup. Ct. N.Y. County 1979).

29. Aetna Clinical Policy Bulletin Number 0615, Subject: Sex Reassignment Surgery (October 15, 2004).

30. CIGNA Coverage Policy Bulletin Number 0266, effective date January 15, 2010 (covers the following for FtMs: initial mastectomy/breast reduction , hysterectomy, salpingo-oophorectomy, colpectomy, and metoidioplasty. Covers the following for MtFs: vaginoplasty, colovaginoplasty, orchiectomy, penectomy, clitoroplasty, and labiaplasty).

covered by a health insurance policy or contract ("policy") solely on the basis that the treatment is for gender dysphoria. Further, an issuer is required to provide an insured with the full range of utilization review appeal rights as described in Article 49 of both the Insurance Law and the Public Health Law (collectively, "Article 49") for any gender dysphoria treatment that is denied based on medical necessity.

In its conclusion at the end, issued Insurance Circular Letter No. 7 (2014) states:

> An issuer of a policy that includes coverage for mental health conditions may not exclude coverage for the diagnosis and treatment of gender dysphoria. Although an issuer may subject gender dysphoria treatment to a medical necessity review, any such review must be performed consistently with the provisions of Article 49.

So, in New York, the full range of treatments for transgender persons will be available to any transgender person with health insurance or a covered dependent of a person with health insurance. Non surgical treatments should be covered proforma. But surgical treatments, especially gender reassignment surgery, will almost certainly require following the Standards of Care of the Harry Benjamin International Gender Dysphoria Association.[31] But responsible surgeons around the world already voluntarily follow those standards of care and the standards of care are for the protection of the transgender person.

Many major U.S. companies now cover sex reassignment surgery in their health care plans along with hormone and other treatments. See Appendix 8, "U.S. Companies That Provide Health Insurance Coverage for Sex Reassignment Surgery." The Human Rights Campaign's 2012 Corporate Equality Index defines qualifying transgendered-inclusive health insurance as:

---

31. World Professional Association for Transgendered Health (formerly the Harry Benjamin International Gender Dysphoria Association), *The Standards of Care for Gender Identity Disorders Sixth Version*, http://www.wpath.org/documents2/socv6.pdf (last visited July 16, 2011).

- Equal health coverage for transgendered individuals without exclusion for medically necessary care
- Insurance contract explicitly affirms coverage and contains no blanket exclusions for coverage
- Insurance contract and/or policy documentation is based on the World Professional Association for Transgendered Health (WPATH) Standards of Care
- Plan documentation must be readily available to employees and must clearly communicate inclusive insurance options to employees and their eligible dependents
- Benefits available to other employees must extend to transgendered individuals. The following benefits should all extend to transgendered individuals, including for services related to gender transition (e.g., medically necessary services related to sex affirmation/ reassignment):
  1. Short-term medical leave
  2. Mental health benefits
  3. Pharmaceutical coverage (e.g., for hormone replacement therapies)
  4. Coverage for medical visits or laboratory services
  5. Coverage for reconstructive surgical procedures related to sex reassignment
  6. Coverage of routine, chronic, or urgent nontransition services
  7. Plan language ensuring "adequacy of network" or access to specialists should extend to transition-related care (including provisions for travel or other expense reimbursements)
- Dollar maximums on this area of coverage must meet or exceed $75,000.
  1. *To secure full credit for benefits criteria, each benefit must be available to all benefits-eligible U.S. employees. In areas where more than one health insurance plan is available, at least one inclusive plan must be available.*[32]

---

32. HUMAN RIGHTS CAMPAIGN, *Corporate Equality Index*, 13–14 (2012), http://sites.hrc.org/documents/CorporateEqualityIndex_2012.pdf (last visited December 8, 2011).

§8.4(f) Public Agencies Having Custody of Minors

A sad but interesting story that is illustrative of the difficulties faced by transgender adults and youths in obtaining needed medical care. The New York Administration for Children's Services (A.C.S.) decided that a transgender child in its custody was not eligible "at this time" for payment for medical procedures to address her gender dysphoria diagnosis and allow her to conform her appearance to her female gender identity. The Supreme Court of New York County held that decision was arbitrary and capricious and rested on the premise that her chronic absences without leave from group homes, and her failure to consistently participate in programs at group homes, were indicators that she would not participate in necessary postoperative care, which had no foundation in the record. Mental health professionals who supported her applications all knew of her chronic absences, yet stated that she needed surgeries and procedures and did not question whether she would follow through with postoperative care. Her medical records showed that she demonstrated commitment and maturity in dealing with her health care, both trans-related and non-trans-related, and there was no indication that she participated in negative behaviors such as drug or alcohol abuse. The mental health professionals in question agreed that she should undergo the surgeries requested, the pediatrician who recommended that petitioner should not undergo the requested procedures was not mental health professional and had not met with her, and A.C.S. failed to refer her second application to the appropriate A.C.S. committee. The failure of A.C.S. to consider her inability to pay for gender affirming surgeries and procedures after foster care in deciding that she was not eligible "at this time" for payment by A.C.S. for medical procedures that would address her diagnosis of gender dysphoria and allow her to conform her appearance to her female gender identity was arbitrary and capricious. Once she aged out of foster care, she appeared to have no chance of raising money necessary to pay for procedures, since she had not completed her G.E.D. and was estranged from her family.[33]

---

33. D.F. v. Carrion, 43 Misc.3d 746, 986 N.Y.S.2d 769 (N.Y. Sup. Ct. N.Y County 2014), citing N.Y. Civ. Proc. Law & R. 7803.

§8.5 The Costs of Treatments Needed by Transgender Persons (Sex Reassignment Surgery, Hormones, etc.)

The original resistance to covering gender identity disorder and its treatments included a fear of the cost of doing so. It also involved societal bias and prejudice. Now, research has shown that the cost of providing needed treatment for transgender persons is really small. The following table from a research study by Mary Ann Horton, Ph.D., shows the average annual cost per person (or "resident" as labeled in the table) subscribing to a health plan to provide mental health therapy, hormone replacement therapy (the hormones [Rx] and the physician fees [MD]), and sex reassignment surgery.

Total Cost per Resident[34]

	MTF	FTM	TOTAL
Cost per resident for therapy	$0.010	$0.005	$0.007
Cost per resident for HRT Rx	$0.107	$0.027	$0.066
Cost per resident for HRT MD	$0.062	$0.031	$0.046
Cost per resident for surgery	$0.055	$0.054	$0.053
Total cost per resident	$0.234	$0.117	$0.172

Even after allowing for medical care cost inflation since the study in 2008, for less than one dollar per subscriber (or "resident" as labeled in the table) per year, full treatment modalities can be provided to transgender persons. And this is to provide care for a group whose numbers exceed the numbers of those whose conditions are fully covered in every health plan (unless excluded as a preexisting condition). From an epidemiological point of view,19 the number of transsexual persons is statistically significant.

---

34. Mary Ann Horton, *The Cost of Transgendered Health Benefits* (9/30/2008) http://www.tgender.net/taw/thb/THBCost-OE2008.pdf (last visited July 29, 2011). *See also* Mary Ann Horton and Elizabeth Goza, *The Cost of Transgendered Health Benefits – Transgendered at Work* (9/30/2008) http://www.tgender.net/taw/thb/THBWorkshopOE2008.pdf (last visited July 29, 2011).

Transgenderism is more common than the following conditions or diseases, which are fully covered by insurance and public health plans:

- Multiple sclerosis has an incidence of 91.7 per 100,000 people = less than 1 per 1,000[35]
- Duchenne and Becker's muscular dystrophy affects about one in every 3,500 to 5,000 newborn males = less than 1 per 1,000[36]
- Amyotrophic lateral sclerosis (ALS or Lou Gehrig's disease) has an incidence of 1 per 100,000 persons = less than 1 per 1,000[37]
- Male-to-female transgenderism affects 1 in 250 to 500 men = 2 to 4 per 1,000[38]

§8.6 Assisted Reproductive Treatments and Artificial Insemination

Transsexuals having kids? Really? Yes, it has happened but perhaps not the way one might envision, and it is likely to happen again. There was a documentary on television in 2011 about a transgender couple: Cai, a female-to-male transgender man, and Emily, a male-to-female transgender woman, who married and wanted to have a child. The female-to-male husband quit taking his testosterone, was artificially inseminated, and became pregnant and had a child. His wife, the male-to-female took extra hormones so that she could lactate and nurse the child, Dante. Emily, however, later had to nurse the baby with the assistance of a device.[39]

That is not the only instance:

---

35. Multiple Sclerosis Information Trust, *All About Multiple Sclerosis* at http://www.mult-sclerosis.org/prev_tab.html (last visited July 16, 2011).

36. Sherri Garcia, *Duchene Muscular Dystrophy* (Centers for Disease Control 2005) at http://www.cdc.gov/excite/ScienceAmbassador/ambassador_pgm/lessonplans/Garcia%20MD.ppt (last visited July 16, 2011).

37. www.amyotrophiclateralsclerosis.org website at http://www.amyotrophiclateralsclerosis.org/statistics.htm (last visited July 16, 2011).

38. Professor Lynn Conway, *How Frequently Does Transsexualism Occur?*, copy in author's files and retrieved from http://ai.eecs.umich.edu/people/conway/TS/TSprevalence.html (last visited July 16, 2011).

39. "Pregnant and Transgendered," Discovery Home & Health (2011).

In the 1990s, Tracy Lagondino underwent certain treatments to conform her body to the male-typical appearance that reflected Langondino's gender identity. After those treatments and a change of name, the law recognized Lagondino—now Thomas Beatie—as male, but that legal reclassification did not require the alteration of ovaries, uterus, or vagina. Beatie subsequently married a woman who was unable to bear children. After stopping male hormone treatment, Beatie twice conceived by insemination with donor sperm, gestated the pregnancies, and had two children. Prior to these births, a transgender man did have a child without a fraction of the media attention that followed Beatie's pregnancy, perhaps because that transman was not recognized as male by the law or married in a legal sense. As these matters are not monitored, other transgender men may have borne children but not brought their choice to public attention. Even so, some transmen now use online networks to discuss options in having children, so more pregnancies in transgender men may be forthcoming.

Both medical ethics and the law have had searching debates about the ethics of helping men and women with nonstandard sexual identities and people in unconventional relationships become parents. Some critics maintain that the rights and welfare of children born to gay and lesbian parents are compromised in serious ways. Law professor Margaret Somerville makes this argument from a secular point of view, while others do so from religious perspectives. These views have not, however, proved an impediment to most lesbian and gay men who want help from fertility clinicians: Western societies have moved toward acceptance of homosexuality in significant ways. With some exceptions, U.S. courts generally have not found a parent's homosexuality to be an impediment to custody and visitation, even in earlier decades when homosexuality was far less accepted than today. In 2008, the California Supreme Court found that a fertility clinic that turned away a lesbian patient had acted in violation of the state's antidiscrimination law. Professional groups in medicine have also moved toward nondiscrimination standards as well. For example, the American Society for Reproductive Medicine issued an ethics advisory that its members should not turn away men and women looking for help in having children because of their sexual orientation. That's remarkable for happening only 33 years after the American Psychiatric Association (APA) walked away from its judgment that homosexuality is a mental disorder.

The debate about homosexuality is, of course, far more settled than the debate about transgender identities. At present, the same psychiatric organization—the APA—that declassified homosexuality as a disorder continues to define "gender identity disorder" (GID) as pathological. But the question about the nature of transgenderism— disease or not?—is not the only question at stake when it comes to health care ethics. In light of the choices made by Thomas Beatie and his wife, it is well worth asking whether transgender people are entitled to the same access to assisted reproductive treatments (ARTs) as everyone else. In fact, one clinic turned Beatie and his wife away when they went looking for help in having children. Is that a defensible option? Should ARTs be withheld, either because people with the psychiatric "disorder" of GID are fundamentally compromised as parents, or because children face unacceptable risks by reason of having transgender parents?[40]

§8.7 Tax Treatment of Medical Care for Transgender Persons

And for those transgender persons who had the money to pay for sex reassignment surgery and other treatments, there was the further indignity of having the Internal Revenue Service take the position that such surgery and treatments were not deductible medical expenses because they were not for the treatment of a disease or were cosmetic surgery within the meaning of Section 213 of the Internal Revenue Code.[41] Then, in 2010, the U.S. Tax Court with all judges participating issued a decision on a vote of 11–5. The Tax Court rejected the IRS's long-standing position. For pur-

---

40. Timothy F. Murphy, *The Ethics of Helping Transgendered Men and Women Have Children*, 53 PERSPECTIVES IN BIOLOGY AND MEDICINE 46–48 (Winter 2010).
41. 26 U.S.C. §§ 213(D)(1)(A) and 213(d)(9)(B).

poses of the statute that provides for medical expense deduction for costs of treating disease, "disease" need not have demonstrated an organic or a physiological origin in an individual. A taxpayer's hormone therapy and sex reassignment surgery treated a disease and were not cosmetic treatments, and thus, the taxpayer was entitled to medical-expense deductions for the cost of those procedures. Reasonable belief in the procedures' efficacy was justified, as evidence established that cross-gender hormone therapy and sex reassignment surgery were well-recognized and accepted treatments for severe gender identity disorder (GID), that hormone therapy and sex reassignment surgery to alter appearance were undertaken by GID sufferers in an effort to alleviate distress and suffering occasioned by GID, and that these procedures had positive results in that regard. The Tax Court denied a deduction for the taxpayer's breast augmentation surgery.[42]

The IRS has now acquiesced in the Tax Court's decision thus making it national policy.[43]

§8.8 Obtaining Recognition of the Transgender Person's New Sex or Gender after Obtaining Hormones and Surgery

Once the transgender person receives medical treatment in the form of hormones and sex change surgery, the transgender person has the problem of having his or her "new" sex recognized.

[O]nce surgical intervention has taken place, whereby his [or her] anatomical sex is made to conform with his [or her] psychological sex, is not his [or her] position identical to that of the pseudo-hermaphrodite who has been surgically repaired? Should not society afford some measure of recognition to the altered situation and afford this individual the same relief as it does the pseudo-hermaphrodite?

[T]he application of a simple formula . . . should be the test of gender, and that formula is as follows: Where there is disharmony

---

42. O'Donnabhain v. Commissioner, 134 T.C. No. 4, at 19–23, 134 T.C. 34, Tax Ct. Rep. (CCH) 58,122, Tax Ct. Rep. Dec. (RIA) 134.4 (U.S. Tax Ct. 2010).

43. I.R.S. Action on Decision 2011-03, 2011 WL 5198999 (November 3, 2011).

between the psychological sex and the anatomical sex, the social sex
or gender of the individual will be determined by the anatomical sex.
Where, however, with or without medical intervention, the psychological sex and the anatomical sex are harmonized, then the social
sex or gender of the individual should be made to conform to the
harmonized status of the individual and, if such conformity requires
changes of a statistical nature, then such changes should be made. Of
course, such changes should be made only in those cases where physiological orientation is complete.[44]

The nonacceptance or recognition of a transgender person's gender
identity has been a particular problem among some feminists. This
is best described in the following quote from an article in *The New
Yorker.*

The dispute began more than forty years ago, at the height of the
second-wave feminist movement. In one early skirmish, in 1973, the
West Coast Lesbian Conference, in Los Angeles, furiously split over a
scheduled performance by the folksinger Beth Elliott, who is what was
then called a *transsexual.* Robin Morgan, the keynote speaker, said:

> I will not call a male "she"; thirty-two years of suffering in this
> androcentric society, and of surviving, have earned me the title
> "woman"; one walk down the street by a male transvestite, five
> minutes of his being hassled (which he may enjoy), and then he
> dares, he *dares* to think he understands our pain? No, in our
> mothers' names and in our own, we must not call him sister.

Such views are shared by few feminists now, but they still have a
foothold among some self-described radical feminists, who have found
themselves in an acrimonious battle with trans people and their allies.
Trans women say that they are women because they feel female—that,
as some put it, they have women's brains in men's bodies. Radical
feminists reject the notion of a "female brain." They believe that if

---

44. Samuel E. Bartos, *Letting "Privates" Be Private: Toward a Right of Gender Self-
Determination*, 15 Cardozo J. L. & Gender 67, 81–82 (2008).

women think and act differently from men it's because society forces them to, requiring them to be sexually attractive, nurturing, and deferential. In the words of Lierre Keith, a speaker at Radfems Respond, femininity is "ritualized submission."

In this view, gender is less an identity than a caste position. Anyone born a man retains male privilege in society; even if he chooses to live as a woman—and accept a correspondingly subordinate social position—the fact that he has a choice means that he can never understand what being a woman is really like. By extension, when trans women demand to be accepted as women they are simply exercising another form of male entitlement. All this enrages trans women and their allies, who point to the discrimination that trans people endure; although radical feminism is far from achieving all its goals, women have won far more formal equality than trans people have. In most states, it's legal to fire someone for being transgender, and transgender people can't serve in the military. A recent survey by the National Center for Transgender Equality and the National Gay and Lesbian Task Force found overwhelming levels of anti-trans violence and persecution. Forty-one percent of respondents said that they had attempted suicide.[45]

---

45. Michelle Goldberg (August 4, 2014), *What Is a Woman: The Dispute Between Radical Feminism and Transgenderism*, THE NEW YORKER, http://www.newyorker.com/magazine/2014/08/04/woman-2 (last visited August 10, 2014).

CHAPTER 9

Personal Safety

The bias and prejudice towards transgender persons leads to an inordinate amount of violence directed toward transgender persons.

§9.1 Indifference to Violence against Transgender Persons

While the following article may seem lengthy to some, the story that it relates is important to an understanding of the problems faced by transgender persons, and especially those transgender persons of color. In his article, *Disposable People*, Bob Moser relates the following sad story:

> In a city with no shortage of desolate neighborhoods, you'd be hard-pressed to find a bleaker spot than the corner of 50th and C streets in Washington, D.C.
>
> On one side, there's a decaying school, its playground barren as a prison yard. Extending up a couple of blocks is a string of deserted apartment buildings with boards and burned-out holes where windows used to be. Just across the way, folks still live in a set of matching brick buildings.
>
> It's a tough place to grow up, especially when you're different. Especially when you're convinced that you're a girl with a boy's anatomy.

Especially when the other kids taunt you and throw bricks at you and you have to quit school because you can't stand it anymore. Especially when you're determined to live openly as a transgender woman, considered by many the lowest of the low.

Stephanie Thomas could have told you all about it. Until last Aug. 12, 2003.

Around 11:30 P.M. the night of the 11th, 19-year-old Thomas and her best pal, 18-year-old Ukea Davis, reportedly told friends they were going to a nearby gas station for cigarettes. Nobody can say for sure where they actually went.

But just about everybody in the city knows that a little after 3 A.M., the friends were sitting in Thomas' Camry at a stop sign on the corner of 50th and C. Almost home. Then a car came up beside them, and the two were pelted with fire from a semiautomatic weapon.

According to an eyewitness report, another car approached after the shooting. A man got out to see what had happened. Davis was already dead. When the man nudged Thomas' shoulder to see if she was still alive, she moaned in confirmation. But her helper fled as the first car returned. The gunman got out and fired more shots, making sure Thomas was dead.

By the time rescue workers reached the bloody car, she was. Like her friend's, Thomas' body had been pumped full of bullets—at least 10 apiece.

A block up 50th, Thomas' mother, Queen Washington, got the news at 5:30 A.M. She'd been well aware that it was dangerous to be transgender in D.C.—or anywhere else in America, for that matter. But she hadn't seen this coming.

"If he'd known somebody was after him, I'd have known," says Washington, a feisty administrative assistant at the federal Bureau of Land Management who never got used to calling Stephanie "she."

"We were tight. He'd come by just that afternoon with his girlfriends, before he went to get his nails done. We kept it real, him and I. He knew I'd always protect him as much as I could."

Washington knew early on that protecting her youngest kid, whose name was Wilbur when she adopted him at three months, wouldn't be easy.

"He was a beautiful child, always very dainty, always very feminine. In first grade, a teacher—a teacher, mind you!—called him gay. I had to immediately go up to the school and get her straight. He came home that day and my neighbor told him gay meant happy. We looked it up in the dictionary. 'See?' I said. 'It's true!'"

. . .

"That's the last picture of him as a boy," his mother says, "before he became who he was." By contrast, she flips to a photo of Stephanie at 18, bear-hugging her mom. "Look at that smile!" she says. "He was a happy person—after he came out. You see? He didn't have those sad eyes no more."

The only thing that would have been worse than the brutal murders, Washington says, would have been never seeing that smile. "At least he had a chance to be who he was," she says. "I told him, God don't make no mistakes. I know you didn't make yourself. Who would make up a life like this? Who would be something the world hates?"

Hate killing victims Stephanie Thomas and Ukea Davis share a headstone, bought by Thomas's mother.

. . .

The best friends' joint funeral was packed. *The Washington Post* devoted a 3,500-word feature to the two lost lives. Local transgendered activists redoubled their efforts to forestall another tragedy. Police vowed to do the same.

. . .

Early on the morning of Aug. 16, four days after the vigil, one of the District's best-known transgendered nightclub performers, 25-year-old Latina immigrant Bella Evangelista, was shot and killed by a man who had paid her for sex. Police arrested 22-year-old Antoine D. Jacobs as he pedaled away from the scene on a bicycle, charging him with first-degree murder and later with a hate crime.

Four nights later, shortly after a vigil was held for Evangelista, police found the dead body of Emonie Kiera Spaulding. The 25-year-old transgendered woman had been brutally beaten, shot, and dumped nude in a stand of scraggly, trash-strewn woods bordering Malcolm X Avenue. Her clothes were found a day later in a nearby dumpster.

Another 22-year-old, Antwan D. Lewis, was arrested a few days later and charged with second-degree murder—but not, so far, with a hate crime.

The same night Spaulding's body was found, another transgendered woman, Dee Andre, survived a shooting near the U.S. Capitol. Alarmed transgendered activists convened a series of community meetings, hoping to calm nerves and band together against the violence.

Instead, the meetings only added to the sense that D.C.'s transgendered community was in a state of emergency: "We heard of at least 14 other assaults happening that same week," says Jessica Xavier, a local activist and volunteer coordinator.

If this wave of crimes could somehow be tied together—if there were a serial perpetrator, or some kind of "trigger" event—the city's transgendered population might be resting a little easier. But the assaults and murders appeared to be isolated cases of hatred. And though the sequence of events was extraordinary, the violence was not.

In 2000, Xavier had conducted the first study of transgendered people in the District. At the time, the results had seemed plenty disturbing. Of the 4,000 transgendered residents Xavier identified, a whopping 17% said they had been assaulted with a weapon because of their gender identity.

Four years later, the violence appeared to be spiraling out of control even more—despite the fact that D.C.'s Metropolitan Police in 2000 had launched an innovative Gay and Lesbian Liaison Unit (GLLU) designed to tamp down the violence.

"We're scared," says Mara Kiesling, executive director of the Washington-based National Center for Transgendered Equality. "This spree of violence made us feel more vulnerable than we deserve to feel. I'm sure it's increased the hopelessness for a lot of people. When you start hearing about 18 events in a week, you don't know what to do."

But if they aren't sure what to do, folks in Washington's transgender community certainly know what to think. "What we're seeing is a war against transgendered women," says Xavier. "And it's not only here—it's happening everywhere in this country."

. . .

While the past year's murders and assaults are "unrelated" in the law-enforcement sense of the term, most of the incidents do have at least one thing in common: "transphobia," which Jessica Xavier calls "the most powerful hatred on the planet."

"We are regarded by most as disposable people," she says.

. . .

One reason it's so tough to prove that anti-transgender murders are hate crimes is that so few are ever solved. Of the 27 murders in 2002 and the first nine months of 2003, arrests had been made in only 7—fewer than one-third—at press time. The general "clearance rate" for murders is almost twice as high, around 60%.

"The police are very slow in solving murders committed against marginalized Americans, whether they're black, Latino, gay, prostitutes, or transgendered," Levin says.

"When more than one of those characteristics is present in a victim"—usually the case in anti-transgendered murders—"they *really* don't act quickly. They're much more likely to form a task force and offer a reward when the victim is a straight, middle-class college student."

. . .

What has made transgender people such popular targets? "It's partly because we're coming out into the daylight," says Toni Collins, who works with Earline Budd at Transgendered Health Empowerment.

Jack Levin, the criminologist, agrees. "There are more transgendered people who are coming out, willing to expose themselves to the possibility of victimization," he says.

"It reminds me of the period beginning in the '80s when gay and lesbian Americans began to come out in larger numbers. They exposed themselves to the risk of being victims of homophobic offenders. The same thing is happening with transgendered people now. They are encountering much the same violence, for much the same reasons."[1]

---

1. Bob Moser, *Disposable People*, INTELLIGENCE REPORT No. 112 (Southern Poverty Law Center Winter 2003) http://www.splcenter.org/get-informed/intelligence-report/browse-all-issues/2003/winter/disposable-people (last visited July 30, 2011).

"Trans people are never killed from 300 yards away with a high-powered rifle; they're always killed up front and personal. . . . People want to see us die. . . . [T]here is a level of almost unhinged deranged violence about gender hate crimes."[2]

"Acts of violence motivated by hate or intolerance violate the fundamental principles and spirit of equality and freedom on which our country was founded." Queens County, New York, District Attorney Richard Brown.[3]

Transgender people are often targeted for hate violence based on their non-conformity with gender norms, their perceived sexual orientation, or both. Hate crimes against transgender people tend to be particularly violent. The Human Rights Campaign estimates that one out of every 1,000 homicides in the U.S. is an anti-transgender hate crime.[4]

Kay Brown, an instructor for "20th Century Transgendered History and Experience" at the Harvey Milk Institute in San Francisco has calculated that transgender individuals living in the United States today have a one in 12 chance of being murdered. In contrast, the average person has about a one in 18,000 chance of being murdered.[5]

In its 2013 research report, the National Coalition of Anti-Violence Programs (NCAVP) made some disturbing findings, which included that[6]:

---

2. Rikki Wilchins, in the A&E film *Transgendered Revolution* (1998).

3. Kaitlyn Kilmetis, *Hate Crime Charges Filed In Gay Bash,* QUEENS TRIBUNE, January 21, 2011, http://www.queenstribune.com/news/News_HateCrimes.html (last visited July 29, 2011).

4. *How Do Transgendered People Suffer from Discrimination?,* HUMAN RIGHTS CAMPAIGN, http://www.hrc.org/issues/1508.htm (last visited July 29, 2011).

5. Kay Brown, instructor for "20th Century Transgendered History and Experience" at the Harvey Milk Institute in San Francisco, WASHINGTON BLADE, December 10, 1999; City of Eugene, Oregon, Human Rights Commission, Research on Gender Identity Code Protections, p. 4, (September 20, 2005), http://www.eugene-or.gov/portal/server.pt/gateway/PTARGS_0_2_57716_0_0_18/0905%20Gender%20Identity%20Research.pdf (last visited July 29, 2011); *More about Transgendered Murder Statistics,* THE HANGED JUROR, http://blog.thejurorinvestigates.com/2009/04/23/more-about-transgendered-murder-statistics.aspx (last visited July 29, 2011); and based on the FBI's "Uniform Crimes Reports, Crime in the United States 2000," showing the murder rate of 5.5 people per 100,000.

6. *National Coalition of Anti-Violence Programs* (2014) 2013 Report on Lesbian, Gay, Bisexual, Transgender and HIV-Affected Hate Violence (©New York Gay and Lesbian Anti-Violence Project, Inc.), p. 9.

- **Transgender women survivors were:**
  - 4 times more likely to experience police violence compared with overall survivors.
  - 6 times more likely to experience physical violence when interacting with the police compared with overall survivors.
  - 2 times more likely to experience discrimination, 1.8 times more likely to experience harassment, and 1.5 times more likely to experience threats and intimidation compared with overall survivors.
  - 1.8 times more likely to experience sexual violence when compared with overall survivors.
- **Transgender survivors were:**
  - 3.7 times more likely to experience police violence compared with cisgender[7] survivors and victims.
  - 7 times more likely to experience physical violence when interacting with the police compared with cisgender survivors and victims.
  - 1.8 times more likely to experience discrimination compared with cisgender survivors and victims.
  - 1.4 times more likely to experience threats and intimidation compared with cisgender survivors and victims.
  - 1.5 times more likely to experience harassment when compared with cisgender survivors.
  - 1.7 times more likely to experience sexual violence when compared with cisgender survivors.
- **Transgender people of color survivors were:**
  - 2.7 times more likely to experience police violence and 6 times more likely to experience physical violence from the police compared with white cisgender survivors and victims.
  - 1.5 times more likely to experience discrimination, 1.5 times more likely to experience threats and intimidation, and 1.5 times more

---

7. "Cisgender" is a term used to identify individuals whose gender identity and gender expression matches the sex they were assigned at birth. NCAVP replaced the term non transgender with "cisgender" in the 2012 report in order for the report language to reflect contemporary language used in the LGBTQ community.

likely to experience sexual violence compared with white cisgender survivors and victims.

- 1.8 times more likely to experience hate violence in shelters compared with white cisgender survivors and victims.
- **Transgender men survivors were:**
  - 1.6 times more likely to experience violence from the police and 5.2 times more likely to experience physical violence perpetrated by the police compared with other survivors.
  - 1.5 times more likely to experience injuries as a result of hate violence and 4.3 times more likely to be the target of hate violence in shelters when compared with other survivors.

So, not only are transgender persons more likely to be the victim of an assault than cisgender persons, they were more likely to be victimized again by the police if they reported the assault to the police. The police are supposed to "protect and serve" all people, but too often the police mistreat not just racial and ethnic minorities when they report a crime but also transgender persons who report a crime. It is no wonder that racial and ethnic minorities, transgender, and other groups who are viewed as being not "normal" are reluctant to report crimes to the police.

§9.2 The Faces of Transgender Violence
Brandon Teena (1973–1994)
Brandon Teena, a 21-year-old transgender man, died in late December 1994 after being shot execution style by two men both of whom had raped Teena the prior week upon discovering that he had female genitalia. Teena's life and death were the subject of the movie *Boys Don't Cry*. The sheriff who investigated the rape and later the murder called Teena "it." The murderers were sentenced to life in prison. They had also killed others present in the home where they killed Teena.[8]

---

8. Anna M. Griffy, The Brandon Teena Story, Justice Junction (2004; Brandon Teena, http://brandon-teena.tk/ (last visited July 29, 2011); Davina Anne Gabriel, *Activists Protest Violence As Lotter Trial Begins*, http://www.tgforum.com/docs/brandon.html (last visited July 29, 2011); and Brandon Teena, Wikipedia, http://en.wikipedia.org/wiki/Brandon_Teena (last visited July 29, 2011).

Thomas Nissen accused John Lotter of committing the murders. In exchange for a reduced sentence, Nissen admitted to being an accessory to the rape and murder. Nissen testified against Lotter and was sentenced to life in prison. Lotter proceeded to deny the veracity of Nissen's testimony, and Lotter's testimony was discredited. The jury found Lotter guilty of murder, and he received the death penalty. Lotter and Nissen both appealed their convictions, and their cases have gone to review. In September 2007, Nissen recanted his testimony against Lotter. He claimed that he was the only one to shoot Teena and that Lotter had not committed the murders. In 2009, Lotter's appeal, using Nissen's new testimony to assert a claim of innocence, was rejected by the Nebraska Supreme Court, which held that since—even under Nissen's revised testimony—both Lotter and Nissen were involved in the murder, the specific identity of the shooter was legally irrelevant.[9]

Brandon Teena's mother sued the county and the sheriff for wrongful death and intentional infliction of emotional distress. The trial court dismissed the action. The Nebraska Supreme Court reversed and held that a special relationship was created that gave rise to a duty of the officers to protect Teena after she reported her rape to the police and offered to aid in the prosecution of the suspects, and the alleged remark of the sheriff that the victim's absence from the scheduled interview reflected poorly on her credibility on rape allegations did not give rise to claim for intentional infliction of emotional distress.[10] On remand, the trial court found the county negligent; awarded economic damages of $6,223.20 and noneconomic damages of $80,000, reduced the damage award on the negligence claim by 85 percent for the murderers' intentional torts and by 1 percent for the victim's negligence; denied recovery on the intentional infliction of emotional distress claim; and awarded "nominal damages" for loss of society, comfort, and companionship. The Nebraska Supreme Court affirmed in part and reversed in part and held that the statute providing for allocation of damages among negligent tortfeasors did not allow for such allocation due to the acts of intentional tortfeasors, and as a matter of law, the county sheriff's conduct toward the victim during the interview was extreme and

---

9. Nebraska v. Lotter, 771 N.W.2d 551, 564 (Neb. 2009).
10. Brandon v. County of Richardson, 252 Neb. 839, 566 N.W.2d 776 (1997).

outrageous as was required to support a claim for intentional infliction of emotional distress, the award of zero damages on the mother's loss of society claim was inadequate as a matter of law. The finding that the victim was 1 percent contributorily negligent was clearly wrong, and the county had a duty to protect the victim, and this duty required more than simply performing a reasonable investigation of her complaint.[11] On remand, the trial court awarded $7,000 on the claim of intentional infliction of emotional distress and $5,000 in damages for loss of society. The Nebraska Supreme Court affirmed and held that the award of $5,000 as damages for loss of society was supported by competent evidence of a relationship between the victim and her family and was not clearly wrong, and the award of $7,000 for intentional infliction of emotional distress bore a reasonable relation to evidence and was not clearly wrong.[12]

Gwen Araujo (1985–2002)

Gwen Araujo, a 17-year-old transgender woman, died on October 3, 2002, after several men strangled her with a rope and buried her body about 150 miles away from a Newark, California, house party after one of the alleged assailants' girlfriend announced that Araujo had male genitalia. The murderers tried to escape responsibility by using the "gay panic" defense—that is, finding out that Gwen was still anatomically male produced such fear that it caused them to be extremely violent. Her story was the subject of a Lifetime television movie, *A Girl Like Me: The Gwen Araujo Story.*

The accused were Michael Magidson, Jaron Nabors, José Merél, and Jason Cazares. On September 12, 2005, after the jury announced that it had deadlocked on the third defendant, the verdicts were announced. The defendant on whom the jury had deadlocked was Cazares. Magidson and Merél were each convicted of second-degree murder but not convicted of the hate crime enhancement allegations. Nabors was sentenced to eleven years. Merél and Magidson were sentenced to fifteen years to life. Their convictions and sentences were affirmed on appeal.[13]

---

11. Brandon ex rel. Estate of Brandon v. County of Richardson, 261 Neb. 636, 624 N.W.2d 604 (2001).

12. Brandon v. County of Richardson, 264 Neb. 1020, 653 N.W.2d 829 (2002).

13. People v. Merel, 2009 WL 1314822 (Cal.App. 1st Dist. 2009).

At Araujo's mother's request, a judge posthumously changed Araujo's legal name from Eddie to Gwen on June 23, 2004.[14]

PFC Barry Winchell (1978–1999)

In 1999, Specialist Justin Fisher and others took Private First Class (PFC) Barry Winchell to a Nashville club, The Connection, which featured performers. Here, Winchell met a male-to-female transgender showgirl named Calpernia Addams. The two began to date. Fisher began to spread rumors of the relationship at Fort Campbell, Kentucky, where both men served. Winchell then became a target of ongoing harassment, which his superiors did little to stop.

The harassment was continuous until the weekend of July 4, 1999, when Winchell and fellow soldier, Calvin Glover, fought after Winchell accused Glover of being a fraud. Both were drinking beer throughout the day. Glover was soundly beaten by Winchell, and Fisher harassed Glover about being beaten by "a fucking faggot' like Winchell." Fisher and Winchell had their own history of physical altercations as roommates in the barracks at Fort Campbell. Fisher continued to goad Glover. Subsequently, Glover took a baseball bat from Fisher's locker and struck Winchell in the head with the baseball bat as he slept on a cot outside near the entry to the room Winchell shared with Fisher in the early hours of July 5, 1999. Winchell died of massive head injuries on July 6, 1999, at Vanderbilt University Medical Center. Glover was later convicted for the murder of Winchell. Fisher was convicted of lesser crimes regarding impeding the subsequent criminal investigation, and both were subsequently incarcerated at the United States Disciplinary Barracks.

The murder charges against Fisher were dropped, and he was sentenced in a plea bargain to twelve and a half years, denied clemency in 2003, released to a halfway house in August 2006, and released from all custody

---

14. Information about Gwen Araujo was obtained from the Lifetime television movie, *A Girl Like Me: The Gwen Araujo Story;* Women's History Month: Gwen Araujo, Feminists for Choice, http://feministsforchoice.com/womens-history-month-gwen-araujo.htm (last visited July 29, 2011); Murder of Gwen Araujo, Wikipedia, http://en.wikipedia.org/wiki/Murder_of_Gwen_Araujo (last visited July 29, 2011).

in October 2006. Glover is serving a life sentence. Glover's conviction and sentence were affirmed on appeal.[15]

PFC Barry Winchell was murdered because he dated a transgender woman. The 2003 Showtime film *Soldier's Girl* is based on Winchell's murder and the events leading up to the brutal slaying.[16] As PFC Winchell's story shows, the violence is not limited to transgender persons but also extends to their significant others, families, friends, and allies (SOFFAs). Ms. Addams, who starred in LOGO's *Trans American Love Story*, is also a decorated war veteran and a long-time advocate for transgender rights. She also appeared in the Academy Award-nominated film *TransAmerica* and on the hit television series *Deadwood* and *CSI*.[17]

§9.3 Gender-Based Violence and Hate Crimes Laws

A hate crime occurs when the perpetrator of a crime intentionally selects a victim because of who the victim is. Hate crimes rend the fabric of our society and fragment communities because they target an entire community or group of people, not just the individual victim.

§9.3(a) State Hate Crime Laws

Ten states and the District of Columbia have hate crime laws that address gender identity-based violence. Those states are

- California[18]
- Connecticut[19]
- District of Columbia[20]

---

15. United States v. Glover, 2002 WL 34571438 (Army Ct. Crim. App. 2002).

16. Information about Barry Winchell was obtained from viewing the Showtime film *Soldier's Girl*; *Army Did Not Protect Son, Parents Claim*, WASHINGTON POST, January 10, 2000; Kenneth Turan, *Star-crossed Love*, WASHINGTON POST, May 31, 2003; and Barry Winchell, Wikipedia, http://en.wikipedia.org/wiki/Barry_Winchell (last visited July 29, 2011).

17. PFLAG Launches New Ad Campaign with Calpernia Addams, Highlighting Organization's Commitment to the Transgender Community—"This is Our Love Story" Campaign Will Debut This Summer, retrieved from http://community.pflag.org/Page.aspx?pid=892 (last viewed August 10, 2014).

18. Cal. Penal Code § 422.55.

19. CONN. GEN. STAT. §§ 53a-181j- 53a-181l.

20. D.C. CODE §§ 22-3701 – 3702,22-3704 and § 2-1401.02.

- Hawaii[21]
- Maryland[22]
- Minnesota[23]
- Missouri[24]
- New Jersey[25]
- New Mexico[26]
- Vermont[27]
- Washington[28]

§9.3(b) Federal Hate Crimes Law

The Hate Crimes Prevention Act (HCPA) was initially introduced in the House and Senate in 1997. During the subsequent twelve years, Congress passed various versions of the HCPA but was ultimately unsuccessful in advancing the bill for the president's signature. This changed during the 111th Congress, when versions of the HCPA were introduced by Representatives John Conyers (D-MI) and Mark Kirk (R-IL) in the House and Senators Edward Kennedy (D-MA), Patrick Leahy (D-VT), Arlen Specter (D-PA), Susan Collins (R-ME), and Olympia Snowe (R-ME) in the Senate. On April 29, 2009, the House of Representatives passed hate crimes legislation (H.R. 1913) by a vote of 249–175. On July 16, 2009, the Senate voted 63–28 to proceed with hate crimes legislation (S. 909) as an amendment (S. Amend. 1511) to the Department of Defense (DoD) authorization bill (S. 1390). The DoD authorization bill then passed the Senate with hate crimes legislation attached as an amendment on July 23, 2009.

As part of the final negotiations between the House and Senate, the conferees honored the memory of two victims of hate crimes by naming the hate crimes provision of the conference report the Matthew Shepard and

---

21. Hawaii Rev. Stat § 846–51.
22. Md. Ann. Code, Crim. Law §10-301, *et seq.*
23. Minn. Stat. Ann. §363A.03, §609.2231(4), §609.595(1a), §609.748, and §611A.79.
24. Mo. Rev. Stat. § 557.035.
25. N.J. Stat. Ann. § 2C:16-1.
26. N.M. Stat. Ann. § 31-18B-1, *et seq.*
27. Vt. Stat. Ann. tit. 13 § 1455.
28. Wash. Rev. Code § 9A.36.080.

James Byrd Jr. Hate Crimes Prevention Act.[29] Matthew Shepard was a gay college student who was tortured and murdered in Laramie, Wyoming, and James Byrd Jr., was an African-American man who was dragged to death in Jasper, Texas. The act has been challenged, but found to be constitutional.[30]

Under the act, federal jurisdiction applies if the prohibited conduct occurs:

1. during the course of, or as the result of, the travel of the defendant or the victim across a state line or national border or using a channel, facility, or instrumentality of interstate or foreign commerce;

2. the defendant uses a channel, facility, or instrumentality of interstate or foreign commerce in connection with the conduct described in subparagraph (A);

3. in connection with the conduct described in subparagraph (A), the defendant employs a firearm, dangerous weapon, explosive or incendiary device, or other weapon that has traveled in interstate or foreign commerce; or

4. the conduct described in subparagraph (A) interferes with commercial or other economic activity in which the victim is engaged at the time of the conduct or otherwise affects interstate or foreign commerce.[31]

While it is great to have a national hate crime law that protects transgender individuals, the problem with any federal law like the Matthew Shepard and James Byrd, Jr. Hate Crimes Prevention Act is the interstate commerce connection that is required. Also, it is purely a criminal statute and no civil remedy is provided.

Violence against transgender persons is not just a problem in the United States, but it is an international problem. On March 26, 2007, a group of human rights experts launched the Yogyakarta Principles on the Application of Human Rights Law in Relation to Sexual Orientation and Gender Identity. The Principles are intended as a coherent and comprehensive identification of the obligation of states to respect, protect, and fulfill the human

---

29. Matthew Shepard & James Byrd, Jr. Hate Crimes Prevention Act, Pub. L. No. 111-84, Div. E, 123 Stat. 2190, 8 U.S.C. § 249(a)(1).

30. United States v. Jenkins, 2012 WL 4887389 (E.D. Ky. 2012) and United States v. Beebe, 807 F.Supp.2d 1045 (D. N.M. 2011).

31. 8 U.S.C. § 249(a)(2)(B).

rights of all persons regardless of their sexual orientation or gender identity. Since their launch, the Principles have attracted considerable attention on the part of states, United Nations, actors, and civil society. It is likely that they will play a significant role within advocacy efforts and, whether directly or otherwise, in normative and jurisprudential development.

Those who transgress gender norms are particularly likely to be targeted for violence. The [organization] "Transgendered Day of Remembrance" estimates that one transgender person is killed every month in the U.S. In Nepal, métis (people born as men who identify as women) have been beaten by police with batons, gun butts, and sticks; burnt with cigarettes; and forced to perform oral sex.

Transgender people are "often subjected to violence . . . in order to 'punish' them for transgressing gender barriers or for challenging predominant conceptions of gender roles," and transgender youth have been described as "among the most vulnerable and marginalized young people in society." As one Canadian report underlines:

The notion that there are two and only two genders is one of the most basic ideas in our binary Western way of thinking. Transgender people challenge our very understanding of the world. And we make them pay the cost of our confusion by their suffering.[32]

Defenders (of the rights of lesbian, gay, bisexual, transgender, and intersex persons [LGBTI]) have been threatened, had their houses and offices raided, they have been attacked, tortured, sexually abused, tormented by regular death threats and even killed. . . . In numerous cases from all regions, police or government officials are the alleged perpetrators of violence and threats against defenders of LGBTI rights. In several of these cases, the authorities have prohibited demonstrations, conferences and meetings, denied registration of [organizations] working for LGBTI rights and police officers have, allegedly, beaten up or even sexually abused these defenders of LGBTI rights.[33]

---

32. Michael O'Flaherty & John Fisher, *Sexual Orientation, Gender Identity and International Human Rights Law: Contextualising the Yogyakarta Principles*, 8 Oxford Human Rights L. Rev. 207, 209 (2008).

33. *Id.* at 213.

The Yogyakarta Process

The United Nations High Commissioner for Human Rights, Louise Arbour, has expressed concern about the inconsistency of approach in law and practice. In an address to a lesbian, gay, bisexual, and transgender forum, she suggested that although the principles of universality and nondiscrimination apply to the grounds of sexual orientation and gender identity, there is a need for a more comprehensive articulation of these rights in international law, "[i]t is precisely in this meeting between the normative work of States and the interpretive functions of international expert bodies that a common ground can begin to emerge."

Furthermore, commentators have suggested that international practice could also benefit from the application of more consistent terminology to address issues of sexual orientation and gender identity. While some Special Procedures, treaty bodies and States have preferred speaking of "sexual orientation" or "gender identity," others speak of "lesbians," "gays," "transgender," or "transsexual" people, and still others speak of "sexual preference" or use the language of "sexual minorities." In addition, issues of gender identity have been little understood, with some mechanisms and States referencing transsexuality as a "sexual orientation" and others frankly acknowledging that they do not understand the term.

It is in this context of such diverse approaches, inconsistency, gaps, and opportunities that the Yogyakarta Principles on the application of international human rights law in relation to sexual orientation and gender identity were conceived. The proposal to develop the Yogyakarta Principles originated in 2005 with a coalition of human rights NGOs that was subsequently facilitated by the International Service for Human Rights and the International Commission of Jurists. It was proposed that the Principles have a tripartite function. In the first place, they should constitute a "mapping" of the experiences of human rights violations experienced by people of diverse sexual orientations and gender identities. This exercise should be as inclusive and wide ranging as possible, taking account of the distinct ways in which human rights violations may be experienced in different regions of the world. Second, the application of international human rights law to such experiences should be articulated in as clear and precise a manner as possible. Finally, the Principles should spell out in some detail the nature of the obligation on States for effective implementation of each of the human rights obligations.

Principles. They came from 25 countries representative of all geographic regions. They included one former UN High Commissioner for Human Rights (Mary Robinson, also a former head of state), 13 current or former UN human rights special mechanism office holders or treaty body members, two serving judges of domestic courts and a number of academics and activists. Seventeen of the experts were women. The first of the present authors was one of the experts. He also served as [reporter] of the process, responsible for proposing various formulations and capturing various expert views in a single agreed text. The drafting process took place over a period of some 12 months during 2006/07. While much of the drafting was done by means of electronic communications, many of the experts met at an international seminar that took place in Yogyakarta, Indonesia at Gadjah Mada University from 6 to 9 November 2006 to review and [finalize] the text. All of the text was agreed by consensus.

Although initially some participants envisioned a very concise statement of legal principles, expressed in general terms, the seminar eventually reached the view that the complexity of circumstances of victims of human rights violations required a highly elaborated approach. They also considered that the text should be expressed in a manner that reflected the formulations in the international human rights treaties, whereby its authority as a statement of the legal standards would be reinforced.

There are 29 principles. Each of these comprises a statement of international human rights law, its application to a given situation and an indication of the nature of the State's duty to implement the legal obligation. There is some order to the Principles. Principles 1 to 3 set out the principles of the universality of human rights and their application to all persons without discrimination, as well as the right of all people to recognition before the law. The experts placed these elements at the beginning of the text in order to recall the primordial significance of the universality of human rights and the scale and extent of discrimination targeted against people of diverse sexual orientations and gender identities, as well as the manner in which they are commonly rendered invisible within a society and its legal structures. Principles 4 to 11 address fundamental rights to life, freedom from violence and torture, privacy, access to justice and freedom from arbitrary detention. Principles 12 to 18 set out the importance of nondiscrimination in the enjoyment of economic, social and cultural rights, including employment, accommodation, Social Security, education and health. Principles 19 to 21 [emphasize] the importance of the freedom to express oneself, one's identity and one's sexuality, without State interference based on sexual orientation or gender identity, including the rights to participate peaceably in public assemblies and events and otherwise associate in community with others.

Principles 22 and 23 highlight the rights of persons to seek asylum from persecution based on sexual orientation or gender identity. Principles 24 to 26 address the rights of persons to participate in family life, public affairs and the cultural life of their community, without discrimination based on sexual orientation or gender identity. Principle 27 [recognizes] the right to defend and promote human rights without discrimination based on sexual orientation and gender identity, and the obligation of States to ensure the protection of human rights defenders working in these areas. Principles 28 and 29 affirm the importance of holding rights violators accountable, and ensuring appropriate redress for those who face rights violations.

Most of the principles are titled in a manner that directly reflects the provisions of human rights treaties: right to education, highest attainable standard of health, etc. Those that differ are so phrased either to more specifically address a problematic situation (Principle 18, Protection from Medical Abuse), or to better reflect an accepted legal standard that does not derive from any one specific treaty provision (the principles on promotion of human rights—27, effective remedies—28 and accountability—29).

The content of each Principle reflects the particular human rights challenges that the experts identified as well as the precise application of the law for that situation. As such, they vary widely in style and category of contents. However, a general typology for the legal obligations of States can be observed: (i) all necessary legislative, administrative and other measures to eradicate impugned practices; (ii) protection measures for those at risk; (iii) accountability of perpetrators and redress for victims; and, (iv) promotion of a human rights culture by means of education, training and public awareness-raising. It may thus be observed that the Principles take account of the manner in which UN human rights treaty bodies in their General Comments, as well as the theory of rights-based approaches, as discussed earlier, are informing contemporary understanding of the State's implementation obligation.[34]

§9.4 Domestic Violence

How is domestic violence different in queer communities? Further, how is it different in transgender communities?

Domestic violence is not a fun topic. It doesn't warm the heart. It is a bit scary, and sometimes, it happens in our own homes. Many people like to think of violence as something that happens "out there" to others.[35]

Transgender people are the targets of the most vicious and blatant forms of violence. They are routinely abused by the police and medical professionals, in addition to being subjected to random street violence and domestic partner abuse. Intimate partners, often appalled to discover the gender transgression, can verbally, psychologically, physically and sexually abuse the person.[36]

---

34. *Id.* at 231–235.

35. Rich Jentzen, *Domestic Violence within our Community, For Ourselves: Reworking Gender Expression* (October 15, 1999), http://www.forge-forward.org/newsletters/pdf/9911-DV-news.pdf (last visited July 30, 2011).

36. Arlene Istar Lev and S. Sundance Lev, *Sexual Assault in the Transgendered Communities, For Ourselves: Reworking Gender Expression* (October 15, 1999), http://www.forge-forward.org/newsletters/pdf/9911-DV-news.pdf (last visited July 30, 2011).

Societal discomfort with transgenderism has rendered transgender victims of sexual assault, gay bashing, and domestic violence without necessary services. Not all rape crisis centers and domestic violence shelters are prepared to address the issues of transgender people. Medical personnel respond with prejudice and have been known to withhold care to people they perceive to be cross-dressing. The criminal justice and the phobic bigotry, like racist violence, allow us to falsely identify the victims of violence as the provocateurs of the violence. As transgender advocate Dallas Denny said, "Despite the fact that they are much more often victims of violence than they are perpetrators, transgendered persons are frequently portrayed in the media as psychotics and criminals."[37] Given the virulent violence against transgender people by the police, this is especially ironic.

Transgender people are often sexually targeted specifically because of their transgender status. The sexual perpetrator will stalk them, or attack them, infuriated by their cross-gender behavior.

Definition: LGBTQ = Lesbian, gay, bisexual, transgender, and queer, which is an all-encompassing term of art in literature on the subject.

The term *queer* has been reclaimed in a positive way to reflect the diversity of sexual and gender identities, which can include transgender people, intersex people, genderqueers, and people who consider themselves heterosexual and engage in same-sex sex even though they do not identify as bisexual or gay.

It has been difficult to determine the prevalence of this form of abuse. The issue of LGBTQ partner violence has been difficult to research because of the larger homophobic, biphobic, transphobic, and heterosexist context. Most LGBTQ violence is not reported to the police or to mainstream crisis organizations.[38] Lesbians, gay men, bisexuals, transgender and queer

---

37. Dallas Denny, *Violence against transgendered persons: An unrecognized problem*, THE ADVOCATE (April 1992). *See also Sexual Assault in the Lesbian, Gay, Bisexual and Transgendered Communities*, J.C. McClennen & J. Gunther, eds., Same-sex partner abuse: A professional's guide to practice intervention (Mellen Press 1999).

38. *See, e.g.*, Patricia Tjaden and Nancy Thoennes (November 1998), Prevalence, incidence, and consequences of violence against women: Findings from the National Violence Against Women Survey (NCJ 172837), Washington, DC: National Institute of Justice/Centers for Disease Control and Prevention; Tarynn M. Witten and A. Evan Eyler (1999), *Hate crimes and violence against the Transgendered*, 11 PEACE REVIEW: A JOURNAL OF SOCIAL JUSTICE 461–468; and Rebecca L. Stotzer (May-June 2009), *Violence against transgender people: A review of United States data*, 14 AGGRESSION AND VIOLENT BEHAVIOR 170–179.

people may be reluctant to report abuse because they do not want to be seen as betraying the LGBTQ community, or they may be concerned with homophobic or transphobic responses. Thus statistics from official sources are likely to indicate very minimal levels of violence. Many large-scale studies on domestic violence have not included gays and lesbians or even considered the experiences of transgender, intersex, bisexual, or queer people.

I address LGBTQ partner or domestic violence because transgender domestic violence is an understudied area so far, but it shares many of the same dynamics as lesbian and gay domestic violence.

Violence in LGBTQ relationships may be referred to as partner violence, relationship violence, or same-sex/same-gender domestic violence. The term *domestic violence*, however, has been most strongly associated with heterosexual relationships and assumes certain gendered roles (male batterers, female victims). Therefore, it can work against acknowledging violence that occurs in same-sex/same-gender relationships. It is a term that some members of LGBTQ communities cannot relate to because of these roles. However, some researchers and LGBTQ groups continue to use the term *domestic violence* to draw parallels to and make comparisons with heterosexual domestic violence.

Like heterosexual domestic violence, violence in LGBTQ relationships involves the conscious manipulation and control of one person by another through the use of threats, coercion, humiliation, or force. LGBTQ partner violence can take many of the same forms as heterosexual domestic violence. For example, physical abuse can include actions such as hitting, punching, slapping, biting, restraining, and pushing. Sexual abuse may involve forcing someone to have sex against their will, raping someone with an object or weapon, or making demeaning sexual comments. Emotional abuse can include manipulation, isolation, humiliation, lying, threats to kill, threats to commit suicide, racial attacks, and intimidation. Verbal abuse may consist of insults, name-calling, and yelling. Financial abuse may also be part of the dynamic when one person creates debts, steals money, or uses money to control another person. The violence can also be lethal.

Domestic violence victims often feel no one will understand their problem, will not understand why they did not leave sooner, why they did not call police sooner, and so on. Transgender persons who suffer domestic violence have those same feelings, *plus* the added factor of why a "guy wearing a dress" does not fight back (the same thing that is said to gay men who are domestic violence victims).

Finally, when considering violence in LGTBQ relationships it is also important to recognize the larger backdrop of violence and oppression in many LGBTQ people's lives. For many people, domestic violence is just one form of violence that they have experienced.

> Statistical research for violence towards the transgendered population is still in its infancy. The preliminary data of transgendered and intersexed individuals gathered by the Gender, Violence, and Resource Access Survey found that 50% of respondents had been raped or assaulted by a romantic partner (Courvant and Cook-Daniels, 1998). Eyler and Witten (1999) have begun a longitudinal study of violence against the transgendered community, and the preliminary data clearly show physical and sexual violence perpetrated on those who express cross-gender behavior. Our transphobic bigotry, like racist violence, allows us to falsely identify the victims of violence as the provocateurs of violence.
>
> . . .
>
> Our societal discomfort with transgenderedism, has rendered transgendered victims of sexual assault, gay-bashing, and domestic violence without necessary services. Rape Crisis Centers and domestic violence shelters are unprepared to address the issues of transgendered people. Medical personnel respond with judgment and have been known to withhold care to people they perceive to be cross-dressing. The criminal justice and the legal systems often re-traumatize victims. The complexity of issues facing the transgendered person who is sexually assaulted can only be addressed by broad changes in the delivery system and extensive education regarding the needs of this community.[39]

---

39. Arlene Istar Lev & S. Sundance Lev, *Sexual Assault in the Transgendered Communities, For Ourselves: Reworking Gender Expression* (October 15, 1999), http://www.forge-forward. org/newsletters/pdf/9911-DV-news.pdf (last visited July 30, 2011).

The Violence Against Women Act of 1994[40] was amended by the Violence Against Women Reauthorization Act of 2013[41] to provide coverage to lesbians and MtF transgender persons. Of course, federal legislation like this may or not apply at the local level. And, whether by statutory definition or by policy or simply practice of the local courts and/or police, state domestic violence laws may or may not apply to lesbians and MtF transgender persons.

The passage in 2014 of legislation including LGBTQ communities under the Violence Against Women Act is a landmark victory. But there is still no general mandate for all states to fund LGBTQ programming, and LGBTQ and HIV-affected communities still face larger barriers in accessing shelter and services. Intersections of race, class, and other marginalized identities exacerbate inaccessibility. A 2013 report by the Williams Institute found that 7.6 percent of lesbian couples, compared with 5.7 percent of married different-sex couples, are in poverty. African American same-sex couples have poverty rates more than twice the rate of different-sex couples. The National Center on Transgender Equality found that transgender people experience poverty at twice the national rates and that transgender people of color experience poverty at four times the national rates.[42] LGBTQ people may be nearly twice as likely to experience Inter Personal Violence (IPV) as non-LGBTQ people, but bisexual people are nearly twice as likely to experience IPV as those identified as gay or lesbian.[43] Transgender people are at much higher risk for IPV and sexual violence than non transgender people.[44] This high rate of violence is exacerbated by institutional discrimination in service provision. In a landmark 2010 study by NCAVP and the National Center for Victims of Crime, surveying 648 domestic violence agencies, sexual assault centers, prosecutors' offices, law enforcement agencies, and child victim services, 94 percent of respondents said they were not serving

---

40. Pub. L. No. 103-322, 108 Stat. 1902 *et seq.*

41. Pub. L. No. 113-4.

42. Grant, Jaime M., Lisa A. Mottet, Justin Tanis, Jack Harrison, Jody L. Herman, and Mara Keisling. (2011) *Injustice at Every Turn: A Report of theNational Transgender Discrimination Survey,* http://www.thetaskforce.org/downloads/reports/reports/ntds_full.pdf (last visited August 21, 2013).

43. Zahnd, E. G., Grant, D., Aydin, M., Chia, Y. J., & Padilla-Frausto, D. I. (2010) *Nearly four million California adults are victims of intimate partner violence.* Los Angeles: UCLA Center for Health Policy Research.

44. Stotzer, Rebecca. (2009). Violence against transgender people: A review of United States data. *Aggression and Violent Behavior, 14,* 170–179.

LGBTQ survivors of IPV and sexual violence.[45] Lambda Legal has reported that overall, LGBTQ survivors of IPV are reluctant to seek services utilized by heterosexual women such as law enforcement or victim services due to the perceived risk of re-victimization.[46,47]

Individual stories about transgender victims of domestic violence are difficult to find, but one such story follows.

> Claudia is an African-American male-to-female transsexual woman who was sexually molested before her transition by her then wife. When Maria returned home early one evening and discovered Claudia dressed in female clothes, she flew into a rage. She began beating Claudia, cursing, and calling her sexually abusive names. Claudia was ashamed to have been caught, and passively accepted this behavior. This infuriated Maria even more, who began sexually molesting Claudia, while degrading both her feminine appearance, and her masculine body. Maria raped Claudia and then left the marriage.[48]

Traditional opposite sex domestic violence has the same cyclic characteristics as LGBTQ or even just transgender domestic violence. The current understanding of abuse, represented by the Power and Control Wheel, evolved out of many discussions with battered women and batterers through the Domestic Abuse Intervention Project in Duluth, Minnesota.

---

45. National Center for Victims of Crime and NCAVP, *Why It Matters: Rethinking Victim Assistance for Lesbian, Gay, Bisexual, Transgender, and Queer Victims of Hate Violence & Intimate Partner Violence*, http://www.avp.org/documents/WhyItMatters.pdf (last visited July 12, 2013).

46. Davidson, Meghan M. and Alysondra Duke. "Same-Sex Intimate Partner Violence: Lesbian, Gay, and Bisexual Affirmative Outreach and Advocacy." *Journal of Aggression, Maltreatment & Trauma*. 18: 795–816, 2009.

47. *National Coalition of Anti-Violence Programs* (2014) 2013 Report on Lesbian, Gay, Bisexual, Transgender and HIV-Affected Hate Violence (©New York Gay and Lesbian Anti-Violence Project, Inc.), p. 14.

48. Arlene Istar Lev & S. Sundance Lev, *Transgendered Victims of Sexual Assault*, SAME-SEX PARTNER ABUSE: A PROFESSIONAL'S GUIDE TO PRACTICE INTERVENTION, J.C. McClennen & J. Gunther, eds. (1999 Mellen Press).

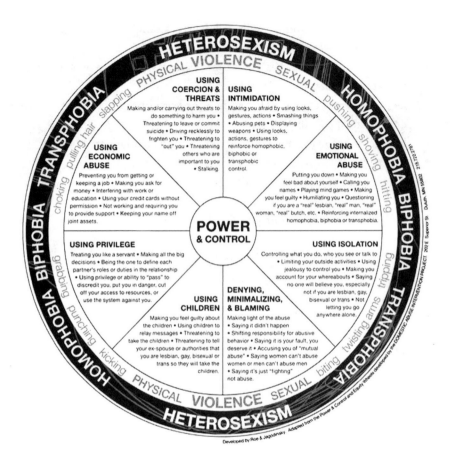

Power and Control Wheel

Tactics used against transgender victims

- Using pronouns not preferred by you or calling you "it"
- Calling you pejorative names
- Ridiculing how your body looks
- Telling you that you are not a real man/woman
- Telling you that nobody would believe you because "you're transgendered"
- Ridiculing or belittling your identity as a bisexual, trans, femme, butch, genderqueer

- Claiming they are more "politically correct" and using their status as an L, G, B, and/or T person against you
- Claiming they know what's best for you, how you should dress or wear makeup (or not), etc.
- Denying access to medical treatment or hormones or coercing you to not pursue medical treatment
- Hiding or throwing away hormones, binders, clothes, etc.
- Eroticizing/fetishizing your body against your will
- Touching body parts you don't want touched, or calling them by terms they know you find offensive
- Telling you they thought you liked "rough sex" or "this is how real men/women like sex"
- Telling you that nobody will ever love you
- Telling you that you don't deserve better and/or would never find a better partner
- Threatening to "out" you to your employer, friends, or family members
- Negating your personal decisions
- Threatening to take the children or turn them against you
- Forbidding you to talk to others about transgender topics

Tactics used by transgender abusers
- Claiming they are just being "butch" or that "it's the hormones" (to explain their violent behavior)
- Ridiculing or belittling your identity as a bisexual, trans, femme, butch, genderqueer
- Claiming that your identity "undermines" or is "disrespectful" of theirs
- Charging you with "not being supportive" if you ask to discuss questions of transitioning timing and/or expense
- Denying that you are affected by the transition or by being partnered with a trans person
- Accusing you of not allowing her to have a "proper adolescence"
- Forbidding you to talk to others about transgender topics
- Telling you that you would harm the L, G, B, and/or T community if you exposed what was happening
- Negating your personal decisions

- Claiming they are more "politically correct" and using their status as an L, G, B, and/or T person against you[49]

Below is advice to those concerned about domestic violence in the LGBT context, including "Red Flags."

"Red Flags" of a Battering Personality

If you are uncertain whether your partner is abusive or if you want to be able to tell at the beginning of the relationship if the other person has the potential to become abusive, there are behaviors you can look for, including the following:

1. **JEALOUSY:** An abuser will always say that jealousy is a sign of love. Jealousy has nothing to do with love; it's a sign of possessiveness and lack of trust. In a healthy relationship, the partners trust each other unless one of them has legitimately done something to break that trust.

2. **CONTROLLING BEHAVIOR:** At first, the batterer will say this behavior is because they are concerned for your safety, a need for you to use time well or to make good decisions. Abusers will be angry if you are "late" coming back from the store or an appointment; you will be questioned closely about where you went, who you talked to. As this behavior gets worse, the abuser may not let you make personal decisions about the house, your clothing, or going to church. They may keep all the money; or may make you ask permission to leave the house or room.

3. **QUICK INVOLVEMENT:** Many domestic violence victims only knew their abuser for a few months before they were living together. The abuser may come on like a whirlwind, claiming "you're the only person I could ever talk to" and "I've never felt loved like this by anyone." Abusers are generally very charming at the beginning of the relationship. You will be pressured to commit in such a way that later you may feel very guilty if you want to slow down involvement or break up. If you are newly out, be careful; abusers often target those they know are new

---

49. FORGE: For Ourselves: Reworking Gender Expression, *Transgendered/SOFFA: Domestic Violence/Sexual Assault Resource Sheet.*

to the GLBT community because it is a time when you are vulnerable and may not know very many people in the community.

4. **UNREALISTIC EXPECTATIONS:** Abusive people will expect their partner to meet all their needs: the perfect partner, lover, and friend. They say things like "if you love me, I'm all you need and you're all I need." You are supposed to take care of everything for them; emotionally, physically, and sometimes economically.

5. **ISOLATION:** The abusive person tries to cut the partner off from all resources. If you have same-sex friends, you are a "whore," a "slut," or "cheating." If you are close to family, you're "tied to the apron strings." The abuser will accuse people who are supportive of causing trouble and may restrict use of the phone. They will gradually isolate you from all of your friends. They may not let you use a car (or have one that is reliable) and may try to keep you from working or going to school. Some abusers will try to get you into legal trouble so that you are afraid to drive or go out.

6. **BLAMES OTHERS FOR PROBLEMS:** If your partner is chronically unemployed, someone is always doing them wrong or is out to get them. They may make mistakes and then blame you for upsetting them so that they can't concentrate on their work. They will tell you that you are at fault for almost anything that goes wrong.

7. **BLAMES OTHERS FOR FEELINGS:** Abusive people will tell you, "you made me mad" and "I can't help being angry." Although they actually make the decision about how they think or feel, they will use feelings to manipulate you. Abusers see themselves as the "victim" in the relationship and do not take responsibility for their own feelings or behaviors.

8. **HYPERSENSITIVITY:** Abusers are easily insulted and may take the slightest setback as a personal attack. They will rant and rave about the injustice of things that are really just a part of living, such as having to get up for work, getting a traffic ticket, or being asked to help with chores.

9. **CRUELTY TO ANIMALS OR CHILDREN:** This is a person who punishes animals brutally or is insensitive to their pain. They may expect children to be capable of things beyond their ability. They may tease children and younger brothers and sisters until they cry. They may be

very critical of other people's children or any children you bring into the relationship. Your partner may threaten to prevent you from seeing children you have no biological rights to, or punish children to get even with you. About 60% of people who beat their partner also beat their children.

10. **"PLAYFUL" USE OF FORCE IN SEX:** This kind of person may like to act out fantasies where the partner is helpless. They let you know that the idea of rape is exciting. They may show little concern about whether you want to have sex, and use sulking or anger to manipulate you. They may start having sex with you while you are sleeping, or demand sex when you are ill or tired. They may want to "make up" by having sex after they have just been physically or verbally abusive to you.

11. **VERBAL ABUSE:** In addition to saying things that are meant to be cruel, this can be seen when the abuser degrades or curses you, belittling any of your accomplishments. They may accuse you of not being a "real" lesbian or gay man. If you aren't out, they may threaten to out you to family members or your employer. The abuser will tell you that you are stupid and unable to function without them. They may wake you up to verbally abuse you, or not let you go to sleep.

12. **RIGID SEX ROLES:** Abusers expect the partner to play the "female" role, to serve them, and insist that you obey them in all things. The abuser sees you as unintelligent, inferior, responsible for menial tasks, and less than whole without the relationship. They will often tell you that no one else would want you or that you are nothing without them. They will remind you of everything they have done for you.

13. **DR. JEKYLL AND MR. HYDE:** Many victims are confused by their abuser's sudden changes in mood and may think it indicates a special mental problem. Abusers may be nice one minute and explode the next. Explosiveness and moodiness are typical of people who beat their partners. Many victims feel if their partner would just quit drinking or using drugs, the violence would stop. This is usually not the case. Abusive people continue the abuse, even after they stop using alcohol or drugs, unless they also seek help for their abusive behavior.

14. **PAST BATTERING:** These people say they have hit a partner in the past, but the previous partner made them do it. You may hear from

relatives or ex partners that the person has been abusive. A batterer will beat any person they are with if they are with that person long enough for violence to begin; situational circumstances do not make a person an abusive personality.

15. **THREATS OF VIOLENCE:** This could include any threat of physical force meant to control you: "I'll slap your mouth off," "I'll kill you," "I'll break your neck." Most people do not threaten their mates, but a batterer will say "everyone talks like that," or "it didn't mean anything."

16. **BREAKING OR STRIKING OBJECTS:** This behavior is used as a punishment (breaking loved possessions) but is used mostly to terrorize you into submission. The abuser may beat on the table with their fist or throw objects around. This is not only a sign of extreme emotional immaturity but indicates great danger when someone thinks they have the "right" to punish or frighten their partner.

17. **ANY FORCE DURING AN ARGUMENT:** A batterer may hold you down, restrain you from leaving the room, push you, or shove you. They may pin you to the wall, saying, "You're going to listen to me!"

What to Do If You Are a Victim of Domestic Violence

It can be extremely difficult for GLBT victims to admit that domestic violence is an issue in their relationship. Even once they have admitted to themselves that there is a problem, they are often at a loss at where to turn to for help. They may be fearful of receiving a homophobic response from those they seek assistance from.

In most states, domestic violence shelters at least train their staff to be sensitive to GLBT issues when working with victims of domestic violence. In larger cities, there are often domestic violence shelters just for GLBT victims.

Call your local domestic violence shelter and ask what services they offer to GLBT clients. If you aren't satisfied with what they offer, ask for a referral to a domestic violence shelter in the largest city near you.

Also, you don't have to out yourself in order to get help if you choose not to. The fact that you are a victim of domestic violence is enough for you to receive assistance. Do what you need to do to feel safe. Domestic violence advocates and counselors know that you have already been through a lot and won't pressure you to answer questions you don't want to answer about the name or gender of your abuser.

Please don't give up in reaching out for help. Even in small towns, it is possible for you to find help from people sensitive to GLBT clients.[50]

Service Impacts on Trans/SOFFA Clients

Transgender people and significant other, friends, families, and allies (SOF-FAs) who have been abused have fewer services available to them.

- Many transgender/SOFFA individuals do not want to challenge the myth of community nonviolence.
- As an already oppressed minority, trans+/SOFFAs are often hesitant to address issues that many fear will further "taint" the community. The LGBT community often wonders why they need to take on this issue as well as the others facing the community.
- The "battered women's" movement often avoids the fact that women batter, and men are victims. The pervasiveness of this myth has led police, hospital workers, and people in the criminal justice system to deny male victims or female perpetrators. (This is further "muddied" when people are not clearly "male" or "female.")
- Transgender and SOFFA individuals may be cautious in approaching medical providers, police, or the courts due to past experiences related to gender. These individuals may fear revictimization through transphobia, degradation, hostility, or accusations from these service providers/public safety workers.
- Shelters are typically "male-" or "female"-only. Transgender people and SOFFAs may not be allowed entrance into shelters or emergency housing facilities due to their gender/genital/legal status.
- Because transness is eroticized and sexualized, many providers believe that S&M is a common practice among transgendered people. The belief that all trans+ people want to be objectified and abused, totally denies the prevalence of DV in relationships involving a trans person.
- Even in larger cities, service providers who specifically outreach to transgendered/SOFFA people may be limited. Many victims fear losing their privacy or not being able to maintain anonymity within care settings.

---

50. *Gay, Lesbian, Bisexual and Transgendered Domestic Violence*, http://www.rainbow-domesticviolence.itgo.com/ (last visited August 6, 2011).

- There have been many custody cases lately involving trans+ people. The risk of losing custody of a child might influence a trans+ or SOFFA individual from coming forward about abusive behavior.
- The isolation that accompanies domestic violence can be compounded by being trans or in a relationship with a trans+ partner in a transphobic society. Silence about domestic violence within the trans+/SOFFA community further isolates the victim, giving more[51]

---

51. FORGE: For Ourselves: Reworking Gender Expression, *Transgendered/SOFFA: Domestic Violence / Sexual Assault Resource Sheet.*

CHAPTER 10

Employment

§10.1 The Research Studies

Like violence against transgender persons, employment discrimination against transgender persons is pervasive. A study conducted between 1996 and 1997 found that 37 percent of transgender individuals surveyed had experienced employment discrimination.[1] In 2009, a National Transgendered Discrimination Survey found:

- **Double the rate of unemployment:** Survey respondents experience unemployment at twice the rate of the population as a whole.
- **Near universal harassment on the job:** Ninety-seven percent of those surveyed reported experiencing harassment or mistreatment on the job.
- **Significant losses of jobs and careers:** Forty-seven percent had experienced an adverse job outcome, such as being fired, not hired, or denied a promotion.

---

1. Emilia L. Lombardi, Riki Anne Wilchins, Dana Priesing & Diana Malouf, *Gender Violence: Transgendered Experiences with Violence and Discrimination*, 42 J. OF HOMOSEXUALITY 89 (2001).

- **High rates of poverty:** Fifteen percent of transgender people in the sample lived on $10,000 per year or less—double the rate of the general population.
- **Significant housing instability:** Nineteen percent of the sample have been or are homeless, 11 percent have faced eviction, and 26 percent were forced to seek temporary space.[2]

In another report in 2011, the Williams Institute reported even larger numbers regarding discrimination against transgender persons. When surveyed separately, transgender respondents report even higher rates of employment discrimination and harassment than LGB people.

- As recently as 2011, 78 percent of respondents to the largest survey of transgender people to date reported experiencing at least one form of harassment or mistreatment at work because of their gender identity; more specifically, 47 percent had been discriminated against in hiring, promotion, or job retention.
- Consistently, 70 percent of transgender respondents to a 2009 California survey and 67 percent of transgender respondents to a 2010 Utah survey reported experiencing employment discrimination because of their gender identity.[3]

The following table from the Williams Institute study is eye opening.

2. National Center for Transgendered Equality and the National Gay and Lesbian Task Force, *National Transgendered Discrimination Survey* (November 2009) at http://transequality.org/Resources/NCTE_prelim_survey_econ.pdf (last visited July 31, 2011).

3. Brad Sears & Christy Mallory, *Documented Evidence of Employment Discrimination & Its Effects on LGBT People*, 7–8, THE WILLIAMS INSTITUTE OF THE U.C.L.A. SCHOOL OF LAW (July 2011).

Results of Recent Non-probability Surveys Measuring Employment Discrimination against Transgender People (2005–2010)[4]

Study	Year(s) Data Collected	Population	Method	% Reporting Discrimination/ Harassment
Transgendered Law Center (2009)	2005	Transgendered people in California (n = 646)	Non-probability sample	70% over the lifetime
One Colorado (2010)	2010	LGBT people in Colorado (n = 4,600)	Non-probability sample	52% over the lifetime (transgendered only)
Rosky, C., *et al.* (2011)	2010	Transgendered People in Utah (n = 27)	Non-probability sample	67% over the lifetime
Grant, J., *et al.* (2011)	2008–2009	Transgendered People in U.S. (n = 6,450)	Non-probability sample	78% had experienced at least one form of harassment or mistreatment; 47% discriminated against in hiring, promotion, or job retention
Herman, J. (2011)	2008–2009	Transgendered people in Massachusetts	Non-probability sample	76% over the lifetime

§10.2 States with Nondiscrimination Statutes That Include Gender Identity

Seventeen states and the District of Columbia ban discrimination in employment on the basis of gender identity or gender expression.

1. California[5]
2. Colorado[6]

---

4. *Id.*
5. CAL. GOV. CODE §§ 12926 and 12949.
6. COLO. REV. STAT. § 24-34-401, 402.

3. Connecticut[7]
4. District of Columbia[8]
5. Hawaii[9]
6. Illinois[10]
7. Iowa[11]
8. Maine[12]
9. Massachusetts[13]
10. Minnesota[14]
11. New Hampshire[15]
12. New Cities and Nondiscrimination Ordinances Jersey[16]
13. New Mexico[17]
14. Oregon[18]
15. Rhode Island[19]
16. Vermont[20]
17. Washington[21]
18. Massachusetts[22]

---

7. CONN. GEN. STAT. § 46a-81c to m.

8. D.C. CODE §§2-1401.01, 2-1401.02, and §§2-1402.11, 2-1402.21, 2-1402.31, 2-1402.41, 2-1402.71, and 2-1402.73.

9. HAW. REV. STAT. § 368-1, *et seq.*

10. 775 ILL. COMP. STAT. 5/1-102 and 5/1-103.

11. IOWA CODE §§216.2 and 216.6.

12. ME. REV. STAT. ANN. tit. 5 §4553 and §4571.

13. MASS. GEN. LAWS ANN. ch. 151B, §§ 1 and 4. While gender identity is not explicitly included in the state's anti-discrimination law, several courts and the state Commission Against Discrimination have ruled that transgendered individuals can pursue an anti-discrimination claim under the category of sex or disability discrimination. Jette v. Honey Farms Mini Market, 2001 Mass. Comm. Discrim. LEXIS 50 (Mass. Comm. Against Discrimination 2001).

14. MINN. STAT. §363A.01 to §363A.41.

15. N.H. REV. STAT. ANN. § 354-A:1 (2002). While gender identity is not explicitly included in the state's anti-discrimination law, the New Hampshire Superior Court ruled that transgendered individuals can pursue an anti-discrimination claim under the law's disability discrimination category. Jane Doe v. Electro-Craft Corp., 1988 WL 1091932 (N.H. Super. Ct. 1988).

16. N.J. STAT. ANN. § 10:2-1, § 10:5-1-49.

17. N.M. STAT. ANN. §§ 28-1-2, 7, 9.

18. ORE. REV. STAT. ANN. § 659A.004.

19. R.I. GEN. LAWS § 28-5-3, § 28-5-7, § 34-37-4, § 34-37-4.3, § 11-24-2.

20. VT. STAT. ANN. tit. 21 § 495, tit. 9 § 4503, tit. 8 § 10403, § 4724, tit. 3 § 963.

21. WASH. REV. CODE §§ 49.60.130–175, 176, 178, 180, 190, 200, 215, 222–225, 300; WASH. ADMIN. CODE § 356-09-020.

22. Mass. Bill H.3810 (enacted November 16, 2011), amending MASS. GEN. LAWS, Ch. 4, § 7 (effective July 1, 2012).

§10.3 Counties with or Laws That Include Gender Identity

At least 120 cities and counties in twenty-six states prohibit employment discrimination on the basis of gender identity in employment ordinances that govern all public and private employers in those jurisdictions. Some of those cities and counties that prohibit discrimination on the basis of gender identity do so only for city and county employees, companies that contract with the city or county, or vendors to the city or county. Those cities and counties are shown in Appendix 7, "Cities and Counties with Employment Nondiscrimination Ordinances That Include Gender Identity or Expression." If you are or your client is in one of those locales and suffers discrimination, go online and find the jurisdiction's codified laws or ordinances or go down to the city hall or other government building and ask to see them and get a copy.

§10.4 Federal Employment Nondiscrimination Laws

There are three basic federal discrimination laws that might apply to employment discrimination against transgender persons. These are the Americans with Disabilities Act,[23] the Civil Rights Act of 1871,[24] and Title VII of the Civil Rights Act of 1964.[25] They are discussed separately below. For federal employees and employees of companies with contracts with the federal government, there is no federal statute other than the interpretations of Title VII, except Executive Orders. On July 21, 2014, President Obama signed an Executive Order[26] (E.O.), which amended E.O. 11478, Equal Employment Opportunity In The Federal Government, and E.O. 11246, Equal Employment Opportunity by substituting "sexual orientation, gender identity" for "sexual orientation" in E.O. 11478 and by substituting "sex, sexual orientation, gender identity, or national origin" for "sex, or national origin" in

---

23. 42 U.S.C.A § 12101, *et seq.*
24. 42 U.S.C.A. § 1983. *See* Smith v. City of Salem, 378 F.3d 566 (6th Cir. 2004) (recognizing that allegations by a city fire department employee, who was born male and subsequently was diagnosed with gender identity disorder, that employee who alleged that he had been discriminated against based upon his gender non-conforming behavior and appearance, sufficiently alleged a claim of sex discrimination grounded in the Equal Protection Clause of the 14th Amendment under 42 U.S.C. § 1983), and Kastl v. Maricopa County Community College Dist., not reported in F.Supp.2d, 2004 WL 2008954 (D. Ariz. 2004) (denying Rule 12(b)(6) motion to dismiss transgender plaintiff's claims under Title VII and 42 U.S.C. § 1983).
25. 42 U.S.C.A § 2000e, *et seq.*
26. E.O. 13672, 79 Fed.Reg. 42971, 2014 WL 3591762 (July 21, 2014).

E.O. 11246. This change only applies to federal agencies and to companies
with contracts with the federal government.

§10.4(a) Americans with Disabilities Act

To address the issue so far, the courts have uniformly held that the Americans with Disabilities Act[27] does not apply to persons with gender identity
disorder because the act states in relevant part: "Under this chapter, the term
'disability' shall not include . . . [t]ransvestism, transsexualism, pedophilia,
exhibitionism, voyeurism, gender identity disorders not resulting from physical impairments, or other sexual behavior disorders."[28] Most transgender
persons are glad that we are not classified as "disabled." Although because
we have so few protections from employment discrimination, we are as a
practical matter disabled in that we are shut out of the job market without
recourse. It should be noted that the exclusion by the federal law has not
been adopted by the states with similar laws. In one Connecticut case, the
court found that a transsexual city employee had a chronic physical disability and was physically disabled under the Connecticut Commission on
Human Rights and Opportunities statutes. Thus the employee's claim of
discrimination based on her physical disability of being transsexual was a
cognizable claim under the statutes. The employee was prescribed medication before her surgery, continued to take the medications post-surgery, and
would be under the care of a physician for the rest of her life. A "chronic
physical handicap" was considered, by universal dictionary definition, one
that was marked by long duration and not acute. The fact that one could
not detect a physical disability by observing the employee was irrelevant.[29]
Also, a New York court held that the gender identity disorder condition of
a resident of a foster care facility was a "disability" within the meaning of

---

27. 42 U.S.C.A § 12101, *et seq.*
28. 42 U.S.C.A § 12211(b)(1). *See also* 49 C.F.R. § 39.3(5)(i), 49 C.F.R. § 37.3(5)(i), 41
C.F.R. § 60–741.3(e)(1), 29 C.F.R. § 1630.3(d)(1), 29 C.F.R. § 37.4(1)(i), 29 C.F.R. § 34.2(1)
(i), 28 C.F.R. § 36.104(5)(i), and 28 C.F.R. § 35.104(5)(i). *See* Johnson v. Fresh Mark, Inc.,
337 F. Supp. 2d 996 (N.D. Ohio 2003), Oiler v. Winn-Dixie Louisiana, Inc., not reported in
F.Supp.2d, 2002 WL 31098541 (E.D. La. 2002), and Doe v. United Consumer Financial Services, 2001 WL 34350174 (N.D. Ohio 2001).
29. CONN. GEN. STAT. ANN. § 46a-60 and Commission on Human Rights & Opportunities v. City of Hartford, 2010 WL 4612700, 50 Conn. L. Rptr. 750 (Conn. Super. 2010).

the Human Rights Law in that the condition was clinically diagnosed by physicians using medically accepted standards.[30]

§10.4(b) Title VII of the Civil Rights Act of 1964

The application of the ban on sex discrimination under Title VII of the Civil Rights Act of 1964[31] to employment discrimination against transgender persons has been uneven. The cases that have had success in asserting Title VII claims for sex discrimination on behalf of transgender persons have been able to do so using a theory or argument that discrimination against transgender persons is because of sex stereotyping, which the U.S. Supreme Court held was a form of sex discrimination in the landmark case of *Price Waterhouse v. Hopkins*.[32] This approach has been the subject of several scholarly articles.[33]

However, citing *Price Waterhouse v. Hopkins*, the Equal Employment Opportunity Commission has determined that gender identity discrimination is cognizable under Title VII:

Complainant filed an appeal concerning her equal employment opportunity (EEO) complaint alleging employment discrimination in violation of Title VII of the Civil Rights Act of 1964 (Title VII), as amended, 42 U.S.C. § 20003, et seq. For the following reasons, the Commission finds that the Complainant's complaint of discrimination based on gender identity, change of sex, and/or transgender status is cognizable under Title VII and remands the complaint to the Agency for further processing.

. . .

Thus, we conclude that intentional discrimination against a transgender individual because that person is transgender is, by definition,

---

30. N.Y. Exec. L. §§ 292 and 296. Doe v. Bell, 194 Misc. 2d 774, 754 N.Y.S.2d 846 (N.Y. Sup. Ct. N.Y. County 2003).

31. 42 U.S.C.A § 2000e, *et seq.*

32. Price Waterhouse v. Hopkins, 490 U.S. 228, 109 S. Ct. 1775, 104 L.Ed. 2d 268 (1989).

33. *See, e.g.,* Amanda S. Eno, *The Misconception of "Sex" in Title VII: Federal Courts Reevaluate Transsexual Employment Discrimination Claims,* 43 Tulsa L. Rev. 765 (2008); Ilona M. Turner, *Sex Stereotyping Per Se: Transgendered Employees and Title VII,* 95 Cal. L. Rev. 561 (2007); and James D. Esseks, *Sex Stereotyping Claims Brought by Lesbian, Gay, Bisexual, or Transgendered Plaintiffs,* 799 PLI/Lit 529 (Practising Law Institute 2009).

discrimination "based on . . . sex," and such discrimination therefore violates Title VII.[34]

The U.S. Courts of Appeals and District Courts that have recognized and accepted sex stereotyping as enunciated in *Price Waterhouse v. Hopkins* as a basis for applying Title VII to transgender persons' claims of employment discrimination are shown in the list below. If the court has recognized a sex-stereotyping claim under Title VII, the term *Recognized* is used beside the court, and a footnote gives the citation and some information about the case. If the court has not recognized a sex-stereotyping claim under Title VII, the term *Not Recognized* is used beside the court, and a footnote gives the citation and some information about the case. If there is no notation at all, that particular court has not addressed the issue. There is disagreement between the circuits on this issue, and in a few, there is even disagreement between the district courts in the circuit.

- U.S. Court of Appeals for the First Circuit
- U.S. District Court for the District of
  - Maine
  - Massachusetts—Recognized[35]
  - New Hampshire—Recognized[36]
  - Puerto Rico—Recognized as to a straight woman[37]
  - Rhode Island

---

34. Macy v. Holder, E.E.O.C. Dec. 0120120821, 2012 WL 1435995, at 1 and 11 (April 20, 2012). The same result was reached in Hart v. Lew, 973 F.Supp.2d 561, 97 Empl. Prac. Dec. ¶ 44,920 (D. Md. 2013), which involved an I.R.S. employee (complaint stated a claim for sex discrimination under Title VII, where complaint alleged that supervisors made improper remarks or took improper actions on the basis of employee's sex, that these incidents were motivated by animus or discomfort with employee's status as transsexual or with her status as female).

35. Centola v. Potter, 183 F. Supp. 2d 403 (D. Mass. 2002) (denying summary judgment) and Ianetta v. Putnam Invs., Inc., 142 F. Supp. 2d 131 (D. Mass. 2001) (recognized claim but found that employer nevertheless had a legitimate reason for termination).

36. Bilunas v. Henderson, not reported in F.Supp.2d, 2000 WL 639329 (D. N.H. 2000) (denying summary judgment).

37. Vargas Caban v. Caribbean Transp. Services, not reported in F.Supp.2d, 2005 WL 3560689 (D. Puerto Rico 2005) ("The [Supreme] Court had also previously determined that a sexual harassment claim could exist if the employee was harassed for not complying with socialized gender expectations ('sex stereotyping')").

- U.S. Court of Appeals for the Second Circuit—Recognized as to gays and lesbians[38] and as to a straight man and woman[39]
- U.S. District Court for the District of
  - Connecticut
  - New York—Recognized[40]
  - Vermont
- U.S. Court of Appeals for the Third Circuit—Recognized as to a gay man[41]

---

38. *See* Dawson v. Bumble & Bumble, 398 F.3d 211, 218 (2nd Cir. 2005) (gay employee "may have claim" but court nevertheless expressed concern that a "gender stereotyping claim" should not be used to "bootstrap protection for sexual orientation into Title VII."); and Zalewska v. County of Sullivan, 316 F.3d 314 (2nd Cir. 2003) (forcing female employee to wear pants—court found no discriminatory intent existed with respect to the challenged policy, but nonetheless noted that discrimination based on a failure to conform to gender norms was prohibited by the Equal Protection Clause).

39. Miller v. City of New York, 177 Fed. Appx. 195 (2nd Cir. 2006) (holding that there were material issues of fact that plaintiff, a "non-muscular man with a disability," was subjected to a hostile work environment where he alleged that his supervisor "made his life at work miserable by claiming that [plaintiff] was not a 'real man' or a 'manly man'" and assigning plaintiff heavy manual labor tasks he could not perform because of his disability in order to 'toughen [him] up'); and Back v. Hastings on Hudson Union Free School Dist., 365 F.3d 107, 119 (2nd Cir. 2004) (holding that it is impermissible discrimination under the Equal Protection Clause to suppose "that a woman *will* conform to a gender stereotype" as well as to suppose "that a woman is unqualified for a position because she does *not* conform to a gender stereotype").

40. Tronetti v. TLC Healthnet Lakeshore Hosp., 909 F.Supp.2d 758, 2003 WL 22757935 (W.D. N.Y. 2003) (transgendered employee who was in the process of transitioning from male to female was advised to avoid wearing overtly feminine attire and thereafter was harassed, subjected to demeaning rumors concerning her sexuality, and ultimately forced to resign based upon unfounded charges. The court held that plaintiff's Title VII claim against his employer, insomuch as it was based on alleged discrimination for failing to "act like a man," was actionable and denied Rule 12(b)(6) motion to dismiss.); and Samborski v. West Valley Nuclear Services Co., 909 F.Supp.2d 758, 1999 WL 1293351 (W.D. N.Y. 1999) (lesbian employee alleged she encountered verbal harassment of an anti-lesbian nature from her male co-workers, who subjected her to constant offensive statements because she did not meet her male co-workers' expectations of what a woman should look like. The court agreed finding her exposure to working conditions to which her fellow male employees were not were evidence of disparate treatment based on sex.).

41. Bibby v. Philadelphia Coca-Cola Bottling Co., 260 F.3d 257, 262–63 (3rd Cir. 2001) (court declined to find the plaintiff, who alleged he had been harassed based upon his sexual orientation, had a cognizable claim under Title VII, but recognized that a plaintiff may be able to prove a claim of sex discrimination under Title VII by showing that the "harasser's conduct was motivated by a belief that the victim did not conform to the stereotypes of his or her gender."); and Prowel v. Wise Business Forms, Inc., 579 F.3d 285 (3rd Cir., Aug. 28, 2009) (gay man alleged that his co-workers called him names, derided his looks, left him notes with slurs based upon his sexual orientation, among other behaviors. Third Circuit reversed summary judgment finding the evidence could support a claim of harassment on account of his failure to conform to gender stereotypes.).

- U.S. District Court for the District of
  - Delaware
  - New Jersey
  - Pennsylvania—Recognized[42]
  - U.S. Virgin Islands
- U.S. Court of Appeals for the Fourth Circuit
- U.S. District Court for the District of
  - Maryland—Recognized[43]
  - North Carolina
  - South Carolina
  - Virginia
  - West Virginia
- U.S. Court of Appeals for the Fifth Circuit
- U.S. District Court for the District of
  - Louisiana—Not Recognized[44]
  - Mississippi
  - Texas—Recognized[45]
- U.S. Court of Appeals for the Sixth Circuit—Recognized[46]

---

42. Mitchell v. Axcan Scandipharm, Inc., 909 F.Supp.2d 758, 2006 WL 456173 (W.D. Pa. 2006) (transgendered employee alleged he was fired after he announced his intention to transition from male to female and began presenting himself as female to customers. The court found that plaintiff had "sufficiently pleaded claims of gender discrimination" under Title VII because the "facts show[ed] that his failure to conform to sex stereotypes of how a man should look and behave was the catalyst behind defendant's actions" and denied the Rule 12(b)(6) motion to dismiss.) See also Bianchi v. City of Philadelphia, 183 F. Supp. 2d 726 (E.D. Pa. 2002) (recognizing sex stereotyping claim exists, but holding that employee did not allege that his alleged harassers' had targeted him because he failed to conform to their idea of masculinity).

43. Finkle v. Howard County, Md., ___ F.Supp.2d ___, 2014 WL 1396386 (D.Md. 2014).

44. Oiler v. Winn-Dixie, not reported in F.Supp.2d, 2002 WL 31098541 (E.D. La. 2002) (transgendered plaintiff who only cross-dressed during his off-hours was fired from his truck driver job with a grocery chain. Plaintiff sued his employer for gender discrimination. The court found that being "trans-gendered" or suffering from a gender identity disorder was not a characteristic based on "biological sex" and, as a result, was not entitled to Title VII protection.).

45. Lopez v. River Oaks Imaging & Diagnostic Group, Inc., 542 F. Supp. 2d 653 (S.D. Tex. 2008) (transgendered applicant had an offer of employment rescinded after discovering the plaintiff was biologically male but presented as female during the interview process. The court denied summary judgment.).

46. Barnes v. City of Cincinnati, 401 F.3d 729, 737 (6th Cir. 2005) (court affirmed verdict for transgendered plaintiff, an Ohio police officer demoted due to undergoing a gender transition, award of $320,511 and award of $527,888 attorneys' fees and $25,837 in costs. Court stated that plaintiff's "failure to conform to sex stereotypes concerning how a man

- U.S. District Court for the District of
  - Kentucky
  - Michigan
  - Ohio—Recognized[47]
  - Tennessee—Recognized but not as to a transgender person[48]
- U.S. Court of Appeals for the Seventh Circuit—Not Recognized[49]
- U.S. District Court for the District of
  - Illinois—Recognized as to an effeminate man[50]
  - Indiana—Recognized and Not Recognized[51]
  - Wisconsin
- U.S. Court of Appeals for the Eighth Circuit—Recognized as to a man perceived as gay[52]

---

should look and behave was the driving force behind [his employer's] actions."); Smith v. City of Salem, 378 F.3d 566, 573 (6th Cir. 2004) (court reversed summary judgment for employer as to claim by a male-to-female transsexual of sex stereotyping under Title VII. Plaintiff, who was a lieutenant in the fire department, had worked for seven years without any negative incidents, but city disciplined plaintiff and tried to force him to quit while he was in the early stages of transitioning from male to female.).

47. Doe v. United Consumer Financial Services, 2001 WL 34350174 (N.D. Ohio 2001) (court denied motion to dismiss finding that, since the employee may have been fired, at least in part, because her appearance and behavior did not fit into her company's sex stereotypes, dismissal of her claims under Title VII was improper. Transgendered employee began transitioning from male to female by changing her name and assuming a female identity. Her employer investigated her background and interrogated her about her name change and new gender at a meeting. Plaintiff was told the next day that the employer no longer required her services.).

48. Rhea v. Dollar Tree Stores, Inc., 395 F. Supp. 2d 696 (W.D. Tenn. 2005) (two gay employees were found to have properly pled a Title VII claim for gender discrimination. In so doing, the district court recognized that plaintiffs could validly assert a claim under Title VII for sex stereotyping discrimination and gender non-conforming behavior and appearance.).

49. Ulane v. Eastern Airlines, Inc., 742 F.2d 1081 (7th Cir. 1984) (the court of appeals reversed the district court and held that Title VII does not protect transsexuals.).

50. Jones v. Pacific Rail Services, 2001 WL 127645 (N.D. Ill. 2001) (court determined that offensive locker room banter about the non transgendered employee's effeminate appearance stated a valid Title VII claim.).

51. Creed v. Family Express Corp., not reported in F.Supp.2d, 2007 WL 2265630 (N.D. Ind. 2007) (transgendered employee who was terminated after being told that "she could no longer present herself in a feminine manner at work" stated a claim of discrimination based on sex because of her "failure to comply with male stereotypes"). *But see* Sweet v. Mulberry Lutheran Home, not reported in F.Supp.2d, 2003 WL 21525058 (S.D. Ind. 2003) (following the pre-Price Waterhouse v. Hopkins case of Ulane v. Eastern Airlines, Inc., 742 F.2d 1081 (7th Cir. 1984)).

52. Schmedding v. Tnemec Co., Inc., 187 F.3d 862, 865 (8th Cir. 1999) (according to the court of appeals, plaintiff's allegations that his "perceived sexual preference," his co-workers' rumors that falsely labeled him as homosexual in an effort to debase his masculinity, and other

- U.S. District Court for the District of
  - Arkansas
  - Iowa
  - Minnesota
  - Missouri—Recognized[53]
  - Nebraska
  - North Dakota
  - South Dakota
- U.S. Court of Appeals for the Ninth Circuit—Recognized as to an effeminate man,[54] a gay man,[55] and mixed as to a transgender person[56]

---

derogatory comments and acts toward him were on account of his sex, thereby implicating Title VII's prohibitions. Dismissal of his complaint was reversed.). *See also* Lewis v. Heartland Inns of America, L.L.C., 591 F.3d 1033 (8th Cir. 2010). However, in a pre-Price Waterhouse v. Hopkins case the Eighth Circuit held that the word "sex" in the Title VII ban on sex discrimination in employment is to be given its plain meaning and does not encompass discrimination based on transsexualism. Sommers v. Budget Marketing, Inc., 667 F.2d 748 (8th Cir. 1982).

53. Broadus v. State Farm Ins. Co., not reported in F.Supp.2d, 2000 WL 1585257 (W.D. Mo. 2000) (transgendered African American in the process of transitioning from a female to a male claimed he was harassed and ultimately forced to resign his position because his supervisor treated him differently because he did not conform to a stereotype of how a woman should look and sexual orientation. The court granted summary judgment to the employer while confirming that, if and when sexual stereotyping plays a role in an employment decision, such disparate treatment is actionable under Title VII. Nevertheless, the court determined that plaintiff had failed to present evidence that his supervisor had created a hostile work environment.).

54. Nichols v. Azteca Restaurant Enterprises, 256 F.3d 864, 874–75 (9th Cir. 2001) (the court found that a four-year pattern of verbal abuse toward a male employee based upon his effeminate behavior was harassment because of sex in violation of Title VII.).

55. Rene v. MGM Grand Hotel, Inc., 305 F.3d 1061, 1069 (9th Cir. 2002) (the *en banc* court reviewed *en banc* the panel's decision to uphold a grant of summary judgment on grounds Title VII did not prohibit discrimination on grounds of sexual orientation, and reversed the panel's decision, finding that plaintiff's sexual orientation was immaterial to whether he could sustain a cause of action under Title VII. Rather, the fact that the plaintiff had undergone severe and pervasive offensive physical conduct of a sexual nature and sexual assaults—including repeated groping of him by his co-workers—that were unwelcome was sufficient to sustain a claim of harassment under Title VII.).

56. Schwenk v. Hartford, 204 F.3d 1187, 1202 (9th Cir. 2000) (relying on Title VII sex stereotyping case law, the court of appeals concluded that violence in the form of an attempted rape against a transsexual prisoner was violence because of gender under the Gender Motivated Violence Act a/k/a Violence Against Women Act (VAWA), 42 U.S.C. § 13981 and 42 U.S.C. § 1983). However, VAWA's civil remedy provision was later declared unconstitutional as exceeding Congress' power under the Commerce Clause in United States v. Morrison, 529 U.S. 598, 120 S. Ct. 1740, 146 L.Ed. 2d 658 (2000). *See also* Nichols v. Azteca Restaurant Enterprises, Inc., 256 F.3d 864, 874–875 (9th Cir. 2001) in which the court stated that "*Price Waterhouse* sets a rule that bars discrimination on the basis of sex stereotypes" and "To the extent [Ninth

- U.S. District Court for the District of
  - Alaska
  - Arizona—Recognized[57]
  - California
  - Guam
  - Hawaii
  - Idaho
  - Montana
  - Nevada
  - Northern Mariana Islands
  - Oregon—Recognized as to a lesbian[58]
  - Washington
- U.S. Court of Appeals for the Tenth Circuit—Not Recognized[59]
- U.S. District Court for the District of
  - Colorado
  - Kansas—Recognized as to a straight woman[60]

Circuit precedent] conflicts with *Price Waterhouse*, . . . [it] is no longer good law." Straight man who was harassed with terms referring to him as "she" and "her" stated viable claim.

57. Kastl v. Maricopa County Community College Dist., not reported in F.Supp.2d, 2004 WL 2008954 (D. Ariz. 2004) (Court denied motion to dismiss and found that a male-to-female transsexual professor who was discharged because she refused to use the men's room stated a valid Title VII sex discrimination cause of action. According to the court, because the employer had created restrooms for each sex and the plaintiff had alleged she was required to use the men's restroom because she failed to conform to the employer's expectations regarding a woman's behavior or anatomy.) However, the court later granted summary judgment to the employer on the merits. *See* Kastl v. Maricopa County Community College Dist., not reported in F.Supp.2d, 2006 WL 2460636 (D. Ariz. 2006).

58. Heller v. Columbia Edgewater Country Club, 195 F. Supp. 2d 1212, 1224 (D. Or. 2002) (lesbian claimed she was subject to harassment and then terminated by her employer because she was a lesbian. The court denied the employer's motion for summary judgment concluding that the plaintiff had stated claims under Title VII, which prohibits harassment based on a perception that the person "did not conform to [the defendant's] stereotype of how a woman ought to behave.").

59. Etsitty v. Utah Transit Authority, 502 F.3d 1215 (10th Cir., Sept. 20, 2007). (A transgendered woman was fired from her job as a bus driver because the employer feared the public might be offended by her transgendered identity. The court affirmed summary judgment for her employer and determined that Title VII's protections prohibiting sex discrimination did not protect transgendered people.).

60. Abdul-Hakim v. Goodyear Tire & Rubber Co., 455 F. Supp. 2d 1267 (D. Kan. 2006) (statements indicating "antiquated notions concerning women in the workplace, including a belief that women were not to be taken seriously in the workplace and that women did not

- New Mexico
- Oklahoma
- Utah
- Wyoming
- U.S. Court of Appeals for the Eleventh Circuit[61]
- U.S. District Court for the District of
  - Alabama
  - Florida—Not Recognized as to a straight man[62]
  - Georgia—Recognized in a 42 U.S.C. § 1983 action[63]
- U.S. Court of Appeals for the D.C. Circuit
  - U.S. District Court for the District of Columbia—Recognized[64]

---

belong in the workplace but should remain in the home to raise children" could reasonably support a finding of discriminatory animus based on sex stereotyping).

61. Glenn v. Brumby, 663 F.3d 1312 (11th Cir. 2011) (holding that a Georgia General Assembly's Office of Legislative Counsel supervisor did not have sufficiently important governmental interest to justify terminating employee based on the supervisor's purported concern that other women might object to transgendered state employee's restroom use was not sufficiently important governmental interest under the Fourteenth Amendment to justify terminating employee because of her gender non-conformity, where concern was based on speculation, and discrimination against a transgendered individual because of her gender-nonconformity is sex discrimination in violation of the Fourteenth Amendment of the U.S. Constitution's equal protection clause, whether it is described as being on the basis of sex or gender).

62. Mowery v. Escambia County Utilities Authority, not reported in F.Supp.2d, 2006 WL 327965 (N.D. Fla. 2006) (The court granted the employer's motion for summary judgment on a Title VII claim of sex discrimination, despite the plaintiff offering evidence of sexually-oriented, homophobic comments about a straight man. The district court rejected arguments "by some commentators who characterize sex and sexual orientation as 'intricately' interrelated.").

63. Glenn v. Brumby, 724 F. Supp. 2d 1284 (N.D. Ga. 2010), aff'd 663 F.3d 1312 (11th Cir. 2011) (transgendered employee of Georgia General Assembly's Office of Legislative Counsel brought a 42 U.S.C. § 1983 action against her former supervisor and state officials, alleging that she was discriminated against on the basis of sex and her medical condition, in violation of Fourteenth Amendment. Even though the case was brought under § 1983, the court treated it like it was a Title VII case including invoking the seminal Title VII case of McDonnell Douglas Corp. v. Green, 411 U.S. 792, 93 S. Ct. 1817, 36 L. Ed. 2d 668 (1973). The court held that discrimination against transgendered individuals because of their failure to conform to gender stereotypes constitutes discrimination on basis of sex for equal protection purposes. The court found that the defendant violated the employee's Fourteenth Amendment rights and set the matter for determining a remedy.).

64. Schroer v. Billington, 577 F. Supp. 2d 293, 295–300 (D. D.C. 2008) (A retired transgendered Colonel with Special Forces and Special Operations experience was denied job of Specialist in Terrorism and International Crime with the Congressional Research Service (CRS) at the Library of Congress after informing CRS officials of her name change and intent to transition from male to female. "In refusing to hire Diane Schroer because her appearance and background did not comport with the decision maker's sex stereotypes about how men

The court in *Schroer v. Billington* was the first court to discuss comprehensively sex stereotyping as to a transsexual in a Title VII case as the following excerpt demonstrates.

> Imagine that an employee is fired because she converts from Christianity to Judaism. Imagine too that her employer testifies that he harbors no bias toward either Christians or Jews but only "converts." That would be a clear case of discrimination "because of religion." No court would take seriously the notion that "converts" are not covered by the statute. Discrimination "because of religion" easily encompasses discrimination because of a *change* of religion. But in cases where the plaintiff has changed her sex, and faces discrimination because of the decision to stop presenting as a man and to start appearing as a woman, courts have traditionally carved such persons out of the statute by concluding that "transsexuality" is unprotected by Title VII. In other words, courts have allowed their focus on the label "transsexual" to blind them to the statutory language itself.
>
> . . .
>
> The decisions holding that Title VII only prohibits discrimination against men because they are men, and discrimination against women because they are women, represent an elevation of "judge-supposed legislative intent over clear statutory text." [citation omitted] In their holdings that discrimination based on changing one's sex is not discrimination because of sex, *Ulane*, *Holloway*, and *Etsitty* essentially reason "that a thing may be within the letter of the statute and yet not within the statute, because not within its spirit, nor within the intention of its makers." [citation omitted] This is no longer a tenable approach to statutory construction. [citation omitted] Supreme Court decisions subsequent to *Ulane* and *Holloway* have applied Title VII in ways Congress could not have contemplated. . . . . .

---

and women should act and appear, and in response to Schroer's decision to transition, legally, culturally, and physically, from male to female, the Library of Congress violated Title VII's prohibition on sex discrimination.") The court ultimately awarded Schroer $491,190.80. Schroer v. Billington, not reported in F.Supp.2d, 2009 WL 1543686 (D. D.C. 2009).

For Diane Schroer to prevail on the facts of her case, however, it is not necessary to draw sweeping conclusions about the reach of Title VII. Even if the decisions that define the word "sex" in Title VII as referring only to anatomical or chromosomal sex are still good law—after that approach "has been eviscerated by *Price Waterhouse*" [citation omitted]—the Library's refusal to hire Schroer after being advised that she planned to change her anatomical sex by undergoing sex reassignment surgery was *literally* discrimination "because of . . . sex."[65]

Legislation to remedy the shortfall and uneven application of Title VII as to transgender persons, gay men, and lesbians is needed. In 2007, the Employment Non-Discrimination Act (ENDA) of 2007, a bill that would have banned employment discrimination on the basis of sexual orientation and gender identity was introduced in the House of Representatives.[66] In addressing discrimination in the workplace, the Health, Employment, Labor and Pension (HELP) Subcommittee held two historic hearings. On September 5, 2007, Congressman Rob Andrews chaired a legislative hearing to discuss the need for ENDA, which would extend civil rights protections to lesbians, gays, bisexuals, and transgender (LGBT) persons in the workplace. Later that year, the House of Representatives passed for the first time in history a bill to extend workplace protections to the LGBT community. On June 26, 2008, the HELP Subcommittee focused solely on workplace discrimination against transgender Americans. Two alternate bills were later introduced: one that prohibited employment discrimination, preferential treatment, and retaliation on the basis of sexual orientation by employers with fifteen or more employees, which was passed by House,[67] and another that banned only gender identity discrimination.[68] None of those bills was enacted.[69]

Interestingly, even though there isno federal law prohibiting discrimination on the basis of gender identity or expression, the Assistant Secretary of

---

65. Schroer v. Billington, 577 F. Supp. 2d 293, 306–308(D. D.C. 2008).
66. See H.R.2015, 110 Cong., 1st Sess. (2007).
67. H.R. 3685, 110 Cong., 1st Sess. (2007).
68. H.R. 3686, 110 Cong., 1st Sess. (2007).
69. *See* House Report No. 110–923, pp. 39–40 (December 19, 2008), 110th Congress 2nd Sess. 2008, 2008 WL 5427306.

Agriculture for Administration is tasked with the responsibility "to provide for diversity and inclusion" by establishing, directing and providing policy and oversight "for a Department wide Special Emphasis Program (SEP) including: Women, African Americans, Hispanics, Asian/Pacific Islanders, Native Americans, Disabled, and Gay/Lesbian/Bisexual/Transgendered."[70]

§10.4(c) The Civil Rights Act of 1871
The Civil Rights Act of 1871[71] provides:

> Every person who, under color of any statute, ordinance, regulation, custom, or usage, of any State or Territory or the District of Columbia, subjects, or causes to be subjected, any citizen of the United States or other person within the jurisdiction thereof to the deprivation of any rights, privileges, or immunities secured by the Constitution and laws, shall be liable to the party injured in an action at law, suit in equity, or other proper proceeding for redress, except that in any action brought against a judicial officer for an act or omission taken in such officer's judicial capacity, injunctive relief shall not be granted unless a declaratory decree was violated or declaratory relief was unavailable. For the purposes of this section, any Act of Congress applicable exclusively to the District of Columbia shall be considered to be a statute of the District of Columbia.

The two essential elements of an action under the Civil Rights Act of 1871[72] are (1) whether the conduct complained of was committed by a person acting under color of state law, and (2) whether this conduct deprived a person of rights, privileges, or immunities secured by the Constitution or laws of the United States.[73] Thus, usually, only employees of state and local governments or agencies can maintain an action under that act and satisfy the under color of state law requirement. The deprivation of a federal right is

---

70. 7 C.F.R. §§ 2.24(a)(4)(xv)(A) and 2.919a)(15).
71. 42 U.S.C. § 1983.
72. Id.
73. Parratt v. Taylor, 451 U.S. 527, 535, 101 S. Ct. 1908, 1913, 68 L. Ed. 2d 420 (1981).

usually a deprivation of the equal protection of the laws guaranteed by the Fourteenth Amendment of the U.S. Constitution.

While the Civil Rights Act of 1871 was originally used to attempt to remedy racial discrimination,[74] the courts have held that there is no valid reason why it cannot be used to remedy sex discrimination claims as well.[75]

Two cases have recognized sex discrimination claims by transgender employees under the Civil Rights Act of 1871.[76] However, only one reported case has gone to judgment for a transgender employee under the act. In an action under the Civil Rights Act of 1871, the U.S. District Court for the Northern District of Georgia held that a supervisor of the Georgia General Assembly's Office of Legislative Counsel discriminated against a transgender employee on the basis of sex and her medical condition (gender identity disorder), in violation of the Fourteenth Amendment of the U.S. Constitution when it discharged her. The court held that none of the reasons asserted by the supervisor of the transgender employee of the Georgia General Assembly's Office of Legislative Counsel for terminating the transgender employee—namely, avoidance of lawsuits against the state for invasion of privacy or sexual harassment relating to the transgender employee's use of multi-person women's restrooms in the Capitol Building and concerns regarding the operation of the Office of Legislative Counsel and preserving the confidence of state legislators—did not present an "exceedingly persuasive" justification for the transgender employee's termination sufficient to

---

74. *See* Burnett v. Grattan, 468 U.S. 42, 104 S. Ct. 2924, 82 L. Ed. 2d 36 (1984) and Crawford v. Carroll, 529 F.3d 961 (11th Cir. 2008) (involving racial discrimination in employment claim by black state employee).

75. *See* Back v. Hastings On Hudson Union Free School Dist., 365 F.3d 107 (2nd Cir. 2004) (involving sex discrimination in employment claim by public school employee) holding, *inter alia*, that "sex plus" or "gender plus" discrimination is actionable in an action under 42 U.S.C. § 1983 and that stereotyped remarks can be evidence that gender played a part in an adverse employment decision). *See also* Sischo-Nownejad v. Merced Community College Dist., 934 F.2d 1104 (9th Cir. 1991).

76. *See* Smith v. City of Salem, 378 F.3d 566 (6th Cir. 2004) (recognizing that allegations by a city fire department employee, who was born male and subsequently was diagnosed with gender identity disorder, that employee who alleged that he had been discriminated against based upon his gender non conforming behavior and appearance, sufficiently alleged a claim of sex discrimination grounded in the Equal Protection Clause of the Fourteenth Amendment under 42 U.S.C. § 1983), and Kastl v. Maricopa County Community College Dist., 2004 WL 2008954 (D. Ariz. 2004) (denying Rule 12(b)(6) motion to dismiss transgendered plaintiff's claims under Title VII and 42 U.S.C. § 1983).

survive heightened scrutiny review of the employee's equal protection claim based on gender discrimination. However, those same reasons were held sufficient to survive intermediate scrutiny of the transgender employee's medical discrimination claims.[77] The court awarded the employee reinstatement, restoration of seniority, and enjoined the defendant from future discriminatory conduct on the basis of sex against the plaintiff after she returned to the workplace.[78] Even though the case was brought under § 1983, the court treated it like a Title VII case including invoking the seminal Title VII case of *McDonnell Douglas Corp. v. Green*.[79] The court held that discrimination against transgender individuals because of their failure to conform to gender stereotypes constitutes discrimination on the basis of sex for equal protection purposes. The court found that the defendant violated the employee's Fourteenth Amendment rights and set the matter for determining a remedy. The court noted that an employee is not required to sue under Title VII of the Civil Rights Act of 1964 but may instead sue one who is acting or has acted under color of state law under the Civil Rights Act of 1871. Thus, ordinarily this remedy is only available to persons whose employer was or is a state, county (or Parish in Louisiana), or municipal employer or an agency of one of those governmental units.

---

77. Glenn v. Brumby, 724 F. Supp. 2d 1284 (N.D. Ga. 2010), *aff'd* 663 F.3d 1312 (11th Cir. 2011).

78. Glenn v. Brumby, 2010 WL 3731107 (N.D. Ga. 2010), *aff'd* 663 F.3d 1312 (11th Cir. 2011).

79. 411 U.S. 792, 93 S. Ct. 1817, 36 L. Ed. 2d 668 (1973).

CHAPTER 11

Immigration

U.S. law does not explicitly prohibit transgender people from visiting or immigrating to the United States. Transgender people should face no significant or systemic difficulties in obtaining the vast majority of visas (e.g., tourists, students, employees of a company based in the United States).

Many transgender people have immigrated to the United States due to their marriage to a U.S. citizen or permanent resident. However, due to the legal difficulties that some transgender people occasionally face in getting recognition of their marriage, couples in which one partner is transgender are strongly encouraged to seek legal information and advice before applying for marriage-based immigration. See Chapter 6, "Family Law," § 6.1 "Marriage." Immigrants in the U.S. face a range of challenges and hostilities, and the current broken immigration system violates basic standards of decency through indefinite detention, separation from partners, and the denial of medically necessary health care. Because of sometimes-unclear documentation, challenges to their marital status, and blatant discrimination, transgender immigrants face additional hardships.

Section 3 of the Defense of Marriage Act, Pub. L. No. 104-199, 110 Stat. 2419, 2419 (1996), 1 U.S.C.A. § 7, is no longer an impediment to the recognition of lawful same-sex marriages and spouses under the Immigration and Nationality Act if the marriage is valid under the laws of the State where it was celebrated. It was declared to be unconstitutional by the U.S. Supreme Court in *United States v. Windsor*.[1] The Board of Immigration Appeals has begun recognizing and applying the *Windsor* decision in immigration cases.[2]

§11.1 Asylum Statutes and Regulations

Anyone who is in the United States and has been harmed, or fears harm, in their home country because they are transgender, or because they don't otherwise conform to gender norms, should strongly consider applying for asylum. Legally, the past harm, or fear of harm (called *persecution*), has to come from the government, or an agency that the government will not or cannot control in the person's home country. The fear also has to be "legitimate," which means that asylum applicants must provide some evidence of the harm they have suffered, harm that other people like them have suffered, or the existence of a policy or practice that would facilitate such harm.

Asylum is available to people who fear harm based, at least in part, on their race, religion, nationality, membership in a particular social group, or political opinion. Many transgender people have received asylum in the United States because, in their individual case, being transgender or gender nonconforming has been found to be a part of a particular social group. Asylum allows a person to stay in the United States, receive a work permit and public benefits, and eventually apply for a green card.

Under the Immigration and Nationality Act,[3] the Secretary of Homeland Security or the Attorney General may grant asylum to an alien who has applied for asylum in accordance with the requirements and procedures established by the secretary of homeland security or the attorney general under this section if the secretary of homeland security or the attorney general determines that such alien is a refugee.[4] On December 6, 2011, President Obama issued a Presidential Memorandum that provides:

> Those LGBT persons who seek refuge from violence and persecution face daunting challenges. In order to improve protection for LGBT

---

1. United States v. Windsor, 570 U.S. ___, 133 S.Ct. 2675 (2013).
2. See e.g.: Matter of Zeleniak, 26 I&N Dec. 158 (BIA 2013).
3. 8 U.S.C. § 1101, *et seq.*
4. 8 U.S.C. § 1158(b)(1)(A).

refugees and asylum seekers at all stages of displacement, the Departments of State and Homeland Security shall enhance their ongoing efforts to ensure that LGBT refugees and asylum seekers have equal access to protection and assistance, particularly in countries of first asylum. In addition, the Departments of State, Justice, and Homeland Security shall ensure appropriate training is in place so that relevant Federal Government personnel and key partners can effectively address the protection of LGBT refugees and asylum seekers, including by providing to them adequate assistance and ensuring that the Federal Government has the ability to identify and expedite resettlement of highly vulnerable persons with urgent protection needs.[5]

To establish that the applicant is a refugee within the meaning of such section, the applicant must establish that race, religion, nationality, membership in a particular social group, or political opinion was or will be at least one central reason for persecuting the applicant. The burden is on the applicant to prove that he or she is a refugee.[6] A spouse or child of an alien who is granted asylum may, if not otherwise eligible for asylum, be granted the same status as the alien if accompanying, or following to join, such alien.[7] When an alien is granted asylum, the attorney general shall not remove or return the alien to the alien's country of nationality (or, in the case of a person having no nationality, the country of the alien's last habitual residence) and shall authorize the alien to engage in employment in the United States and provide the alien with appropriate endorsement of that authorization.[8]

A request or claim for asylum is often based upon the Convention Against Torture and Other Cruel, Inhuman or Degrading Treatment or Punishment[9]

---

5. Presidential Memorandum—International Initiatives to Advance the Human Rights of Lesbian, Gay, Bisexual, and Transgender Persons, December 6, 2011, Sec. 2, 2011 WL 6058595 (December 6, 2011).

6. 8 U.S.C. § 1158(b)(1)(b).

7. 8 U.S.C. § 1158(b)(3).

8. 8 U.S.C. § 1158(c).

9. The Convention Against Torture was ratified by the U.S. Senate with reservation on October 27, 1990. See 136 Cong. Rec. S17486-01, 1990 WL 168442 (October 27, 1990).

that is implemented in U.S. immigration policy by a regulation promulgated by the Department of Homeland Security.[10]

The Affirmative Asylum Procedures Manual of the Asylum Division provides procedures for the handling of asylum applications by transsexuals, which, on their face, are very sensitive and compassionate.

§11.1(a) Adjudications of Transsexual Principal Applicants

An asylum applicant is presumed to be of the gender that he or she claims on the asylum application. Unless there is a strong indication or evidence of a change in the applicant's gender, medically or otherwise, such as prior use of a name normally used by the opposite sex, the Asylum Officer need not make any special inquiry into determining whether an applicant is in fact the gender claimed on the asylum application or a transsexual.

When an asylum applicant is determined to be transsexual, the asylum application of a transsexual principal applicant is considered on its merits. The applicant's status as a transsexual is not taken into account in evaluating the merits of the asylum claim, unless transsexuality is raised by the applicant as part of the asylum claim. However, the Asylum Officer is required to undertake the usual questioning and requests for documentation in order to ascertain the applicant's identity. The Asylum Officer should ascertain, through testimony and/or documentation, a transsexual asylum applicant's identity, including gender and name at birth and the current outwardly assumed gender, including whether there is any documentation of the assumed gender, such as a re-issued birth certificate, legal name change, or medical records of SRS or other transgendered-related medical treatment.

The Asylum Officer must be sensitive to the transsexual asylum applicant's particular situation, the likelihood that he or she may have experienced stress and/or trauma surrounding issues of gender identity, and the potentiality for increased cultural and language barriers to effective communication. "[A]s in the context of any other

---

10. *See* 8 C.F.R. § 208, *et seq.*

adjudication, all CIS officers shall perform their duties in a manner that accords maximal respect, sensitivity, and consideration when adjudicating any petition, application, or document request filed by, or on behalf of, a transsexual individual." *Id., at 4*. For further guidance, *see* AOBTC Basic Training Materials, *Interviewing Part IV: Inter-Cultural Communication and Other Factors That May Impede Communication at an Asylum Interview*; and *Female Asylum Applicants and Gender-Related Claims*.

The Asylum Office processes and issues the decision based on the applicant's name and gender at birth, unless the asylum applicant submits medical and/or other documentation establishing a gender change via SRS and, where applicable, a legal name change. There must be documentation of SRS in order to change the applicant's gender of record. If contemporary documentation of the surgery is unavailable where, for example, the surgery took place in the applicant's home country and the applicant cannot reasonably be expected to obtain the documentation, a current medical evaluation concluding that the applicant has previously undergone SRS is acceptable. Documentation of pre-surgery treatment alone, such as hormone therapy, is insufficient to support a change in the applicant's gender of record. For example, an applicant who was born a male but who provides documentation of SRS shall be recorded and issued documentation as a female, under a new name if there is documentation of a legal name change. Alternatively, USCIS policy would not allow a change in gender of record for a female who is undergoing hormone treatments and presents herself as male, but who has not undergone SRS. If the applicant has not had SRS and/or cannot provide medical documentation of SRS, Asylum Office personnel issue documents reflecting the gender of the applicant at birth. If the applicant cannot provide evidence of a legal name change Asylum Office personnel should contact HQASM Operations for guidance. Guidance is currently being sought from the USCIS Office of Chief Counsel regarding other applicant-requested name changes. Whether or not an asylum applicant has changed his or her name legally, security checks that are conducted by name must be conducted on all names used by the applicant.

If an applicant presents as and/or claims a different gender than his or her anatomical gender at birth, but will not or has not undergone SRS, Asylum Office personnel must explain to the applicant USCIS policy that the gender of record and documentation cannot be changed to a new gender unless there is documentation of SRS. However, Asylum Office personnel should, as a matter of courtesy, respect the applicant's preferences with respect to being referred to as "him" or "her," or "Mr." or "Ms." in verbal communication.

§11.1(b) Dependents of Transsexual Applicants

A transsexual asylum applicant may include his or her children in an asylum application in accordance with current guidance and regulations without regard to his or her transsexuality. Similarly, an asylum principal applicant may include a transsexual child in his or her asylum application, without regard to the child's transsexuality. Guidelines in the previous section for determining identity and gender apply.

Because of the legal prohibition on recognition of same-sex marriages for purposes of Federal benefits, USCIS personnel are prohibited from recognizing the marriage of a transsexual individual, who, as a result of having undergone SRS, is now the same gender as his or her claimed spouse, regardless of whether the marriage took place before or after the applicant's change of gender.

See Defense of Marriage Act (DOMA), 1 U.S.C. § 7 (1996).

On the other hand, as stated above, USCIS personnel may recognize the marriage of a transsexual individual, who, after having undergone SRS, married someone of the opposite sex as his or her new sex, and the state in which the couple were married recognized the change in sex of the postoperative transsexual and considered the marriage as having taken place between two heterosexual persons. *Matter of Lovo*, 23 I&N Dec. 746 (BIA 2005); Interim Decision #3512.

For example, a male who undergoes medical treatment or SRS in order to change his gender to female, and later marries a male, may include the male as a spouse on the asylum application, provided the state in which they were married recognized the marriage as having taken place between two heterosexuals. However, a male who marries a female, and later becomes a female, cannot include the female as a spouse on the asylum application.

Again, USCIS personnel should be sensitive to the applicant and his or her claimed spouse. The inability to recognize the marriage for purposes of conferring benefits does not prevent USCIS personnel from verbally referring to the applicant's spouse as husband or wife, for example, in the context of an asylum interview. If Asylum Office personnel encounter a situation where a claimed dependent spouse must be removed from an asylum application under this section, Asylum Office personnel follow the guidance in Section III.E.6.b, *Loss of Derivative Status by Marriage, Divorce, or Death of Principal Applicant*, and may, where appropriate, give the removed spouse a reasonable period of time to file a new asylum application as a principal. The Asylum Office may also entertain a request for a *nunc pro tunc* asylum approval in accordance with the guidance in this manual, if a properly granted derivative asylee spouse loses his or her derivative status prior to adjustment due to a gender change by the derivative or principal, whether or not the spouses have divorced. *See* Section III.E, *Dependents*, for further specific procedures for dependent asylum applicants.[11]

§11.2 Asylum Cases

There is little case law on the subject of transgender persons seeking asylum. In one unsuccessful case, a transsexual Honduran citizen's asylum application was denied by the Board of Immigration Appeals (BIA). The U.S. Court of Appeals held that the BIA's statement about the lack of clear medical hardship evidence was not a distortion of the record because the applicant already had sexual reassignment surgery, and Honduran doctors did not state that hormone treatments and checkups were not available in

---

11. Affirmative Asylum Procedures Manual of the Asylum Division, Office of International Affairs, U.S. Citizenship and Immigration Services (Revised July 2010).

Honduras. The BIA's finding that the applicant's potential difficulty in read-justing to life in Honduras was insufficient to establish extreme hardship was not abuse of discretion.[12]

In a successful case, the applicant applied for asylum based on the argument that, as a gay man with a female sexual identity, he had suffered past persecution and had well-founded fear of future persecution in Mexico. The applicant testified that, at the age of eight, he "realized that [he] was attracted to people of [his] same sex." At the age of twelve, the applicant began dressing and behaving as a woman. He faced numerous reprimands from family and school officials because of his sexual orientation. His mother registered him in a state-run Mexican school and informed the school authorities about what she deemed to be his "problem," referring to his sexual orientation. School authorities directed the applicant to stop socializing with two gay friends. The father of a schoolmate grabbed the applicant by the arm and threatened to kill him for "perverting" his son. He was even prevented from attending a school dance because of the way he was dressed. Shortly after the dance, the school asked the applicant's mother to consent to his expulsion because he was not acting appropriately. He could not enroll in another school because the school refused to transfer his paperwork until he agreed to change his sexual orientation. The applicant's parents threw him out of their home the day after his expulsion.

Beyond his school and family, the applicant also suffered harassment and persecution at the hands of Mexican police officers. On numerous occasions, the Mexican police detained and even strip-searched the applicant because he was walking down the street or socializing with other boys also perceived to be gay. In 1992, the Mexican police twice arrested the applicant and a friend. The police told them that it was illegal for homosexuals to walk down the street and for men to dress like women. The police, however, never charged the applicant with any crime. Police officers sexually assaulted the applicant on two separate occasions. In November 1992, when the applicant was fourteen years old, a police officer grabbed him as he was walking down the street, threw him into the police car, and drove to an uninhabited area. The officer demanded that the applicant take off

---

12. Miranda v. Immigration and Naturalization Service, 51 F.3d 767 (8th Cir. 1995).

his clothes. Threatening him with imprisonment if he did not comply, the officer forced the applicant to perform oral sex on him. The officer also threatened to beat and imprison the applicant if he ever told anyone about the incident.

Approximately two weeks later, when the applicant was at a bus stop with a gay friend one evening, the same officer pulled up in a car, accompanied by a second officer. The officers forced both boys into their car and drove them to a remote area, where they forced the boys to strip naked and then separated them. One of the officers grabbed the applicant by the hair and threatened to kill him. Holding a gun to his temple, the officer anally raped the applicant. The applicant believes that his friend was also raped, although his friend refused to talk about the incident. Even before the boys could get dressed, the police officers threatened to shoot if they did not start running. The boys were left stranded in an abandoned area. A few months after the second assault, in February 1993, the applicant was attacked with a knife by a group of young men who called him names relating to his sexual orientation. He was hospitalized for a week while recovering from the attack.

The applicant fled to the United States in October 1993, when he was fifteen years old. He was arrested within a few days of his entry. When the applicant returned to Mexico to live with his sister, she enrolled him in a counseling program, which ostensibly attempted to "cure" his sexual orientation by altering his female appearance. The program staff cut his hair and nails, and forced him to stop taking female hormones. The applicant remained in the program from late January to late March 1994. Because his sister saw no changes in him, she brought the applicant home to live with her. Soon thereafter, however, she forced the applicant out of her house because he was not "cured" of his gay sexual orientation, despite his change in appearance. He again sought refuge in the United States.

The applicant testified that while he was walking down the street in San Diego dressed in women's clothing, a man in a car pulled up and offered money in exchange for sex. The applicant said he would not have sex but asked the man for a ride. When the car turned the corner, police officers were waiting to arrest him. The applicant was held in jail in San Diego for a week.

After a number of attempts to reenter the United States, the applicant last entered on or around October 12, 1994, without inspection. He filed an application for asylum and withholding of deportation on February 22, 1995. At his asylum hearing, the applicant presented the testimony of a professor at San Diego State University and an expert in Latin American history and culture. The professor, who has lived for extended periods of time in Mexico and elsewhere in Latin America, testified that certain homosexuals in Latin America are subjected to greater abuse than others. He testified that it is "accepted in most of Latin America a male before he marries may engage in homosexual acts as long as he performs the role of the male." A male, however, who is perceived to assume the stereotypical female—that is, passive—role in these sexual relationships is "ostracized from the very beginning and is subject to persecution, gay bashing as we would call it, and certainly police abuse." He testified that these gay men with female sexual identities in Mexico are "heavily persecuted by the police and other groups within the society. . . . [They are] a separate social entity within Latin American society and in this case within the nation of Mexico." According to the professor, it is commonplace for police to "hit the gay street . . . and not only brutalize but actually rape with batons . . . homosexual males that are dressed or acting out the feminine role." He also testified that gay men with female sexual identities are likely to become scapegoats for Mexico's present economic and political problems, especially since the recent collapse of the Mexican economy. He specifically noted that the applicant is "a homosexual who has taken on a primarily 'female' sexual role." Based on his expert knowledge, review of the applicant's case, and interaction with the applicant, he opined that the applicant would face persecution if he were forced to return to Mexico.

The U.S. Court of Appeals reversed the decision of the Board of Immigration Appeals. The court stated:

> The primary issue we must decide is whether gay men with female sexual identities in Mexico constitute a protected "particular social group" under the asylum statute. We conclude as a matter of law that gay men with female sexual identities in Mexico constitute a "particular social group" and that [the applicant] is a member of that group. His female sexual identity is immutable because it is inherent in his identity; in any event, he should not be required to change it. Because

> the evidence compels the conclusion that [the applicant] suffered past persecution and has a well-founded fear of future persecution if he were forced to return to Mexico, we conclude that the record compels a finding that he is entitled to asylum and withholding of deportation.[13]

Immigration officials and Immigration Judges have categorized transgender persons seeking asylum as belonging to a recognized "particular social group" denominated as "effeminate gay males with female gender identities," which may be accurate as to some transgender persons but is not as to many others. Even when characterizing transgender persons as such, Immigrations Judges have declined to allow the asylum claim of transgender persons in that group because they said that if returned to their country of origin, they would hide or cease their gender-nonconforming behaviors to try to avoid persecution. However, the Board of Immigration Appeals has rejected such decisions.

> On appeal, the respondent asserts that the Immigration Judge mischaracterized her proffered social group, which consists of effeminate gay males with female gender identities. We agree that the Immigration Judge provided an unclear analysis on the issue of nexus given his conflicting findings and references to non-binding case law as to whether the respondent demonstrated membership in a particular social group pursuant to the above designation, as well as on-account of being a homosexual. Specifically, while the Immigration Judge held that the respondent's proffered group "would possibly qualify for asylum," he found that respondent was not included in this group because she admitted that she would "change the way she lives" and hide her sexual orientation out of fear if returned to Mexico, . . . However, we find that the respondent established the validity of the aforementioned social group, as well as her membership therein, and the fact that she would hide her female identity or sexual orientation due to fear for her safety does not negate the immutability of such characteristics.[14]

---

13. Hernandez-Montiel v. I.N.S., 225 F.3d 1084, 1087 (9th Cir. 2000).
14. Matter of M-G-O-, AXXX XXX 611 (BIA February 4, 2014).

In an interesting case, the petitioner, a U.S. citizen, married the beneficiary, a native and citizen of El Salvador, in North Carolina on September 1, 2002. On November 20, 2002, the petitioner filed a visa petition on behalf of the beneficiary based on their marriage. The record reflects that when the petitioner was born in North Carolina on April 16, 1973, she was of the male sex. However, an affidavit from a physician reflects that on September 14, 2001, the petitioner had surgery that changed her sex designation completely from male to female. In support of the visa petition, the petitioner submitted, among other documents, her North Carolina birth certificate, which lists her current name and indicates that her sex is female; the affidavit from the physician verifying the surgery that changed the petitioner's sex designation; a North Carolina court order changing the petitioner's name to her current name; the North Carolina Register of Deeds marriage record reflecting the marriage of the petitioner and the beneficiary; and a North Carolina driver's license listing the petitioner's current name and indicating that her sex is female. In a decision dated August 3, 2004, the Nebraska Service Center (NSC) director denied the visa petition filed by the petitioner to accord the beneficiary immediate relative status as her husband. In support of his denial, the NSC director stated that defining marriage under the immigration laws is a question of federal law, which Congress clarified in 1996 by enacting the Defense of Marriage Act (DOMA). Pursuant to the DOMA, to qualify as a marriage for purposes of federal law, one partner to the marriage must be a man and the other partner must be a woman. The NSC director concluded that "since the petitioner and beneficiary were born of the same sex, their marriage is not considered valid for immigration purposes and the beneficiary is not eligible to be classified as the spouse of the petitioner." Then the Board of Immigration Appeals engaged in an analysis of DOMA and whether a postoperative transsexual's marriage is a same-sex marriage.

Neither the DOMA nor any other Federal law addresses the issue of how to define the sex of a postoperative transsexual or such designation's effect on a subsequent marriage of that individual. The failure of Federal law to address this issue formed the main basis for the

NSC director's conclusion that this marriage cannot be found valid for immigration purposes.

However, with regard to one of the specific issues we are facing in this case, that is whether the DOMA applies to invalidate, for Federal purposes, a marriage involving a postoperative transsexual, it is notable that Congress did not mention the case of *M.T. v. J.T.*, 355 A.2d 204 (N.J. Super. Ct. App. Div. 1976), which recognized a transsexual marriage. Nor did it mention the various State statutes that at the time of consideration of the DOMA provided for the legal recognition of a change of sex designation by postoperative transsexuals. Rather, Congress's focus, as indicated by its consistent reference to homosexuals in the floor discussions and in the House Report, was fixed on, and limited to, the issue of homosexual marriage.

Furthermore, a specific statement in the House Report's section-by-section analysis provides support for the conclusion that Congress did not consider transsexual marriages to be per se violative of the DOMA. . . .[15]

We have long held that the validity of a marriage is determined by the law of the State where the marriage was celebrated. The State of North Carolina considers the petitioner to be a female under the law and deems her marriage to the beneficiary to be a valid opposite-sex marriage. We find that the DOMA does not preclude our recognition of this marriage for purposes of Federal law. As the NSC director did not raise any other issues regarding the validity of the marriage, we conclude that the marriage between the petitioner and the beneficiary may be the basis for benefits under section 201(b)(2)(A)(i) of the Act. Accordingly, the petitioner's appeal will be sustained, and the visa petition will be approved.[16]

Evidentiary support for a claim of asylum may be found in the U.S. Department of State, Bureau of Democracy, Human Rights and Labor, Country

---

15. *In re* Lovo-Lara, 23 I. & N. Dec. 746, 749–750, Interim Decision 3512, 2005 WL 1181062 (Bd. Immigration App. 2005).
16. *Id.*

Reports on Human Rights Practices[17] for the current year. Those reports contain findings as to the treatment of many categories of persons in most, if not all, of the countries of Earth.

A resource for transgender immigrants seeking asylum is Immigration Equality, which is a national organization that works to end discrimination in immigration law against those in the lesbian, gay, bisexual, and transgender community and immigrants who are living with HIV or AIDS. Incorporated in 1994, Immigration Equality helps those affected by discriminatory practices through education, outreach, advocacy, and the maintenance of a nationwide resource network and a heavily trafficked website. Immigration Equality also runs a pro bono asylum program and provides technical assistance and advice to hundreds of lawyers nationwide on sexual orientation, transgender, and HIV-based asylum matters.

§11.3 Safety and Health Care of Immigration Detainees

In 2007, a postoperative transgender individual contacted a prisoner advocacy organization. The individual was in Immigration and Customs Enforcement (ICE) detention awaiting resolution of the individual's asylum case. ICE detention officials had confiscated the individual's prescription hormones, a standard part of the individual's healthcare regimen since long before the individual's detention, which was necessary for maintaining the individual's health and transition between genders. Repeated requests to ICE's medical staff for more hormones had been refused, and the individual wanted to know what to do to get the hormone therapy restored.

This posed a very perplexing problem even for organizations and firms routinely involved in transgender rights, prisoner rights, and asylum law. Frustratingly for the individual client, no one had a quick or easy answer. Initial research showed that, unlike the Federal Bureau of Prisons (BOP) or the California Department of Corrections and

---

17. Those reports can be accessed on the U.S. Department of State's website at http://www.state.gov/g/drl/rls/hrrpt/ (last visited August 2, 2011).

Rehabilitation (CDCR), which have established regulations concerning how Gender Identity Disorder (GID) will be treated, ICE regulations had no such policy. It appeared that medical treatment decisions were largely discretionary, and had the potential to vary from detention center to detention center. In the absence of a regulation or policy to cite when arguing for proper transgender healthcare procedures, the individual was left in an uncertain position, stuck in ICE detention for an indeterminate amount of time, with no clear course of action to restore hormone therapy and avoid the degenerative health effects caused by hormone deprivation. Advocates working on the case were also frustrated because, at the time, there were no practitioner's guides or articles suggesting a course of action to help the client. This story is but one demonstration of the veritable legal black hole in which transgender persons in ICE detention now find themselves.[18]

Sexual abuse in immigration detention centers is far too common. The Krome Avenue Detention Center in Miami, Florida, the Varick Street Immigration Detention Center in New York City, and the Port Isabel Service Processing Center in Los Fresnos, Texas, have been extensively investigated and reported on. Rape and sexual abuse charges have been extensively reported. In one case from the Krome Avenue Detention Center in Miami, the officer who was assigned the investigation from the INS Office of Internal Audit told the Florida Immigrant Advocacy Center (FIAC) that a woman who complained of sexual abuse "was just another person making false accusations against Immigration." No disciplinary action was taken, and when the incident was mentioned at a meeting with the FIAC, one supervisory official began to laugh. Pervasive sexual abuse and sexual harassment of detainees at the Port Isabel Service Processing Center included numerous instances of detention officers trading favors and privileges for sex with detainees or coercing detainees into sex. No personnel were disciplined.

The INS contracted with the privately owned Esmor Corporation (now known as Corrections Service Corporation) to run its 300-bed facility in

---

18. Dana O'Day-Senior, *The Forgotten Frontier? Healthcare for Transgendered Detainees in Immigration and Customs Enforcement Detention*, 60 Hastings L. J. 453 (2008).

Elizabeth, New Jersey, in 1993. The INS contracts gave Esmor control of medical care, food services, laundry services, and selection of staff to run the facility and guard detainees. For several years, the INS left Esmor largely free from oversight. Esmor went to great lengths to keep costs down and profits up, resulting in harmful, substandard conditions. Officers at the understaffed facility were often inadequately trained and insufficiently supervised. Described by one Congressional observer as the worst immigration detention center in the nation, Esmor's food was spoiled, its medical care was inadequate, the cells smelled of human waste, and beatings were doled out to those who requested cleaning supplies. Sexual abuse of detainees by officers was rampant. After a riot at Esmor in June 1995 forced the facility's closure, detainees were transferred to the Union County jail, where they faced physical and sexual assault at the hands of a group of two dozen officers. The officers used pliers to remove a detainee's pubic hair during a strip search, forced detainees to put their heads in toilets, encouraged the detainees to engage in homosexual activity and to touch each others' genitals, and forced detainees to kneel on the floor nude and chant, "America is number one."[19]

And this abuse includes transgender detainees as is evidenced by the case of Christina Madrazo.

Case Study: Christina Madrazo

Christina Madrazo, a Mexican national and a preoperative transsexual, was raped twice by a guard at Krome Detention Center in Miami, Florida. The officer who attacked her, Lemar Smith, was the same man responsible for bringing her meals and watching over her cellblock.

Madrazo was initially placed in solitary confinement when she arrived at Krome, because center officials were unsure whether to house her with men or women. She felt isolated and afraid of Smith, who was much larger than she was.

---

19. Stop Prisoner Rape, *No Refuge Here: A First Look at Sexual Abuse in Immigration Detention*, pp. 4–7 (2004), http://www.justdetention.org/pdf/norefugehere.pdf (last visted August 6, 2011).

Smith attacked Madrazo in her cell, attempting to force her to perform oral sex on him. He then sodomized her until he heard another person approaching.

"My fear was incredible," Madrazo recalls. "I didn't know if anybody would help me or protect me. Nobody had given me simple human treatment since they took me there."

After speaking with a psychiatrist at the center and a visitor from the Mexican consulate, Madrazo decided to report the rape.

The night after she filed the report, Smith was allowed back into Madrazo's cell to serve her dinner. Later, he returned and raped her a second time.

"I wanted to scream, but I couldn't," Madrazo recalled. "He told me if I say anything, I'm gonna pay. I felt so angry, so impotent. He called me a bitch and said I deserved it, like he was glad."

Madrazo was sent to a psychiatric hospital for several weeks before being released from custody. One month after her release, Smith was indicted on two counts of felony rape and two counts of sex with a ward. He was sentenced to eight months in jail and one year of probation.

Madrazo filed suit against the United States in connection with the attack, settling her claim in November 2003.[20]

A study "Sexual Abuse in U.S. Immigration Detention by Just Detention International" in 2009 noted:

Unlike criminal defendants, immigration detainees have no right to an attorney. This lack of legal assistance makes it unlikely that survivors of sexual abuse in immigration detention have access to someone who is able to explain their rights and to advocate on their behalf. In addition, after being traumatized by a sexual assault, non-citizen detainees often have difficulty speaking out due to cultural isolation, language barriers, and limited literacy.

. . .

---

20. *Id.* at p. 5.

Similar to the dynamics of sexual violence in prisons, jails, and the community at-large, immigration detainees from marginalized populations are at greatest risk for sexual abuse. In particular, lesbian, gay, bisexual, transgendered, and queer (LGBTQ) individuals, youth, and detainees living with mental illness or disabilities are disproportionately targeted.

Regardless of citizenship status, all detainees retain their basic human right to be free from sexual abuse. Sexual violence in immigration detention is a form of torture, prohibited by international treaties ratified by the U.S., such as the Convention Against Torture and Other Cruel, Inhuman and Degrading Treatment or Punishment (CAT) and the International Covenant on Civil and Political Rights (ICCPR). In addition, non-citizens retain constitutional protections while in U.S. immigration detention, including the right not to be subject to cruel and unusual punishment, such as sexual violence.[21]

This is the same problem faced by transgender prisoners in federal, state, and local jails in the United States. This topic is more thoroughly discussed in Chapter 12, "Criminal Justice and Corrections."

---

21. *Sexual Abuse in U.S. Immigration Detention*, JUST DETENTION INTERNATIONAL (January 2009), http://www.justdetention.org/en/factsheets/immigrationfactsheet.pdf (last visited August 6, 2011).

Criminal Justice and Corrections

The concerns for transgender persons in the criminal justice system primarily relate to their treatment in jails and prisons. There are two concerns: safety and health care. These will be addressed separately.

However, how transgender persons are treated before being incarcerated is a problem since law enforcement officials often refuse to recognize their transgender status and give them the respect that they deserve. The following is a documented example. Male U.S. Marshals who conducted "in custody" strip searches of a pretrial detainee, a transgender woman, who had undergone sex reassignment surgery and had her sex legally changed to female, were held to not be entitled to qualified immunity from transgender detainee's unlawful search claim under 42 U.S.C.A. § 1983. A reasonable officer would have known that a cross-gender search of a female detainee by male United States Marshals Service (U.S.M.S.) employees that included intimate physical contact, exposure of private body parts, and verbal harassment, all in front of male detainees and male U.S.M.S. employees, in the absence of an emergency, was unreasonable.[1]

---

1. Shaw v. District of Columbia, 944 F.Supp.2d 43 (D. D.C. 2013).

§12.1 Safety of Transgender Inmates

Inmates have a constitutional right to adequate housing.[2] When dealing with male-to-female transgender inmates, however, the determination of what is adequate is often a problem. The issue is not that transgender inmates are or should be entitled to any kind of special housing, rather it is whether they will be housed with male or female inmates. This situation was recognized by the U.S. Supreme Court, which held that prison officials who were involved in transferring a female transsexual prisoner to a maximum security facility in which she was allegedly raped and assaulted by other prisoners could be held liable if it were proven that they had shown deliberate indifference to the transsexual prisoner's safety, in violation of her Eighth Amendment rights.[3] In *Farmer v. Brennan*,[4] the Court found that the transgender inmate was safer in administrative segregation, but did not address whether that was proper or not.[5]

A prison inmate sued a guard and a prison supervisor, alleging that her privacy and Eighth Amendment rights were violated by a guard's disclosure that she was transsexual. The U.S. District Court granted judgment notwithstanding the verdict in favor of the defendants on a privacy claim and dismissed an Eighth Amendment claim on grounds of qualified immunity. The U.S. Court of Appeals for the Second Circuit reversed in part and held in part that the transsexual inmate had a privacy right of confidentiality in her medical records and that there was no qualified immunity from the claim that the guard and supervisor were deliberately indifferent to the safety of the inmate, in violation of her Eighth Amendment rights, as a result of the disclosure of the inmate's transsexual status. However, the supervisor had qualified immunity on the confidentiality claim, as there was no clearly established right to the confidentiality of prison medical records at time in question.[6]

---

2. Farmer v. Brennan, 511 U.S. 825, 832, 114 S. Ct. 1970, 128 L. Ed. 2d 811 (1994).

3. *Id.*

4. *Id.*

5. The issue was not raised. The question presented to the Supreme Court was: "Does the 'deliberate indifference' standard adopted in City of Canton, Ohio v. Harris, 489 U.S. 378 (1989), govern Eighth Amendment claims regarding failure to protect prisoners from assault?", Petitioner's Brief, at i. 1993 WL 625980.

6. Powell v. Schriver, 175 F.3d 107 (2nd Cir. 1999).

The plaintiff, a transgender inmate, is undergoing hormone therapy and has a feminine appearance. The plaintiff contends that he informed the defendants that Rogers State Prison was not a safe place to house inmates like him. The plaintiff alleged that another inmate sexually assaulted him after he (the plaintiff) informed defendant Hooks of his concern about his safety. He also alleges that he was placed in protective custody with this same inmate, who once again sexually assaulted him. According to the plaintiff, all three defendants failed to take reasonable steps to ensure his safety. It was held that the complaint stated a cause of action.[7]

In a very interesting case, the Connecticut Superior Court granted the motion to transfer a transgender juvenile inmate to the Commissioner of Correction at the Connecticut Correctional Institution, Niantic, as a transgendered female. She was ordered to be held in isolation for no more than 72 hours. She was to be examined, evaluated, and classified under the appropriate State and Federal statues, guidelines, rules, and procedures. This transfer was to be reviewed by the court every six months to determine whether it should be continued or terminated, unless the Commissioner of the Dept. of Correction has already exercised the powers granted under Conn. Gen. Stat. § 17a–13 by removing such person from the John R. Manson Youth Institution, Cheshire, or the Connecticut Correctional Institution, Niantic. Such transfer was to terminate upon the expiration of the commitment in the juvenile matter.[8]

Jails and prisons also have a duty under the Eighth Amendment to the U.S. Constitution to provide for their inmates' safety.[9] This duty includes protecting inmates from rape, sexual assault, and battery by other inmates and by staff.[10]

The biggest problem with prison rape and violence is the indifference of too many who are in control of the prisons. Massachusetts Department of Correction spokesman Anthony Carnevales said, "Well, that's prison . . .

---

7. Green v. Hooks, not reported in F.Supp.2d, 2013 WL 1620727 (S.D. Ga. 2013).

8. In re Doe, not reported in A.3d, 2014 WL 2600505 (Conn. Super. 2014).

9. Farmer v. Brennan, *supra* note 1.

10. Farmer v. Brennan, 511 U.S. 825, at 833–834.

I don't know what to tell you." In that offhand remark, he was expressing what many feel in their hearts but are loathe to admit—"they deserve it."[11]

Prison rape and violence are issues of control and domination. This is illustrated by the statement of a Minnesota inmate before the Congressional committee considering the enacted Prison Rape Elimination Act of 2003[12] (PREA). "Most of the prisoners who rape are spending 5 to life. And are a part of a gang. They look for a smaller, weaker individual. And make that person into a homosexual then sell him to other inmates of gangs. Anywhere from a pack of cigarettes to 2 cartons . . . No one cares about you or anyone else."[13] A New York inmate related the following to the Committee. "When a man finally gets his victim, he protects him from everyone else, buys him anything, the victim washes his clothes, his cell, etc. In return, the entire prison knows that this guy has a 'BITCH' or 'girl.' Now I've seen this happen many times. The response from the guards is 'the strong survive,' 'who cares,' or they join in the teasing and tormenting. But someone who is not 'protected' has other problems. I've seen inmates attacked by two or three men at a time and forced to the floor, while three men hold him down the fourth rapes him. I've known two men who have hung themselves after this."[14] These statements are supported by the findings of the Congress in enacting the PREA. "Young first-time offenders are at increased risk of sexual victimization. Juveniles are 5 times more likely to be sexually assaulted in adult rather than juvenile facilities—often within the first forty-eight hours of incarceration."[15] When representing a transgender defendant in a criminal case, the practitioner should, when feasible, argue for alternative sentencing other than incarceration since most correctional facilities can only offer administrative segregation to the transgender inmate to protect the inmate from prison rape and other violence

---

11. Testimony of Pat Nolan before the U.S. House of Representatives Committee on the Judiciary, Subcommittee on Crime, Terrorism, and Homeland Security, April 29, 2003, p. 92, hearing on the Prison Rape Reduction Act of 2003.

12. 42 U.S.C. § 15601, *et seq.*

13. Inmates Testimony to Human Rights Watch presented to the U.S. House of Representatives Committee on the Judiciary, Subcommittee on Crime, Terrorism, and Homeland Security, April 29, 2003, p. 20, hearing on the Prison Rape Elimination Act of 2003.

14. *Id.*

15. 42 U.S.C. § 15601(4).

and administrative segregation is the same as solitary confinement—which is an enhanced punishment usually reserved for inmates who fail to follow the rules in the general prison population.

In its findings for he PREA, Congress stated: "Prison rape often goes unreported, and inmate victims often receive inadequate treatment for the severe physical and psychological effects of sexual assault—if they receive treatment at all."[16] "Insufficient research has been conducted and insufficient data reported on the extent of prison rape. However, experts have conservatively estimated that at least 13 percent of the inmates in the United States have been sexually assaulted in prison. Many inmates have suffered repeated assaults. Under this estimate, nearly 200,000 inmates now incarcerated have been or will be the victims of prison rape. The total number of inmates who have been sexually assaulted in the past 20 years likely exceeds 1,000,000."[17] A U.S. Department of Justice report documented 8,210 allegations of sexual violence in prisons in 2004.[18] The seriousness of this problem is illustrated by the fact that the PREA was passed by a *unanimous* vote in both houses of Congress.[19] The legislation mandates that a U.S. Department of Justice report be published annually.[20]

On May 17, 2012, the U.S. Department of Justice released a final rule regarding implementation of the PREA. Due to a Presidential Memorandum issued that same day, other federal departments with confinement facilities are required to work with the attorney general to issue rules or procedures that will satisfy the requirements of the PREA. The standards set forth in the final rule are binding on the Federal Bureau of Prisons. With regard to states, those that do not comply with the standards are subject to a five percent reduction in funds they would otherwise receive for prison purposes from the department unless the governor certifies that five percent of such funds will be used to enable compliance in future years. No organization responsible for the accreditation of correctional facilities may receive any

---

16. 42 U.S.C. § 15601(6).

17. 42 U.S.C. § 15601(2) Findings by the Congress in passing the Prison Rape Elimination Act of 2003.

18. Allen J. Beck and Timothy A. Hughes, U.S. Dept. of Justice, Bureau of Justice Statistics, *Sexual Violence Reported by Correctional Authorities, 2004*, NCJ210333 (July 2005).

19. 42 U.S.C. § 15601, *et seq.*

20. 42 U.S.C. § 15603.

federal grants unless it adopts accreditation standards consistent with the standards set forth in the final rule. The rule is also binding on state and local facilities that house federal inmates. The rule adopts the following definitions:

> *Gender nonconforming* means a person whose appearance or manner does not conform to traditional societal gender expectations.
>
> *Inmate* means any person incarcerated or detained in a prison or jail.
>
> *Intersex* means a person whose sexual or reproductive anatomy or chromosomal pattern does not seem to fit typical definitions of male or female. Intersex medical conditions are sometimes referred to as disorders of sex development.
>
> . . .
>
> *Transgendered* means a person whose gender identity (i.e., internal sense of feeling male or female) is different from the person's assigned sex at birth.[21]

The screening process shall take into consideration "whether the inmate is or is perceived to be gay, lesbian, bisexual, transgendered, intersex, or gender nonconforming."[22] That screening information shall be used:

> (c) In deciding whether to assign a transgendered or intersex inmate to a facility for male or female inmates, and in making other housing and programming assignments, the agency shall consider on a case-by-case basis whether a placement would ensure the inmate's health and safety, and whether the placement would present management or security problems.
>
> (d) Placement and programming assignments for each transgendered or intersex inmate shall be reassessed at least twice each year to review any threats to safety experienced by the inmate.

---

21. 28 C.F.R. § 115.5.
22. 28 C.F.R. § 115.41.

(e) A transgendered or intersex inmate's own views with respect to his or her own safety shall be given serious consideration.

(f) Transgendered and intersex inmates shall be given the opportunity to shower separately from other inmates.

(g) The agency shall not place lesbian, gay, bisexual, transgendered, or intersex inmates in dedicated facilities, units, or wings solely on the basis of such identification or status, unless such placement is in a dedicated facility, unit, or wing established in connection with a consent decree, legal settlement, or legal judgment for the purpose of protecting such inmates.[23]

The rule also requires that personnel be trained in how "to communicate effectively and professionally with residents, including lesbian, gay, bisexual, transgender, intersex, or gender nonconforming residents."[24] In summary, the new Department of Justice rule appears to be a very positive step not only in protecting transgender and other inmates from sexual abuse but in treating transgender inmates with respect.

The danger to transgender inmates comes not just from other inmates. For example, in 2010, a New York City corrections officer was arrested and charged with forcing a transgender inmate to engage in a sex act with him at a Manhattan jail.[25]

Sexual abuse of lesbian, gay, bisexual, transgender, and queer (LGBTQ) inmates constitutes one of the most rampant and ignored human rights violations in the U.S. today. In a 2007 academic study, funded by the California Department of Corrections and Rehabilitation and conducted at six California men's prisons, *67 percent of inmates who identified as LGBTQ reported having been sexually assaulted* by another inmate during their incarceration, *a rate that was 15 times higher than for the inmate population overall.* Of the hundreds of

---

23. 28 C.F.R. § 115.42.

24. 28 C.F.R. § 115.231(a)(9).

25. Anahad O'Connor, *Guard Held in Sexual Attack on Transgendered Inmate*, N.Y. TIMES (October 7, 2010), http://www.nytimes.com/2010/10/08/nyregion/08inmate.html (last visited August 3, 2011).

survivors who contact JDI [Just Detention International] every year, approximately 20 percent self identify as gay, bisexual or transgendered.[26] [emphasis added]

California recognized the problem of prisoner rape within its correctional facilities. On September 22, 2005, Governor Arnold Schwarzenegger signed the Sexual Abuse in Detention Elimination Act.[27] This act is not specifically for transgendered inmates, but it does include some provisions that would appear to be helpful to transgender inmates:

> The Department of Corrections and Rehabilitation inmate classification and housing assignment procedures shall take into account risk factors that can lead to inmates and wards becoming the target of sexual victimization. §2636(a)
>
> Inmates and wards who file complaints of sexual abuse shall not be punished, either directly or indirectly, for doing so. If a person is segregated for his or her own protection, segregation must be non-disciplinary. §2637(b)
>
> Staff shall not discriminate in their response to inmates and wards who are gay, bisexual, or transgendered who experience sexual aggression, or report that they have experienced sexual abuse. §2637(e)

The problem with using administrative segregation housing for other than disciplinary reasons is that inmates are confined to their cells for twenty-one to twenty-four hours a day and often have little or no human contact except for highly limited (and often unpleasant) interactions with facility staff.[28] In segregation, a prisoner gets at most an hour a day out of his or her cell for exercise, and it has been known to be as little as five to ten minutes a day.[29] Inmates in segregation get at most one shower per week, and

---

26. Just Detention International, *Fact Sheet, LGBTQ Detainees Chief Targets for Sexual Abuse in Detention* (2009), http://www.justdetention.org/en/factsheets/JD_Fact_Sheet_LGBTQ_vD.pdf (last visited August 6, 2011).

27. CAL. PENAL CODE § 2635, *et seq.*, A.B. 550, 2005 Cal. Legis. Serv. Ch. 303.

28. Gabriel Arkles, *Safety and Solidarity Across Gender Lines: Rethinking Segregation of Transgendered People in Detention*, 18 TEMP. POL. & CIV. RTS. L. REV. 515, 538–539 (2009).

29. Hesitt v. Helms, 459 U.S. 460, 480, 103 S. Ct. 864, 74 L. Ed. 2d 675 (1983).

it is not uncommon for showers to be less frequent than that.[30] Access to the prison library, educational classes, laundry, and other prison facilities is either very restricted or totally denied to inmates in isolation. Medical care is also known to be restricted and even denied to inmates in segregation.[31] Emotional distress has been found to occur when an inmate is placed in such solitary confinement.[32] Solitary confinement, even when not used as a punishment, still amounts to punishment. It is punishment in excess of what would be imposed if the inmate were not transgender, and it is, thus, cruel and unusual punishment to automatically place transgender inmates into solitary confinement when they have committed no breach of prison rules.[33]

§12.2 Health Care for Transgender Inmates

The U.S. Supreme Court has held that every inmate, regardless of gender identity, is entitled to reasonable medical care.[34] Dr. Lori Kohler, a transgender medicine expert, argues that the lack of access to medical care, whether from an internist or a specialist, is attributable to the attitude of the medical profession.[35]

Thus, it is not surprising that medical care for transgender inmates is generally so lacking. This is because of the well-known situation that prison health care lags behind that available to nonincarcerated individuals. Some of this is attributable to public apathy toward inmate care, and some is attributable to legislatures' desire to spend as little as possible on prisoner care, including health care.

Within the need for and right to reasonable medical care in prison, transgender inmates have specific essential needs—that is, hormonal medications

---

30. *Id.*

31. Estelle v. Gamble, 429 U.S. 97, 114 n. 8, 97 S. Ct. 285, 50 L. Ed. 2d 251 (1976).

32. *See* Cox v. Cook, 420 U.S. 734, 735, 95 S. Ct. 1237, 43 L. Ed. 2d 587 (1975).

33. Meriwether v. Faulkner, 821 F.2d 408, 415 (7th Cir. 1987), *cert. den.* 484 U.S. 925 (1987) ("The Eighth Amendment prohibits punishments which involve the unnecessary and wanton infliction of pain, are grossly disproportionate to the severity of the crime for which an inmate was imprisoned, or are totally without penological justification."); *see also* Veal v. Lane, 14 F.3d 605 (7th Cir. 1993).

34. Farmer v. Brennan, 511 U.S. 825, 832, 114 S. Ct. 1970, 128 L. Ed. 2d 811 (1994).

35. Kaiser Family Foundation, *Transcript of 17th National HIV/AIDS Update Conference: Vulnerable Communities Track: Forging New Ground: Transgendered Issues and Corrections Medicine,* pp. 11–14 (April 12, 2005).

under the relevant Standards of Care.[36] This has been held to include hormone therapy for transgender inmates.[37] One court held that the prisoner's "[gender identity disorder] diagnosis constitutes a serious medical need."[38] That court also entered a permanent injunction requiring the prison to ensure that a prisoner received consistent and timely ongoing treatment for her gender identity disorder in accordance with the Standards of Care promulgated by the World Professional Association for Transgendered Health and applicable community standards.[39]

For male-to-female transgender persons this would be a testosterone suppressant and estrogen at a dosage similar to one prescribed for a postmenopausal woman. For the female-to-male transgender person the need is for an estrogen suppressant and testosterone. There is evidence that access to cross gender hormone therapy "not only improves people's quality of life, but it actually will improve their adherence to treatment for chronic disease."[40] And, unlike sex or gender reassignment surgery, these medications are inexpensive. The most commonly prescribed antiandrogen drug is Spironolactone, which is the generic version of the name-brand drugs Aldactone, Novo-Spiroton, Aldactazide, Spiractin, Spirotone, Verospiron, and Berlactone. The most commonly prescribed estrogen is Estrace, which is available in generic form as Estradiol. Both of these generic versions of these drugs are available at Walmart for $4.00[41]—which means that a prison health plan could acquire them for that or less.

To complete the treatment provided by the Standards of Care, preoperative transsexuals need sex or gender reassignment surgery. At present, this surgery is only available from a handful of specialized surgeons in

---

36. World Professional Association for Transgendered Health (formerly the Harry Benjamin International Gender Dysphoria Association), *The Standards of Care for Gender Identity Disorders*, http://www.wpath.org/documents2/socv6.pdf (last visited August 3, 2011).

37. Brooks v. Berg, 270 F. Supp. 2d 302, at 305 (N.D. N.Y. 2003), and Brooks v. Berg, 289 F. Supp. 2d 286, at 287 (N.D. N.Y. 2003).

38. Soneeya v. Spencer, 851 F. Supp.2d 228, 231–232 (D. Mass. 2012).

39. Soneeya v. Spencer, *supra*, at 252.

40. Kaiser Family Foundation, *supra* note 31, pp.17–18.

41. WalMart $4 Prescription Program (June 5, 2008) http://i.walmart.com/i/if/hmp/fusion/genericdruglist.pdf (last visited August 3, 2011).

the United States (in Arizona,[42] California,[43] Colorado,[44] and Florida[45]), a two-surgeon clinic in Montreal, Canada,[46] one in New Zealand,[47] one in Spain,[48] one in the United Kingdom,[49] one in Brussels,[50] and several clinics in Thailand.[51] At this time in the United States, no correctional system has a policy of paying for sex or gender reassignment surgery. However, the U.S. District Court for Massachusetts on September 4, 2012, became the first court to order that a prison system provide sex reassignment surgery to an inmate. In that case, the court ordered the Massachusetts Department of Correction to provide sex reassignment surgery to Michelle L. Kosilek, a male-to-female transgender inmate. The court held:

> Kosilek has proven, however, that the Commissioner's purported security concerns are a pretext to mask the real reason for the decision to deny him sex reassignment surgery—a fear of controversy, criticism, ridicule, and scorn. Therefore, Kosilek has proven that the DOC is violating his rights under the Eighth Amendment. He has also established that this violation will continue if the court does not now order

42. Toby R. Meltzer, M.D., *see* http://www.tmeltzer.com/ (last visited August 3, 2011).

43. Gary J. Alter, M.D., *see* http://www.altermd.com/Transsexual%20Surgery/male_to_female.htm (last visited August. 3, 2011); and Michael L. Brownstein, M.D., *see* http://www.brownsteinmd.com/ (last visited August 3, 2011).

44. Dr. Marci L. Bowers, M.D. [who is a male-to-female transsexual herself], *see* http://www.marcibowers.com/grs/history.html (last visited August 3, 2011).

45. The Reid Center for Genital Surgery, *see* http://www.srsmiami.com/ (last visited August 3, 2011).

46. Pierre Brassard, M.D., & Maud Belanger, M.D., *see* http://www.grsmontreal.com/anglais.html (last accessed August 3, 2011).

47. Peter Walker, M.D. at Southern Cross Trust Hospital, http://www.plasticsurgery.co.nz/ (last accessed visited August 3, 2011).

48. Sáenz de Cabezon, M.D., *see* http://www.saenzdecabezon.com/angl/fresp.html (last visited August 3, 2011).

49. James Bellringer at Charing Cross Hospital & Parkside Hospital, *see* http://www.bellringers.pwp.blueyonder.co.uk/ (last visited August 3, 2011).

50. Transsexual Women Resources, *Sexual Reassignment Surgery* at http://www.annelawrence.com/srsindex.html (last visited August 3, 2011).

51. Choomchoke Janwimaluang, M.D., at Ban Don Hospital, *see* http://www.srsthailand.com/ (last visited August 3, 2011); and Sanguan Kunaporn, M.D. at Phuket International Hospital, *see* http://phuket-plasticsurgery.com/ (last visited August 3, 2011).

the DOC to provide the treatment its doctors have prescribed. Therefore, such an injunction is being issued.[52]

The District Court in *Kosilek* was affirmed by a three-judge panel of the
First Circuit.[53] But the First Circuit granted en banc review and reversed.
The en banc court gave great deference to the security concerns of the
Massachusetts Dept. of Corrections.[54]

After the *Kosilek* case, a preoperative transsexual inmate filed an action
under 42 U.S.C.A. § 1983 alleging that state prison officials' continued denial
of consideration for her request for sex reassignment surgery as treatment for
her gender identity disorder constituted deliberate indifference to her serious
medical need in violation of the Eighth Amendment. The U.S. District Court
dismissed the complaint. The U.S. Court of Appeals for the Fourth Circuit
reversed and held that the inmate stated a plausible Eighth Amendment claim.[55]

Until 2001, Canada did not provide sex or gender reassignment surgery
to its inmates. Now it does as a result of a recent decision by the Canada
Human Rights Tribunal.[56] The tribunal reasoned that the Correctional Services of Canada (CSC) Health Service Policy's "blanket prohibition on access
to sex reassignment surgery is discriminatory on the basis of both sex and
disability."[57] Based on personal dealings with transgender persons in Canada,
the surgery is classified as elective and nonemergency, so to get it under the
Canadian national health plan one must go on a waiting list. The persons
that I talked to when I was in Montreal for my surgery stated that the waiting period was two to three years, which they and I considered reasonable.

The rationale for making sex or gender reassignment surgery available
to Canadian inmates would not apply in the United States because there is

52. Kosilek v. Spencer, 889 F.Supp.2d 190, 198 (D. Mass. 2012), post-judgment order
2013 WL 204696 (D. Mass. 2013), aff'd Kosilek v. Spencer, 740 F.3d 733 (1st Cir. 2014), rev'd
on reh. *en banc* Kosilek v. Spencer, ___ F.3d ___, 2014 WL 7139560 (1st Cir. 2014) . See also:
Kothmann v. Rosario, 558 Fed.Appx. 907 (11th Cir. 2014) (prisoner stated a claim for deliberate indifference, and prisoner's right to hormone therapy was clearly
53. Kosilek v. Spencer, 740 F.3d 733 (1st Cir. 2014)
54. Kosilek v. Spencer, ___ F.3d ___, 2014 WL 7139560 (1st Cir. 2014)
55. De'lonta v. Johnson, 708 F.3d 520 (4th Cir. 2013).
56. Kavanagh v. Canada, 41 C.H.R.R. D/119, 2001 Carswell Nat. 3807, at ¶¶ 198 and
200 (Canada Human Rights Tribunal 2001).
57. Kavanagh v. Canada, *supra* note 49 at § 198.

no national health plan in the United States. Surgery is excluded from most group insurance plans in the United States except at a number of large U.S. companies. A list of those companies is in Appendix 8. Due to the budget problems of most correctional systems and the cost of the surgeries and associated travel to what is likely to be an out-of-state surgeon, most correctional systems in the United States are likely to resist paying for such surgeries. In fact, Wisconsin enacted the Inmate Sex Change Prevention Act, which specifically prohibited its prison system from paying for either hormones or surgery for transgender inmates. However, the U.S. District Court for the Eastern District of Wisconsin declared the law unconstitutional as violating prisoners' rights under the Eighth Amendment to the U.S. Constitution as to hormonal treatment.[58]

In 2011, as a result of a suit by Vanessa Adams,[59] the Federal Bureau of Prisons changed its policy towards transgender inmates. Previously, the policy had been to only continue treatment for inmates that had begun before commitment to the Bureau of Prisons. The new policy was outlined in a Memorandum for Chief Executive Officers dated May 31, 2011. That memo provided in pertinent part:

> This memorandum provides additional clarification for the evaluation and treatment of inmates with Gender Identity Disorder (GID), and should be read in conjunction with guidance provided in June, 2010 (attached). This memorandum should be distributed and implemented immediately, and applies to inmates currently in Bureau of Prisons (BOP) custody. This memorandum will be incorporated into the national program statement as soon as possible.
>
> Inmates with a possible diagnosis of GID, including inmates who assert they have GID, will receive thorough medical and mental health evaluations from medical professionals with basic competence in the assessment of the DSM-IV/ICD-10 sexual disorders and who have participated in BOP's GID training, including the review of

---

58. Fields v. Smith, 712 F.Supp. 2d 830 (E.D. Wis. 2010).
59. Adams v. Federal Bureau of Prisons, 716 F.Supp.2d 107 (D. Mass. 2010) (denying BOP's motion to dismiss after BOP agreed to provide hormones to Adams).

all available community health records. The evaluation will include an assessment of the inmate's treatment and life experiences during incarceration (including hormone therapy, completed or in-process surgical interventions, real life experience consistent with the inmates gender identity, private expressions that conform to the preferred gender, and counseling). If a diagnosis of GID is reached, a proposed treatment plan will be developed which promotes the physical and mental stability of the patient. The development of the treatment plan is not solely dependent on services provided or the inmate's life experiences prior to incarceration. The treatment plan may include elements or services that were, or were not, provided prior to incarceration, including but not limited to: those elements of the real life experience consistent with the prison environment, hormone therapy and counseling. Treatment plans will be reviewed regularly and updated as necessary.

Current, accepted standards of care will be used as a reference for developing the treatment plan. All appropriate treatment options prescribed for inmates with GID in currently accepted standards of care will be taken into consideration during evaluation by the appropriate medical and mental health care staff. Each treatment plan or denial of treatment must be reviewed by the Medical Director or BOP Chief Psychiatrist. Hormone therapy must be requested through the non-formulary review process, and approved by the Medical Director and/or BOP Chief Psychiatrist. Consultation with the Chief of Psychiatry prior to such approval may be appropriate in some cases.[60]

The most enlightened policy for the treatment of transgender inmates is a proposed policy contained in a Policy Statement by the National Commission on Correctional Health Care in 2009. It provides:

---

60. Memorandum for Chief Executive Officers, Subject: Gender Identity Disorder Evaluation and Treatment, May 31, 2011, from RADM Newton E. Kendig, Assistant Director, Health Services Division and Charles E. Samuels, Jr., Assistant Director, Correctional Programs Division (copy in author's files).

Transgendered people face an array of risks to their health and well-being during incarceration. They are commonly placed in correctional facilities according to their genitals and/or sex assigned at birth, regardless of their safety needs or gender presentation. Incarcerated transgendered people are often targets of physical assault and emotional abuse. The health risks of overlooking the particular needs of transgendered inmates are so severe that acknowledgement of the problem and policies that assure appropriate and responsible provision of health care are needed.

The term transgendered refers to a diverse group of people who identify or express their gender in a way that does not match traditional ideas about the sex they were assigned at birth. Transgendered women are people who were assigned the sex of male at birth and who now identify as women. Transgendered men are people who were assigned the sex of female at birth and who now identify as men. Transgendered people may identify as men, women, neither, both, or as another gender. Transgendered people can be any race, sexual orientation, age, religion, body type, socioeconomic background, or national origin.

The National Commission on Correctional Health Care publishes *Standards* for prisons, jails, and juvenile justice facilities, which address Board approved recommendations for an adequate health care delivery system and address issues such as patient confidentiality, discharge planning, qualified health care professionals, medication availability and delivery, and staff training. Position statements are intended to provide information on the management of specific problems not addressed in the *Standards*.

Position Statement

Prisons, jails, and juvenile justice facilities have a responsibility to ensure the physical and mental health and well-being of transgendered people in their custody. Correctional health staff should manage transgendered inmates in a manner that respects the biomedical and psychological aspects of a Gender Identity Disorder (GID) diagnosis. The National Commission on

Correctional Health Care recommends that the following principles guide correctional health care professionals in addressing the needs of transgendered inmates:

Management

1. The management of medical (e.g., medically necessary hormone treatment) and surgical (e.g., genital reconstruction) transgendered issues should follow accepted standards[61] that have been developed by professionals with expertise in transgendered health. Determination of treatment necessary for transgendered patients should be on a case-by-case basis. Ideally, correctional facility health professionals should be trained in transgendered health care issues. Alternatively, correctional health staff should have access to other professionals with expertise in transgendered health care to help determine appropriate management and provide training in transgendered issues.

2. Because inmate-patients may be under different stages of care prior to incarceration, there should not be blanket administrative policies that restrict specific medical treatments for transgendered people. Policies that make treatments available only to those who received them prior to incarceration, or limit GID treatment to psychotherapy should be avoided. Policies that attempt to "freeze" gender transition at the stage reached prior to incarceration are inappropriate and out of step with medical standards, and should be avoided.

3. Diagnosed transgendered patients who received hormone therapy prior to incarceration should have that therapy continued without interruption pending evaluation by a specialist, absent urgent medical reasons to the contrary. Transgendered inmates who have not received hormone therapy prior to incarceration should be evaluated by a health care provider qualified in the area of transgendered health to determine their treatment needs. When determined to be medically necessary for a particular inmate, hormone therapy should be initiated and sex

---

61. World Professional Association for Transgendered Health (formerly the Harry Benjamin International Gender Dysphoria Association), *The Standards of Care for Gender Identity Disorders*, http://www.wpath.org/documents2/socv6.pdf (last visited August 3, 2011).

reassignment surgery considered on a case-by-case basis. Regular laboratory monitoring should be conducted according to community medical standards.

4. Treatment for genital self-harm, and for complications arising from prior surgery or from forms of self-treatment, should be provided when medically necessary.

5. Correctional health care providers should provide patient education materials to help transgendered patients cope with their diagnosis and treatment.

6. Psychotherapy such as "reparative" therapy or attempts to alter gender identity should not be employed. Reparative therapy inappropriately portrays GID as a mental illness and not a medical condition.

Patient Safety

1. In matters of housing, recreation, and work assignments custody staff should be aware that transgendered people are common targets for violence. Accordingly, appropriate safety measures should be taken, regardless of whether the individual is placed in male or female housing areas.

Discharge Planning

1. Transgendered inmates receiving hormone therapy should receive a sufficient supply upon release to last until a community provider assumes care. Referrals should be made to community-based organizations with sensitive and inclusive services for transgendered people.

2. Correctional policies for management of transgendered inmates should be developed and implemented in partnership with local transgendered communities, particularly current and former inmates, and transgendered service providers, whenever possible.[62]

---

62. National Commission on Correctional Health Care (NCCHC), Position Statement: *Transgendered Health Care in Correctional Settings* (adopted by the NCCHC Board of Directors October 18, 2009), http://www.ncchc.org/resources/statements/transgendered.html (last visited December 21, 2010).

It is hoped that the U.S. Bureau of Prisons and various state, county, and city correctional systems and facilities will adopt this proposed policy. This policy would, if implemented in good faith, address the very real and important concerns of transgender prisoners. In 2011, the U.S. Bureau of Prisons finally ended its policy of freezing an inmate's treatment for gender identity disorder (GID) at whatever level it was at the time of the inmate's incarceration to the Bureau of Prisons. In a memorandum dated May 31, 2011, the Bureau of Prisons new policy can be summarized by its concluding paragraph: "In summary, inmates in the custody of the Bureau with a possible diagnosis of GID will receive a current individualized assessment and evaluation. Treatment options will not be precluded solely due to level of services received, or lack of services, prior to incarceration."[63] This is a step forward for the Bureau of Prisons, but the better policy would be the one in the Position Statement of the National Commission on Correctional Health Care.

Transgender prisoners do not demand or deserve special treatment or rights, but like other prisoners, they can reasonably demand and expect that their unique needs for safety and medical care be met by the jails and prisons in which they are incarcerated. Just like a paraplegic prisoner is entitled to a wheel chair,[64] a toilet that is accessible,[65] and the taking of precautions to prevent decubitus ulcers (i.e., pressure sores and pressure ulcers).[66] Such ulcers or sores can be easily prevented with a special egg carton-shaped cushion.[67] Or, just like a prisoner with mental health problems is entitled to proper medication or therapy.[68] So, a transgender prisoner's medical needs and mental health needs must be met to afford to the prisoner his or her constitutional rights.[69]

---

63. U.S. Bureau of Prisons, Memorandum, Subject: *Gender Identity Disorder Evaluation and Treatment*, dated May 31, 2011, copy in author's files and retrieved from http://www.glad.org/uploads/docs/cases/adams-v-bureau-of-prisons/2011-gid-memo-final-bop-policy.pdf (last visited September 30, 2011).

64. Weeks v. Chaboudy, 984 F.2d 185 (6th Cir. 1993).

65. LaFaut v. Smith, 834 F.2d 389 (4th Cir. 1987).

66. Lawson v. Dallas County, 286 F.3d 257 (5th Cir. 2002).

67. University of Pittsburgh, *An RCT on Preventing Pressure Ulcers With Wheelchair Seat Cushions* (2005, updated 2010), retrieved from website of the National Institutes of Health website at http://clinicaltrials.gov/ct2/show/NCT00178126 (last visited December 23, 2010).

68. Belcher v. City of Foley, 30 F.3d 1390, 1395 (11th Cir. 1994).

69. *See* Fields v. Smith, 712 F.Supp. 2d 830 (E.D. Wis. 2010); Brooks v. Berg, 270 F. Supp. 2d 302 (N.D. N.Y. 2003); and Gammett v. Idaho State Bd. of Corrections, not reported in

However, the case of Anthony Q. Rowe shows there is still a long way to go with respect to transgender inmates receiving medically appropriate treatment. Before his incarceration in 2007, Rowe received treatment from a private physician, which included prescriptions for the following medications: Premetrium 200 mg daily, Aldactone 100 mg daily, and Estradiol 2 mg twice daily. During Rowe's initial evaluation by the Michigan Department of Corrections, the examining physician ordered three medications for Rowe: Premarin 1.25 mg daily, Estradiol 2 mg daily, and Prometrium 200 mg daily. The order for these three medications was deferred pending approval by the regional medical officer. The examining doctor entered a progress note indicating that the regional medical officer denied administration of the three medications. A fourth medication, Aldactone, was ordered and administered to Rowe. Later, the Aldactone was discontinued. Rowe went fifteen months without his needed medications and suffered irreversible hardening of silicone, which is apparently located in various parts of his body. Rowe has "loose silicone" in the hip, cheek, and breasts, and his physical characteristics are maintained by the silicone rather than implants. Yet, the U.S. Magistrate Judge recommended dismissal of his suit seeking an order to have the medications reinstated. It is important to note, that like many states, Michigan outsources its medical care to a for-profit corporate provider, Correctional Medical Services, Inc., which on August 9, 2011, produced 3,042 hits in Westlaw. The company provides or has provided medical care services to half or more of the states and has been sued many, many times. Even allowing for the litigiousness of prisoners, it seems a bad idea to put medical care decisions in the hands of a company that makes a larger profit when it delivers fewer services.[70]

It is too bad that Michigan is in the Sixth Circuit instead of the Seventh Circuit. The Seventh Circuit just affirmed a district court decision that declared unconstitutional and enjoined the enforcement of Wisconsin's

---

F.Supp.2d, 2007 WL 2186896 (D. Idaho 2007) (granting preliminary injunction in favor of transgendered prisoner), Gammett v. Idaho State Bd. of Corrections, not reported in F.Supp.2d, 2007 WL 2684750 (D. Idaho 2007) (denying state's motion for reconsideration and motion to vacate).

70. Rowe v. Correctional Medical Services, Inc., not reported in F.Supp.2d, 2010 WL 3779561 (W.D. Mich. 2010), report approved and adopted and summary judgment granted, not reported in F.Supp.2d, 2010 WL 3779437 (W.D. Mich. 2010).

Inmate Sex Change Prevention Act.[71] The court of appeals made an interesting observation.

> At trial, defendants stipulated that the cost of providing hormone therapy is between $300 and $1,000 per inmate per year. The district court compared this cost to the cost of a common antipsychotic drug used to treat many DOC inmates. In 2004, DOC paid a total of $2,300 for hormones for two inmates. That same year, DOC paid $2.5 million to provide inmates with quetiapine, an antipsychotic drug which costs more than $2,500 per inmate per year. Sex reassignment surgery is significantly more expensive, costing approximately $20,000. However, other significant surgeries may be more expensive. In 2005, DOC paid $37,244 for one coronary bypass surgery and $32,897 for one kidney transplant surgery. The district court concluded that DOC might actually incur greater costs by refusing to provide hormones, since inmates with GID might require other expensive treatments or enhanced monitoring by prison security. In fact, at oral argument before this court, counsel for defendants disclaimed any argument that Act 105 is justified by cost savings.[72]

ACLU lawyer John Knight hailed the ruling as a significant victory: "This was a discriminatory law that cruelly singled out transgendered people by denying them—and only them—the medical care they need . . . too often the medical needs of transgendered persons are not treated as the serious health issues that they are. We are glad that the appeals court has found that medical professionals, not the Wisconsin legislature, should make medical decisions for inmates."[73]

In "an unprecedented move," the Pentagon is trying to transfer convicted national security leaker Pvt. Bradley Manning, who has changed her name to

---

71. WIS. STAT. ANN. § 302.386(5m).

72. Fields v. Smith, 653 F.3d 550, 555–556 (7th Cir. 2011).

73. Kyle Luebke, *Seventh Circuit Court strikes down transphobic Wisconsin law,* LGBTQ Nation (August 9, 2011), http://www.lgbtqnation.com/2011/08/seventh-circuit-court-strikes-down-transphobic-wisconsin-law/ (last visited August 10, 2011).

Chelsea Manning, to a civilian prison so she can get treatment for her gender identity disorder, defense officials said. Manning was convicted of sending classified documents to anti secrecy website WikiLeaks. She has asked for hormone therapy and to be able to live as a woman. "The request was the first ever made by a transgender military inmate and set up a dilemma for the Defense Department: How to treat a soldier for a diagnosed disorder without violating long-standing military policy. Transgender persons are not allowed to serve in the U.S. military and the Defense Department does not provide such treatment, but Manning can't be discharged from the service while serving his 35-year prison sentence." Some officials have said privately that keeping the soldier in a military prison and unable to have treatment could amount to cruel and unusual punishment.[74] While the Dept. of Defense has no policy for treatment of transgender prisoners, the U.S. Bureau of Prisons does.[75]

A new development in corrections has been the use of mental health laws and facilities to continue to incarcerate "sexually violent predators" who have served their prison sentences, but who are then civilly committed to secure mental health facilities to "protect" society. But what are the rights of persons so confined? Case law is just now beginning to develop on that topic.

In one case, the patient/inmate was a resident at the Florida Civil Commitment Center (F.C.C.C.) in Arcadia, Florida. He alleges in a *pro se* filing that the F.C.C.C. and other defendants had violated his rights under the Fifth, Eighth, and Fourteenth Amendments to the U.S. Constitution by failing to formulate or adopt "a policy for the treatment of Transgender People within the Florida Civil Commitment Center." He was sentenced for possession of child pornography and after completing his sentence was civilly committed to F.C.C.C. under Florida's Sexually Violent Predators Act.[76]

---

74. Jelinek, P. and Baldor, L.C. (May 14, 2014) Pentagon OKs Chelsea Manning Transfer for Gender Treatment, http://bigstory.ap.org/article/pentagon-oks-manning-transfer-gender-treatment (last visited August 24, 2014).

75. Memorandum for Chief Executive Officers, Subject: Gender Identity Disorder Evaluation and Treatment, May 31, 2011, from RADM Newton E. Kendig, Assistant Director, Health Services Division and Charles E. Samuels, Jr., Assistant Director, Correctional Programs Division (copy in author's files).

76. Fla. Stat. §§ 394.910–394.913.

He had filed numerous grievances requesting treatment for Gender Identity Disorder (G.I.D.). Even though the Dept. of Children and Families (D.C.F.) knew of his diagnosis of G.I.D. and has ignored his "serious medical need" and has "refused to provide *any* form of therapy for the Plaintiff's Serious Medical Condition of Gender Identity Disorder."

He wrote to Defendant Secretary David Wilkins and inquired as to whether D.C.F. had a policy for treatment of transgender residents. Defendant Wilkins did not express concern for his condition. Rather, he received a letter from Defendant Montaldi who informed the Plaintiff that D.C.F. did not have a specific policy for transgender treatment and services. He had sought outside assistance for his problems.

He wrote a letter to the D.C.F. in which he complained that he wished to begin receiving hormone therapy; wished to be addressed by his female name; and wanted the F.C.C.C. to hire a therapist who specialized in transgender issues to aid him in making the transition to a female. He also requested that the F.C.C.C. provide him with the appropriate hormones, female clothing, and feminine products from an English company that specialized in transgender products. In response, he was advised that the hormone treatment and therapy he requested was not part of the comprehensive treatment plan at the F.C.C.C. and that as he had not been diagnosed with gender identity disorder, his request for hormonal therapy was not considered appropriate. He was also told that addressing him by his female name would be "clinically unwise" and that "any authentic female clothing found in any resident possession would be considered as contraband." In response to a follow-up letter from him, Defendant Montaldi advised him that "D.C.F. does not have a policy for transgender treatment and services."

The District Court declined to dismiss his complaint for declaratory relief. Thus, he was afforded the same rights as one who is confined to a prison.[77]

---

77. Hood v. Department of Children and Families, 2014 WL 757914 (M.D. Fla. 2014).

Glossary of Transgender Terms*

Androgyne: A person who lives without appearing or behaving particularly male or female.

Androgynous (or androgyny): Having both masculine and feminine gender typed traits.

Cross-Dressing (also CD'ing): To wear clothing typically associated with members of the other sex. Someone who cross-dresses is a cross-dresser. According to psychologists, cross-dressers are mostly heterosexuals. However, it is somewhat difficult to distinguish a cross-dresser from a drag queen except by the sexual orientation subcultures.

Drag King: A female who presents as male and, in doing so, purposely takes masculinity to an extreme.

Drag Queen: A male who presents as female and, in doing so, purposely takes femininity to an extreme.

Female to Male (also FtM): A transgender person born as female who is living as or transitioning to male.

---

* These definitions are drawn from the author's own experiences and from handouts used in many programs presented by the author to attorneys for continuing legal education credit, to statewide psychological associations for continuing education credits, college psychology and sociology classes, to employers and their employees to help them deal with transitioning employees, to crisis helpline staffers, to civic organizations, and other groups interested in learning more about gender identity. Some members of the transgender community may look askance at some of the definitions, but that is the way of the world, or as the French say, *c'est la vie.*

Gender: The social phenomena associated with being male or female.

Gender Bend (or gender bender): To remain within a gender role but push the boundaries by engaging in behavior that is atypical for one's gender (e.g., a girl playing football but still retaining a girlie personality).

Gender Dysphoria: Having negative or conflicting feelings about one's sex or gender role. This is the term that was used before gender identity disorder.

Gender Identity: An inner sense that one is or belongs to a particular sex.

Gender Identity Disorder (or GID): A mental condition included in the American Psychiatric Association's Diagnostic and Statistical Manual IV (DSM-IV) referring to a gender identity that is inconsistent with one's biological sex.

Gender Role: The behaviors, traits, thoughts, and dress expected by a culture of members of a particular sex.

Gender Reassignment Surgery (or GRS): See *Sex Reassignment Surgery*.

Harry Benjamin, M.D.: An endocrinologist and early researcher in gender dysphoria (now gender identity disorder) who founded the Harry Benjamin International Gender Dysphoria Association. He created the Standards of Care for transgender persons.

Harry Benjamin International Gender Dysphoria Association (or HBIGDA): The organization of medical and mental health professionals that maintains the standards of care for the treatment of transsexuals. It is since changed its name to the World Professional Association for Transgendered Health.

Harry Benjamin Standards of Care (also Standards of Care): A list of rules dictating what is considered by a consensus of medical and mental health professionals the appropriate way to treat transsexuals.

Hermaphrodite: A person with primary or secondary sex characteristics of both sexes. Note that, though this term continues to be used by mental health professionals, those classified as such often consider it derogatory. The currently preferred term is *intersexed person*.

Hormone Replacement Therapy (or HRT): A term used for the taking of sex-related hormones (e.g., estrogen, testosterone). Most often the term is used for post-menopausal women taking estrogen. The term also applies to a transsexual taking hormones of the target sex.

International Classification of Diseases 9th Edition (or ICD-9): An international version of the DSM. Both the DSM and the ICD closely parallel one another. But the ICD-9 is used more for coding medical insurance claims forms.

Intersex (also intersexuality, intersexual, and intersexed): Having primary or secondary sex characteristics of both sexes. This is the preferred term for intersexed persons advocacy groups benefiting the intersex.

Masculine (also masculinity): A trait, behaviors, thoughts, dress, and other manner viewed by a culture as typical of males. Often a trait is considered masculine if it focuses on instrumental use of the environment.

Male to Female (or MtF): A transgender person born as male who is living as or transitioning to female.

Passing: To succeed at presenting as one's target sex.

Postoperative (or post-op): A transsexual who has completed GRS.

Preoperative (or pre-op): A transsexual who has not yet had GRS.

Primary Sex Characteristics: The genitalia associated with each sex (i.e., penis, vagina).

Real-Life Test: A requirement of the Harry Benjamin Standards of Care that transsexuals live for one year as their target sex before GRS. The most recent version renamed the real-life test as "real-life experience" though it still retains its test-like use.

Secondary Sex Characteristics: Traits linked to biological sex though not directly involved in procreation (e.g., breasts, facial hair).

Sex: A term referring to biological aspects of being male or female: chromosomes, genitalia, hormones, and secondary sex characteristics.

Sex Reassignment Surgery (or SRS): A medical procedure for changing one's primary sex characteristics to be or resemble to primary sex characteristics of one's target sex.

Sexual Orientation: Sexual attraction to a particular group of persons. Typical sexual orientations are to the other sex (heterosexuality) and one's own sex (homosexuality).

Standards of Care for Gender Identity Disorders (formerly the Harry Benjamin Standards of Care [also Standards of Care]): A list of guidelines dictating what is considered by a consensus of medical and mental health professionals the appropriate way to treat transsexuals promulgated by the World Professional Association for Transgendered Health.

Transsexual: One who lives full time in a gender role consistent with his or her inner gender identity whether such person has had sex reassignment surgery or not.

Transgendered or Transgender: An umbrella term referring to anyone whose behavior, thoughts, or traits differ from the societal expectations for his or her biological sex. This group includes cross-dressers, transsexuals, intersexed persons, gay men, lesbian women, and bisexuals.

Transition: The process of switching from one's biological sex to the sex that is consistent with one's inner gender identity.

Transman (and Transmen): A person who was born with female genitalia but whose gender identity is that of a man and whose personal presentation is that of a man.

Transvestite (also transvestism): A psychopathological term that includes cross-dressing but also includes other opposite-sex-related clothing activity.

World Professional Association for Transgendered Health (or WPATH): Formerly the Harry Benjamin International Gender Dysphoria. The organization of medical and mental health professionals that maintains the standards of care for the treatment of transsexuals.

State Laws Relating to Changing One's Name

State	MS Word and PDF Forms Available at http://ambar.org/transgenderbook
Alabama	Alabama Instructions Petition to Change Name Decree Changing Name
Alaska	Alaska Instructions Alaska Superior Court Case Description Form Petition for Change of Name Affidavit of Posting of Name Change Order for Change of Name
Arizona	Arizona Instructions Application for Change of Name for an Adult Order Changing Name for an Adult
Arkansas	Arkansas Instructions Arkansas Instructions for Civil Cover Sheet Arkansas Civil Cover Sheet Arkansas Petition to Change Name Arkansas Decree Changing Name
California	California Instructions Civil Case Cover Sheet Petition For Change Of Name And Gender—Form Nc-200 Attachment To Petition For Change Of Name—Form Nc-110 Order To Show Cause For Change Of Name And Gender—Form Nc-220 Declaration Of Physician Documenting Change Of Gender Through Surgical Treatment—Form Nc-210 Decree Changing Name And Gender—Form Nc-230

State	MS Word and PDF Forms Available at http://ambar.org/transgenderbook
Colorado	Colorado Instructions Name Change Petition Order for Publication of Change of Name Public Notice of Petition for Change of Name Final Decree for Change of Name
Connecticut	Connecticut Instructions Application for Change of Name Affidavit Re Change of Name Order Changing Name
Delaware	Kent County Instructions Kent County Petition for Name Change Kent County Publication Notice Kent County Order Changing Name New Castle County Instructions New Castle County Petition for Name Change New Castle County Publication Notice New Castle County Order Changing Name Sussex County Instructions Sussex County Petition for Name Change Sussex County Publication Notice Sussex County Order Changing Name
District of Columbia	District of Columbia Instructions Superior Court Information Form Application for Change of Name Notice to Creditors Order of Publication Order for Change of Name
Florida	Florida Instructions Petition for Change of Name Final Judgment for Change of Name
Georgia	Georgia Instructions Petition to Change Name Notice of Petition to Change Name Final Order Changing Name
Hawaii	Hawaii Instructions Fact Sheet Petition to Change Name Notice of Change of Name Order Changing Name
Idaho	Idaho Instructions Petition for Name Change Notice of Hearing Order for Name Change

State	MS Word and PDF Forms Available at http://ambar.org/transgenderbook
Illinois	Illinois Instructions Petition to Change Name Legal Notice For Change Of Name Judgment Changing Name
Indiana	Indiana Instructions Appearance By Self-Represented Person In Civil Case Verified Petition for Change of Name Notice of Petition for Change of Name Notice of Filing of Proof of Publication Order for Change of Name
Iowa	Iowa Instructions Petition to Change Name Change of Name Decree
Kansas	Kansas Instructions Civil Information Sheet Petition for Change of Name Notice of Hearing by Certified Mail Notice of Hearing by Publication Order Changing Name
Kentucky	Kentucky Instructions Case Data Information Sheet Petition for Name Change Order Changing Name
Louisiana	Louisiana Instructions Petition to Change Name Name Change Order
Maine	Maine Instructions Petition for Change of Name Order for Change of Name
Maryland	Maryland Instructions Civil Domestic Case Information Report Petition for Change of Name Notice Certificate of Publication Order for Change of Name
Massachusetts	Massachusetts Instructions Petition to Change Name Citation for Change of Name Decree for Change of Name
Michigan	Michigan Instructions Petition to Change Name Order Following Hearing on Petition to Change Name

State	MS Word and PDF Forms Available at http://ambar.org/transgenderbook
Minnesota	Minnesota Instructions Application for Name Change Order Granting Name Change
Mississippi	Mississippi Instructions Petition to Change Name Order Changing Name
Missouri	Missouri Instructions Confidential Case Filing Information Sheet Petition to Change Name Order Changing Name
Montana	Montana Instructions Petition for Name Change Order Setting Name Change Hearing Notice of Hearing on Proposed Name Change Order Granting Name Change
Nebraska	Word Forms: Nebraska Instructions Petition for Name Change Legal Notice of Name Change Decree of Name Change PDF Forms: Nebraska Instructions For Filling Out Petition For Name Change Nebraska Petition For Name Change Nebraska Instructions For Filling Out Legal Notice For Name Change Nebraska Legal Notice of Name Change Nebraska Instructions For Filling Out Decree Of Name Change Nebraska Decree of Name Change Nebraska Instructions For Your Adult Name Change Hearing
Nevada	Nevada Instructions Petition for Change of Name Nevada Clark County Family Court Cover Sheet Affidavit of Petitioner Notice of Petition for Change of Name Order for Change of Name without New Birth Certificate Order for Change of Name with New Birth Certificate
New Hampshire	New Hampshire Instructions Petition for Change of Name Name Change Affirmation Order Changing Name

State	MS Word and PDF Forms Available at http://ambar.org/transgenderbook
New Jersey	New Jersey Instructions Civil Case Information Statement Verified Complaint Proof of Mailing Newspaper Notice Order Fixing Date of Hearing Final Judgment PDF Forms: New Jersey Name Change Packet
New Mexico	New Mexico Instructions Petition for Change of Name Legal Notice Order Changing Name
New York	New York Instructions Petition to Change Name Order Changing Name
North Carolina	North Carolina Instructions Civil Action Cover Sheet Petition for Legal Name Change of an Adult Notice Affidavit of Character Criminal History Record Order Changing the Name of an Adult
North Dakota	North Dakota Instructions Petition for Name Change Notice Affidavit of Petitioner Judgment Changing Name
Ohio	Ohio Instructions Adult Information Form Application for Change of Name of Adult Acknowledgment of Applicant of Sanctions for Failure to Appear at Hearing Entry Setting Hearing and Ordering Notice Notice of Hearing on Name Change Application Judgment Entry for Change of Name of Adult
Oklahoma	Oklahoma Instructions Civil Cover Sheet Petition for Change of Name Order Setting Petition for Hearing Notice of Filing of Petition for Change of Name Order Changing Name

State	MS Word and PDF Forms Available at http://ambar.org/transgenderbook
Oregon	Oregon Instructions Petition for Change of Name Notice of Petition for Change of Name Proof of Posting of Notice of Petition for Change of Name Change of Name Judgment Notice of Name Change Judgment
Pennsylvania	Pennsylvania Instructions Civil Cover Sheet Confidential Information Form Petition for Change of Name Order for Publication Notice of Name Change Decree for Change of Name
Rhode Island	Rhode Island Instructions Authorization for Release of Records Petition for Change of Name Decree Changing Name
South Carolina	South Carolina Instructions Civil Action Cover Sheet Petition for Change of Name and Amendment of Birth Record Order and Certificate of Name and Amendment of Birth Record
South Dakota	South Dakota Instructions Notice of Intent to Change Name Petition to Change Name Judgment Changing Name PDF Forms: Instructions for Change of Name Civil Filing Statement Petition for Change of Name Notice of Hearing for Change of Name Order for Change of Name
Tennessee	Tennessee Instructions Petition for Change of Name Order Changing Name
Texas	Texas Instructions Civil Case Information Sheet Petition to Change Name of Adult Order Changing Name of Adult

State	MS Word and PDF Forms Available at http://ambar.org/transgenderbook
Utah	Utah Instructions Cover Sheet for Civil Actions Dept. of Corrections Certification Regarding Sex Offender Registry Petition for Name Change Request for Hearing Notice of Hearing on Petition for Name Change Order Changing Name PDF Forms: Petition for Name Change Dept. of Corrections Certification Regarding Sex Offender Registry Request for Hearing Notice of Hearing on Petition for Name Change Order Changing Name
Vermont	Vermont Instructions Petition of Adult to Change Name Order Changing Name of Adult PDF Forms: Name Change of Adult Information Petition of Adult to Change Name
Virginia	Virginia Instructions Application for Change of Name Order for Change of Name PDF Forms: Cover Sheet for Filing Civil Actions Application for Change of Name
Washington	Washington Instructions District Court Case Information Cover Sheet Petition for Individual Name Change Order for Individual Name Change
West Virginia	West Virginia Instructions Civil Case Information Statement Petition for Change of Name Notice of Intent to Change Name Order Changing Name
Wisconsin	Wisconsin Instructions Petition for Name Change Notice and Order for Name Change Hearing Order for Name Change PDF Forms: Petition for Name Change Notice and Order for Name Change Hearing Order for Name Change

State	MS Word and PDF Forms Available at http://ambar.org/transgenderbook
Wyoming	Wyoming Instructions Petition for Name Change Notice of Publication Order Granting Name Change

State Laws Relating to Changing Birth Certificates

States change the costs and fees charged, especially when looking for new revenues without raising taxes. So, call the state agency involved or visit its website to get the fees and costs.

Alabama

Alabama will issue an amended birth certificate. The State Registrar of Health Statistics shall amend a birth certificate on receipt of a certified copy of a court order changing the **name** of the person. Upon receipt of a certified copy of an order of a court of competent jurisdiction indicating that the **sex** of an individual born in this state has been changed by surgical procedure and that the name of the individual has been changed, the birth certificate shall be amended.

Documents needed:
* Certified copy of court order changing name
* Certified copy of court order as to sex change

Statutes and Regulations: Ala. Code § 22–9A-19 and Ala. Admin. Code Rule 420–7–1-.16

    State Agency Contact Information:
    Alabama State Board of Health
    Center for Health Statistics
    P.O. Box 5625
    Montgomery, AL 36103–5625

(334) 206–5418

http://www.adph.org/vitalrecords/index.asp?id=1559

Alaska

Upon receipt of a certified copy of a court order changing the **name** of a person born in the state or a person born outside the United States whose adoptive parents are residents of the state at the time of the adoption and upon request of the person or the person's parent, guardian, or legal representative, the state registrar shall amend the birth certificate to reflect the new name.

Documents needed:

- Certified copy of court order

Statutes and Regulations: ALASKA STAT. § 18.50.290 and ALASKA ADMIN. CODE tit. 7, § 05.900

State Agency Contact Information:

Alaska Department of Health and Social Services

Bureau of Vital Statistics

5441 Commercial Boulevard

Juneau, AK 99801

(907) 465–3391

http://dhss.alaska.gov/dph/VitalStats/Pages/default.aspx

Arizona

Arizona will change both the **name** and **sex** and will issue a new birth certificate rather than amend the old one. The original certificate is closed to further inspection.

Documents needed:

- An original letter from the SRS surgeon
- Original or certified copy of the court order for your name change

Statutes and Regulations: ARIZ. REV. STAT. ANN. §§ 36–323 and 36–337 and ARIZ. ADMIN. CODE § R9–19–118 and R9–19–413

State Agency Contact Information:
Office of Vital Records
Arizona Dept. of Health Services
P.O. Box 3887
Phoenix, AZ 85030–3887
(602) 364–1300
http://www.azdhs.gov/vital-records/

Arkansas

Arkansas will change the **name** and will issue a new birth certificate if the court order so specifies. This certificate shall be marked "Court Order." Statutes and regulations only mention changing the name on a birth certificate, but the website of the Division of Vital Records indicates that **sex** can be changed with a court order. *See* http://www.healthy.arkansas.gov/programsServices/certificatesVitalRecords/Pages/ChangingBirthandDeathCertificates.aspx (accessed on 07/31/2011).

Documents needed:

* Court order from a court of competent jurisdiction

Statutes and Regulations: ARK. CODE ANN. § 20–18–307 and ARK. ADMIN. CODE 007.12.1–5.6
   State Agency Contact Information:
   Arkansas Department of Health
   Division of Vital Records
   4815 West Markham Street
   Slot 44
   Little Rock, AR 72205
   (501) 661–2336
   http://www.healthy.arkansas.gov/programsServices/certificatesVitalRecords/Pages/default.aspx

California

California will change the **name** and will issue an amended birth certificate.

Documents required:
- Certified copy of court order changing name

Statutes and Regulations: CALIF. HEALTH & SAFETY CODE, §103405

"Whenever a person has undergone clinically appropriate treatment for the purpose of gender transition," a new birth certificate may be prepared for the person reflecting the change of gender and any change of name accomplished by an order of a court of this state, another state, the District of Columbia, or any territory of the United States. A petition for the issuance of a new birth certificate in those cases shall be filed with the Superior Court of the county where the petitioner resides. "The petition shall be accompanied by an affidavit of a physician attesting that the person has undergone clinically appropriate treatment for the purpose of gender transition, based on contemporary medical standards, and a certified copy of the court order changing the applicant's name, if applicable. The physician's affidavit shall be accepted as conclusive proof of gender change if it contains substantially the following language: 'I, (physician's full name), (physician's medical license or certificate number), am a licensed physician in (jurisdiction). I attest that (name of petitioner) has undergone clinically appropriate treatment for the purpose of gender transition to (male or female). I declare that the foregoing is true and correct to the best of my knowledge.'"

California will issue a new birth certificate changing the sex and name and seal the records relating to the old one and open them only with consent of the applicant or with a court order.

Documents required for Superior Court petition:
- Affidavit of physician as described above
- Certified copy of court order changing name

Statutes and Regulations: CALIF. HEALTH & SAFETY CODE, §§ 103425 to 103440

State Agency Contact Information:
California Department of Public Health – Vital Records
MS: 5103
P.O. Box 997410

Sacramento, CA 95899–7410

(916) 445–2684

http://www.cdph.ca.gov/certlic/birthdeathmar/Pages/default.aspx

Colorado

Colorado will change the **name, sex, or both** on a birth certificate. If only the name is changed, an amended certificate will be issued, but if only the sex or both the name and sex are changed, a new certificate will be issued.

Documents needed:

- A court order changing the name OR
- A certified copy of court order indicating that the sex has been changed by surgical procedure and that such individual's name has been changed

Statutes and Regulations: COLO. REV. STAT. ANN. § 25–2–115 and 5 COLO. CODE REGS. 1006–1:9

State Agency Contact Information:

Colorado Department of Public Health & Environment

4300 Cherry Creek Drive South

Denver, CO 80246–1530

(303) 692–2200

http://www.cdphe.state.co.us/certs/index.html

Connecticut

Connecticut will change the **name** on a birth certificate. The birth certificate is marked "amended," but the item or items amended are not specified. This type of amendment can be accomplished by the local registrar of the town where the birth occurred or the Department of Public Health.

Documents needed:

- A certified copy of court order

Statutes and Regulations: CONN. GEN. STAT. ANN. § 19a-42(f) and CONN. AGENCIES REGS. § 19a-41–9

A person who is a resident of Connecticut and was born in another state or in a foreign jurisdiction, if such other state or foreign jurisdiction requires a court decree to amend a birth certificate to reflect a change in gender, the Connecticut probate courts shall have jurisdiction to issue such a decree. When a person has completed treatment for the purpose of altering his or her sexual characteristics to those of the opposite **sex**, such person may apply to the probate court for the district in which such person resides for a decree that such person's birth certificate be amended to reflect the change in gender. The application to the probate court shall be accompanied by an affidavit from a physician attesting that the applicant has physically changed gender and an affidavit from a psychologist, psychiatrist or a licensed clinical social worker attesting that the applicant has socially and psychologically changed gender. Upon issuance, such probate court decree shall be transmitted to the registration authority of such person's place of birth. Only the Department of Public Health can perform this kind of amendment.

Documents needed for Probate Court:

- Affidavit from a physician attesting that the applicant has physically changed gender
- Affidavit from a psychologist, psychiatrist or a licensed clinical social worker attesting that the applicant has socially and psychologically changed gender

Statutes and Regulations: CONN. GEN. STAT. ANN. §19a-42b and CONN. AGENCIES REGS. § 19a-41–9

State Agency Contact Information:
Connecticut Department of Public Health
State Office of Vital Records
410 Capitol Ave. MS#11VRS
P.O. Box 340308
Hartford, CT 06134–0308
(860) 509–7700
http://www.ct.gov/dph/cwp/view.asp?a=3132&q=388130&dphNav=|46940|

Delaware

Delaware will amend a birth certificate by statute and regulation to change the name.

Documents needed:

- An original or certified copy of the court order for the name change

Statutes and Regulations: DEL. CODE ANN. tit. 16 § 3131 and 16 DEL. ADMIN. CODE 4205–10.0

Upon receipt of a certified copy of an order of a court of competent jurisdiction indicating the sex of an individual born in Delaware has been changed by surgical procedure and whether such individual's name has been changed, the certificate of birth of such individual shall be amended by preparing a new certificate. The item numbers of the entries that were amended shall not, however, be identified on the new certificate or on any certified copies that may be issued of that certificate.

Documents needed:

- An original or certified copy of the court order

Statutes and Regulations: Division of Public Health Office of Vital Statistics Regulation 10.9.4 (found at http://dhss.delaware.gov/dhss/dph/hp/vsregs. html (accessed on 07/31/2011)).

    State Agency Contact Information:
Delaware Office of Vital Statistics
Division of Public Health
417 Federal Street
Dover, DE 19901
(302) 744–4549
http://www.dhss.delaware.gov/dhss/dph/ss/vitalstats.html

District of Columbia—Washington, D.C.

The District of Columbia will not issue a new birth certificate but will amend the original birth certificate. The District will change the person's name, sex, or both.

Documents needed:
- Certified copy of the court order for name change OR
- Certified copy of order of the court indicating that the sex of an individual born in the District has changed by surgical procedure and that such individual's name has been changed

Statutes and Regulations: D.C. CODE ANN. § 7–217 and D.C. MUN. REGS. tit. 29, § 2818; see also *In re Carolyn Ann Taylor*, 2003 WL 22382512 (Super. Ct. 2003) (Superior court statutorily compelled to grant request for change of sex on birth certificate of post-surgery transsexual)

    State Agency Contact Information:
District of Columbia
Vital Records Division
825 North Capitol Street NE
Washington, DC 20002
(202) 671–5000
http://doh.dc.gov/

Florida

Florida will change the **name** on a birth certificate and will attach the name change order to the original birth certificate. However, if the change is by a Florida circuit court that orders the Department of Health to file a new birth certificate, the original birth certificate shall be removed and shall be placed together with the order granting the name change under seal only to be opened by an order from a court of competent jurisdiction.

Documents needed:
- Certified copy of the court order for name change
- Affidavit of Amendment to Certificate of Live Birth, DH Form 430

Statutes and Regulations: FLA. STAT. ANN. §§ 382.003 and 382.016 and FLA. ADMIN. CODE ANN. Rule 64V-1.0033

    State Agency Contact Information:
Florida Department of Health
Bureau of Vital Statistics

P.O. Box 210
1217 Pearl Street
Jacksonville, FL 32231–0042
(904)359–6900
http://www.doh.state.fl.us/planning_eval/vital_statistics/birth_death.htm

Georgia

Georgia will amend the birth certificate to change the **name, sex, or both** of the applicant.

Documents needed:

- An affidavit setting forth (1) information to identify the certificate, (2) the incorrect data as it is listed on the certificate, (3) the corrected entry as it should appear, and (4) an abstract of the evidence which substantiates the amendment of the certificate
- Certified copy of a court order changing the name OR indicating the sex of an individual born in this state has been changed by surgical procedure and that such individual's name has been changed

Statutes and Regulations: GA. CODE ANN. § 31–10–23 and GA. COMP. RULES & REGS. 290–1–3–.25 and 290–1–3–.10

State Agency Contact Information:
Georgia Department of Community Health
Vital Records
2600 Skyland Drive, NE
Atlanta, GA 30319–3640
(404) 679–4702
http://health.state.ga.us/programs/vitalrecords/

Hawaii

Hawaii will change the **sex** and will issue a new birth certificate. When a new certificate of birth is established under this section, it shall be substituted for the original certificate of birth. Thereafter, the original certificate and the evidence supporting the preparation of the new certificate shall be

sealed and filed. Such sealed document shall be opened only by an order
of a court of record.

Documents needed:

- An affidavit of a physician that the physician has examined the birth
  registrant and has determined that the birth registrant has had a sex
  change operation and the sex designation on the birth registrant's birth
  certificate is no longer correct

Statutes and Regulations: HAW. REV. STAT. § 338–17.7

There is no statutory or regulatory procedure for changing one's name on
one's birth certificate in Hawaii. However, the website of the Hawaii State
Department of Health states, "An original entry on a birth . . . certificate
may be amended by either the private request of an individual or an order
of a court of competent jurisdiction. An amendment includes changes, corrections, additions, deletions, or substitutions. An amendment may be made
upon application, but only with the submission of required documentary
evidence in support of the amendment. The evidentiary requirements can
differ, depending on whether the amendment is court-ordered or, if requested
by an individual, whether it materially affects the validity and integrity of
the record." *See* http://hawaii.gov/health/vital-records/vital-records/amend-
ment.html accessed on 07/23/2011. Because a name change is accomplished
under HAW. REV. STAT. § 574–5 by a notarized petition to the lieutenant
governor, one would presumably have to go to court and ask for an order
to change one's name on one's birth certificate.

Documents needed:

- Certified copy of order by lieutenant governor or court of another state

State Agency Contact Information:
Hawaii State Department of Health
Office of Health Status Monitoring
Vital Records Section
P.O. Box 3378
Honolulu, HI 96801–9984

(808) 586–4533

http://hawaii.gov/health/vital-records/vital-records/index.html

Idaho

Idaho will change the **name** on a birth certificate and issue an amended birth certificate. The fact that the name was changed in accordance with a court order must be stated on the certificate.

Documents needed:

- Certified copy of an order of a court of competent jurisdiction changing the name of the person

Statutes and Regulations: IDAHO CODE ANN. § 39–250 and IDAHO ADMIN. CODE Rule 16.02.08.201

State Agency Contact Information:

State of Idaho

Bureau of Vital Records and Health Statistics

450 West State Street

Boise, ID 83702

(208) 334–5988

http://www.healthandwelfare.idaho.gov/Health/VitalRecordsandHealth-Statistics/BirthDeathMarriageDivorceCertificates/tabid/82/Default.aspx

Illinois

Illinois will change the **name** and will issue an amended birth certificate.

Documents needed:

- A certified copy of the name change order

Statutes and Regulations: 410 ILL. COMP. STAT. ANN. 535/22 and ILL. ADMIN. CODE tit. 77 § 500.40

The Illinois statutes and regulations do not deal with changes of sex on a birth certificate. But the website of the Division of Vital Records explicitly states that such changes are available. The website states, "One must have complete gender reassignment surgery before the 'Affidavit by Physician

After the Completion of Gender Reassignment' and the 'Affidavit for a New Birth Certificate After Completion of Gender Reassignment Surgery' can be completed and submitted to this office."

Documents needed:

- The Affidavit for a New Birth Certificate After Completion of Gender Reassignment Surgery is to be completed by the applicant if of legal age or the parent or guardian if not of legal age. This form must be completed in its entirety and notarized.
- The Affidavit by Physician After Completion of Gender Reassignment must be completed by the physician that performed the surgery. This form must be completed in its entirety and notarized.
- If the surgery is performed by a non-U.S. licensed physician, the affidavit must be accompanied by an additional Affidavit by Physician Verifying Completion of Gender Reassignment. The additional affidavit must be completed by a physician licensed to practice within the United States and confirm that the gender reassignment surgery was completed.
- If one would like his or her name changed at this time, a certified copy of the Court Order of Legal Name Change must be submitted to this office as well.

Authority: Illinois Department of Public Health, Division of Vital Records website at http://www.idph.state.il.us/vitalrecords/gender.html accessed on 07/31/2011. Click on Application for Gender Reassignment with Instructions.

State Agency Contact Information:
Division of Vital Records
Illinois Department of Public Health
925 E. Ridgely Avenue
Springfield, IL 62702
(217) 782–6553
http://www.idph.state.il.us/vitalrecords/birth.htm

Indiana

Indiana has no statutory or regulatory authority for amending, changing, or issuing replacement birth certificates when one changes one's name or sex. However, the following was found at the Indiana State Department of Health, Vital Records website:

How can changes be made to a birth certificate?

Please contact the Corrections Section of the ISDH Vital Records office at (317) 233–2700 and ask for instructions for correcting the information.

Documents needed:

- unknown

Authority: Indiana State Department of Health, Vital Records website at http://www.in.gov/isdh/20243.htm#VitalFAQ11 accessed on 07/31/2011

State Agency Contact Information:

Vital Records

Indiana State Department of Health

P.O. Box 7125

Indianapolis, IN 46206–7125

(317) 233–2700

http://www.in.gov/isdh/20243.htm

Iowa

Iowa will change the **name** on the birth certificate and issue an amended certificate. Any new birth certificate issued to a person granted a change of name shall reflect the former name of the person issued the new birth certificate.

Documents needed:

- A certified copy of the court order for the name change

Statutes and Regulations: Iowa Code Ann. §§ 144.39, 674.7 and 674.9, and Iowa Admin. Code 641–102.10(144)

State Agency Contact Information:

Iowa Department of Public Health

Bureau of Vital Records
Lucas Office Building
321 East 12th Street
Des Moines, IA 50319–0075
(515) 281–4944
http://www.idph.state.ia.us/apl/health_statistics.asp

Kansas

Kansas will issue an amended birth certificate changing the **name, sex, or both**. The items recording the registrant's sex may be amended if the amendment is substantiated with the applicant's affidavit that the sex was incorrectly recorded, or with a medical certificate substantiating that a physiological or anatomical change occurred.

Documents needed:

- Authenticated copy of the court order changing name
- Affidavit from applicant documenting dressing and living as new gender OR
- A medical certificate substantiating that a physiological or anatomical change occurred

Statutes and Regulations: KAN. STAT. ANN. § 65–2422a and KAN. ADMIN. REGS. 28–17–20

State Agency Contact Information:
Kansas Office of Vital Statistics
Curtis State Office Building
1000 SW Jackson Street, Suite 120
Topeka, KS 66612–2221
(785) 296–1400
http://www.kdheks.gov/vital/birth.html

Kentucky

Kentucky will change the **name, sex, or both** and will issue an amended birth certificate.

Documents needed:
- Sworn statement by a licensed physician indicating that the gender of the individual has been changed by surgical procedure
- A certified copy of the court order for the name change

Statutes and Regulations: KY. REV. STAT. ANN. § 213.121 and 901 KY. ADMIN. REGS. 5:070

State Agency Contact Information:
Office of Vital Statistics
Kentucky Department for Public Health
Cabinet for Health and Family Services
275 East Main Street 1E-A
Frankfort, KY 40621
(502) 564–4212
http://chfs.ky.gov/dph/vital/birthcert.htm

Louisiana

Louisiana will change **name, sex, or both** and will issue a new birth certificate rather than amend the old one. The original birth certificate and the copy of the petition and judgment received by the registrar shall be sealed in a package and filed in the archives of the vital records registry. This sealed package shall be opened only upon demand of the individual to whom the new certificate was issued and then only by order of the court that rendered the judgment ordering the issuance of the new certificate.

Documents needed:
- An original or certified copy of the order for the name change
- An original or certified copy of the judgment of Louisiana court ordering the issuance of a new birth certificate changing the sex designated thereon from that shown upon the petitioner's original certificate of birth

Statutes and Regulations: LA. REV. STAT. ANN. § 40:62 and LA. ADMIN CODE. tit. 48, § 11107

State Agency Contact Information:

Louisiana Office of Public Health
Vital Records Registry
P.O. Box 60630
New Orleans, LA 70160
(504) 593–5100
http://new.dhh.louisiana.gov/index.cfm/page/649
http://www.dhh.louisiana.gov/

Maine

Maine will change the **name, sex, or both** and will issue a new rather than amended birth certificate.

Documents needed:

*   An affidavit from the surgeon who performed the sex change surgery
*   A certified copy of the court order for the name change

Statutes and Regulations: 10–146 ME. CODE RULES §§ 6, 7, 10 and 11
State Agency Contact Information:
Office of Vital Records
Maine Department of Health and Human Services
244 Water Street
#11 State House Station
Augusta, ME 04333–0011
(207) 287–3181
http://www.maine.gov/dhhs/boh/birth_certificate_application.shtml

Maryland

The Division of Vital Records can change the petitioner's **name, sex, or both** on the petitioner's birth certificate. On receipt of a court order indicating that the sex of an individual born in Maryland "has been changed by surgical procedure," the secretary of health and mental hygiene has to amend that person's Maryland birth certificate accordingly.

Documents needed:

*   A court order indicating that one's name and sex have been changed

- A court order changing one's name

Statutes and Regulations: MD. ANN. CODE, HEALTH-GEN. § 4- 214 and MD. CODE REGS. 10.03.01.02 and 10.03.01.07–1
State Agency Contact Information:
Division of Vital Records
Maryland Department of Health and Mental Hygiene
6550 Reisterstown Road
P.O. Box 68760
Baltimore, MD 21215–0020
(410) 764–3038
http://dhmh.maryland.gov/vsa/SitePages/birth.aspx
http://dhmh.maryland.gov/vsa/SitePages/Home.aspx

Massachusetts
Massachusetts will issue an amended birth certificate as to a **sex** and **name** change.

Documents needed:
- A physician's notarized statement that the person named on the birth record has completed sex reassignment surgery and is not of the sex recorded on said record
- A certified copy of the court order of the legal change of name
- An affidavit executed by the person to whom the record relates

Statutes and Regulations: MASS. GEN. LAWS ANN. 46 § 13
State Agency Contact Information:
Massachusetts Registry of Vital Records and Statistics
150 Mount Vernon Street
1st Floor
Dorchester, MA 02125–3105
(617) 740–2600
http://www.mass.gov/eohhs/gov/departments/dph/programs/health-stats/vitals/

Michigan

Michigan will change the **name** and will issue a new birth certificate rather than amend the old one. The old record is sealed.

Documents needed:

- A certified copy of the court order for the name change

Statutes and Regulations: MICH. COMP. LAWS ANN. §§ 333.2872 and 333.2831

There is no statutory or regulatory authority for it, but Michigan will change the sex on a person's birth certificate according to the Michigan Vital Record Division's website.

Documents needed:

- A completed application to change a Michigan birth record
- A Michigan Vital Record Division's medical affidavit completed by the physician that performed the reassignment surgery certifying that genital sex-reassignment surgery has been successfully completed. The affidavit must be notarized.

NOTE: If one wants to also change his or her first and middle name as a result of reassignment surgery, the physician should designate the changed name on the affidavit. If the physician does not designate the name to be changed at the time one submits the application, it can be done by court order.

Authority: Michigan Vital Record Division's website

http://www.michigan.gov/mdch/0,1607,7–132–4645_4933–13952--,00.html accessed on 07/31/2011

State Agency Contact Information:

Michigan Vital Records Office

Capitol View Bldg, 3rd Floor

201 Townsend Street

Lansing, MI 48913

(517) 335–8660

http://www.michigan.gov/mdch/0,1607,7–132–4645---,00.html

Minnesota

Minnesota's statutes and regulations are not clear about what can be changed. They provide that a "registrant . . . may request a registrar to amend the civil registration information in a birth record. The person requesting the amendment must demonstrate tangible interest in the birth record to be amended. . . . If a court order is presented by a person requesting an amendment, . . . a registrar must add or change information that the court order specifically directs the registrar to add or change. To add or change information that the court order does not specifically direct, the person must present the evidence required" by law or rules. (Office of the State Registrar's website http://www.health.state.mn.us/divs/chs/osr/amend.html accessed on 07/31/2011)

Documents needed:
- A certified copy of the court order

Statutes and Regulations: MINN. RULES 4601.1000
   State Agency Contact Information:
   Office of the State Registrar
   Minnesota Department of Health
   P.O. Box 64499
   St Paul, MN 55164
   http://www.health.state.mn.us/divs/chs/osr/

Mississippi

Mississippi has no specific statutory or regulatory procedure to amend or change a birth certificate due to a name or sex change. The website of the State Registrar of Vital Records states: "To make corrections or to make changes to a birth or death record, contact our Corrections Department at 601–576–7981." (Website of the State Registrar of Vital Records at http://msdh.ms.gov/msdhsite/_static/31,0,109.html (accessed on 07/31/2011)

   State Agency Contact Information:
   Vital Records
   Mississippi Department of Health

2423 North State Street
P.O. Box 1700
Jackson, MS 39215
(601) 576–7981
http://msdh.ms.gov/msdhsite/_static/31.html

Missouri

Missouri will issue an amended birth certificate in the new **name** and **sex**.

Documents needed:

- A certified copy of the court order for the name change or name and sex. Order must indicate that sex has been surgically changed.

Statutes and Regulations: MO. REV. STAT. §193.215 and MO. CODE REGS. ANN. tit. 19 § 10–10.110

State Agency Contact Information:
Missouri Department of Health and Senior Services
Bureau of Vital Records
930 Wildwood
P.O. Box 570
Jefferson City, MO 65102–0570
(573) 751–6387
http://health.mo.gov/data/vitalrecords/index.php

Montana

Montana will change the **name, sex** or **both** on the birth certificate. Montana will issue a new birth certificate if so ordered by the Montana District Court; otherwise, an amended birth certificate will be issued.

Documents needed:

- A certified copy of the Montana District Court order for the name change
- A certified copy of the court order (no state specified) that indicates a surgical sex change and states the full name on the birth certificate and the new name

Statutes and Regulations: MONT. ADMIN. Rule 37.8.311 and MONT. CODE
ANN. § 27–31–101
   State Agency Contact Information:
   Office of Vital Statistics
   Montana Dept. of Public Health and Human Services
   111 N. Sanders, Rm. 209
   P.O. Box 4210
   Helena, MT 59604
   1-(888) 877–1946
   http://www.dphhs.mt.gov/statisticalinformation/vitalrecordsstatistics.
shtml

Nebraska

Nebraska will change the **name** and will issue an amended birth certificate.

Documents Needed:

• A certified copy of the court order for the name change

Statutes and Regulations: NEB. REV. STAT. §§ 71–640 and 71–641 and NEB.
ADMIN. CODE tit. 174 § 006
   State Agency Contact Information:
   Nebraska Vital Records
   1033 O Street, Suite 130
   P.O. Box 95065
   Lincoln, NE 68509–5065
   (402) 471–2871
   http://dhhs.ne.gov/publichealth/pages/vitalrecords.aspx

Nevada

Nevada will indicate a **name** change on a birth certificate.

Documents needed:

• An original or certified copy of the court order for the name change

Statutes and Regulations: NEV. REV. STAT. ANN. § 4440.305

State Agency Contact Information:
Nevada Office of Vital Records
4150 Technology Way, Suite 104
Carson City, NV 89706
(775) 684–4242
http://health.nv.gov/VS.htm

New Hampshire

New Hampshire will change both the **name** and **sex** and will issue a new birth certificate rather than amend the old one for sex and name changes but will issue an amended certificate for name changes only.

Documents needed:

- A certified copy of the court order "advising that such individual born in the state of New Hampshire has had a sex change"
- A certified copy of the court order for the name change

Statutes and Regulations: N.H. REV. STAT. ANN. § and N.H. CODE ADMIN. R. ANN.

State Agency Contact Information:
New Hampshire Division of Vital Records Administration
Archives Building
71 South Fruit Street
Concord, NH 03301–2410
(603) 271–4654
http://www.sos.nh.gov/vitalrecords/Changing_a_Vital_Record.html

New Jersey

New Jersey will show the **name** at birth or marriage, the new name, and the date and manner by which it was obtained, but upon request, only the new name will be shown.

Documents needed:

- A certified copy of the court order for the name change

Fees: Not indicated but are charged for each copy of new birth certificate

   Statutes and Regulations: N.J. Stat. Ann. § 1A:52–4

   State Agency Contact Information:

   New Jersey Bureau of Vital Statistics and Registration

   Attn: Record Modification Unit

   P.O. Box 370

   Trenton, NJ 08625–0370

   (866) 649–8726

   http://www.state.nj.us/health/vital/amend.shtml

New Mexico

New Mexico will change the **name, sex, or both** and will amend the old birth certificate.

Documents needed:

- A certified copy of the court order for the name change
- An affidavit from the surgeon or "the person in charge of an institution . . . indicating that the sex of an individual born in this state has been changed by surgical procedure, together with a certified copy of an order changing the name of the person"

Statutes and Regulations: N.M. Stat. Ann. § 24–14–25

   State Agency Contact Information:

   New Mexico Vital Records

   P.O. Box 26110

   Santa Fe, NM 87502

   1-(866) 534–0051

   http://vitalrecordsnm.org//birth.shtml

New York City

New York City has its own separate Bureau of Vital Statistics. They will issue a new certificate for **name** and **sex** changes. When a new birth certificate is filed, "the original birth certificate, the application for a new birth certificate, and supporting documents shall be placed under physical or electronic seal, and such seal shall not be broken except by order of a court of competent jurisdiction."

Documents needed:

- A certified copy of the court order for the name change
- Proof "satisfactory to the Department has been submitted that such person has undergone convertive surgery." Anecdotal evidence indicates that an original letter from the SRS surgeon and the applicant's psychiatrist or psychologist are satisfactory.

Ordinances and Regulations: RULES OF THE CITY OF NEW YORK, Title 24, §207.01 §207.03, and §207

City Agency Contact Information:
N.Y.C. Department of Health and Mental Hygiene
Office of Vital Records
125 Worth Street, CN4, Rm. 133
New York, NY 10013
(212) 639–9675
http://www.nyc.gov/html/doh/html/services/vr.shtml

New York State

New York State will change the **name** and will issue a new birth certificate. The registrar shall "hold the contents of the original local record confidential along with all papers and copies pertaining thereto. It shall not be released or otherwise divulged except by order of a court of competent jurisdiction." There are anecdotal stories of the Department of Health, Vital Records Section making changes for sex based on sex changes, but there is no statute or regulation to cite as authority.

Documents needed:

A. Form DOH-4380 (12/05) Mail-in Application for Copy of Birth Certificate
B. Form DCH-297 (1/2002) Application for Correction of Certificate of Birth. The application *must* be submitted with copies of either A *or* B:

C. One (1) of the following forms of valid photo-ID:
   - Driver license
   - State issued non driver photo-ID card
   - Passport
   - U.S. Military issued photo-ID
D. Two (2) of the following showing the applicant's name and address:
   - Utility or telephone bills
   - Letter from a government agency dated within the last six (6) months

Statutes and Regulations: N.Y. PUBLIC HEALTH LAW §4138

State Agency Contact Information:

State of New York

Department of Health, Vital Records Section

Certification Unit

Vital Records Section/2nd floor

800 North Pearl Street

Menands, NY 12204

(518) 474–3075

http://www.health.state.ny.us/vital_records/birth.htm

North Carolina

North Carolina will change the **sex** and will issue a new birth certificate rather than amend the old one. "The State Registrar shall place under seal the original certificate of birth, the copy forwarded by the register of deeds and all papers relating to the original certificate of birth. The seal shall not be broken except by an order of a court of competent jurisdiction."

North Carolina will issue an amended birth certificate for a name change according to its website.

Documents needed:

- A notarized statement from the physician who performed the sex reassignment surgery or from a physician licensed to practice medicine who has examined the individual and can certify that the person has undergone sex reassignment surgery
- An original or certified copy of the court order for the name change

Statutes and Regulations: N.C. Gen. Stat. Ann. § 130A-118

Authority: As to name change see North Carolina Vital Records website at http://vitalrecords.nc.gov/vitalrecords/change.htm#namchg accessed on 07/31/2011

State Agency Contact Information:
North Carolina Vital Records
1903 Mail Service Center
Raleigh, NC 27699–1903
(919) 733–3000
http://vitalrecords.nc.gov/vitalrecords/

North Dakota

North Dakota will issue an amended birth certificate for a **name** and **sex** change.

Documents needed:

- A certified copy of the court order for the name change
- An affidavit by a physician that the physician has performed an operation on the person and that by reason of the operation, the sex designation of such person's birth record should be changed

Statutes and Regulations: N.D. Cent. Code § 23–02.1–25 and N.D. Admin. Code §§ 33–04–12–02 and 33–04–12–03

State Agency Contact Information:
North Dakota Department of Health
Division of Vital Records
600 East Boulevard Avenue, Dept. 301
Bismarck, ND 58505–0200
(701) 328–2360
http://www.ndhealth.gov/vital/birth.htm

Ohio

Ohio will change the birth certificate to add a new **name**. Such record shall disclose information that a legal change of name has been granted by the court. The probate court will not hear an application to correct a transsexual's birth certificate where there is no error in the designation of the transsexual's gender as male or female on the original birth certificate. *In re Ladrach*, 32 Ohio Misc.2d 6, 513 N.E.2d 828 (Ohio Probate 1987)

Documents needed:

- A certified copy of the court order for the name change

Statutes and Regulations: OHIO REV. CODE ANN. § 3705.13
   State Agency Contact Information:
Vital Statistics
Ohio Department of Health
246 North High Street, 1st Floor
Columbus, OH 43216
http://www.odh.ohio.gov/vitalstatistics/vitalmisc/vitalstats.aspx

Oklahoma

Oklahoma will issue an amended birth certificate for a **name** change. There is no specific procedure for having the sex changed on a birth certificate, but one possibility is in OKLA. ADMIN. CODE § 310:105–3–3(e), which states: "Any applicant that desires to make a change, alteration or amendment not provided for in paragraphs (a) through (d) of this section may file a petition with the Administrative Hearing Clerk pursuant to" OKLA. ADMIN. CODE § 310:2 "and seek a final decision by an Administrative Law Judge granting the relief requested. The applicant shall bear the burden of proof, by clear and convincing evidence that the proposed change, alteration or amendment sought by the Applicant corrects an error or misstatement of fact as to any non medical information supplied to the State Registrar by the parent(s), facility or attendant."

Documents needed:

- A certified copy of the court order is required.

Statutes and Regulations: OKLA. STAT. ANN. tit. 63 § 1–321
   State Agency Contact Information:
Vital Records Service

Oklahoma State Department of Health
James O. Goodwin Health Center
5051 S. 129th East Ave.
Tulsa, OK 74143–7004
(405) 271–4040
http://www.ok.gov/health/Birth_and_Death_Certificates/

Oregon

Oregon will change the **name, sex or both** on a birth certificate. Oregon will issue amended certificates.

Documents needed:

- A certified copy of the court order changing the name
- A "certified copy of an order of a court of competent jurisdiction indicating that the sex of an individual born in this state has been changed by surgical procedure and whether such individual's name has been changed"

Statutes and Regulations: OR. REV. STAT. § 432.235

State Agency Contact Information:

Oregon Vital Records
P.O. Box 14050
Portland, OR 97293–0050
(971) 673–1190
http://public.health.oregon.gov/BirthDeathCertificates/ChangeVitalRecords/Pages/index.aspx

Pennsylvania

Pennsylvania will change the **name** and issue an amended birth certificate with no mention of being amended. The original birth certificate is amended and sealed so that it is unavailable to the public except with the person's permission or by court order.

Documents needed:

- A certified copy of the court order for the name change

Statutes and Regulations: 35 PA. STAT. ANN. § 450.603 and 28 PA. CODE § 1.3

State Agency Contact Information:
Division of Vital Records
ATTN: Birth Unit
101 South Mercer Street
Central Building, Room 401
P.O. Box 1528
New Castle, PA 16103
(724) 656–3100
http://www.portal.health.state.pa.us/portal/server.pt/community/
birth_certificates/14121/corrections_to_birth_certificates/612936

Rhode Island

Rhode Island will issue an amended birth certificate changing the **name** with a note designating the change of name.

Documents needed:

- A original letter from the SRS surgeon
- A court order is not required
- Affidavit from the applicant

Statutes and Regulations: R.I. GEN. LAWS § 23–3–21 and R.I. Code Rule 31–1–29:35.0

State Agency Contact Information:
Rhode Island Department of Health
Office of Vital Records, Room 101
3 Capitol Hill
Providence, RI 02908–5097
(401) 222–2811
http://www.health.ri.gov/records/howto/getacopy/

South Carolina

South Carolina will amend a birth certificate to reflect a **name** change. It shall be marked "Amended by Court Order." The "existing certificate and court order upon which the new certificate was based are to be sealed and placed in a special sealed file. Such sealed file shall not be subject to inspection except upon order of a court of competent jurisdiction."

Documents needed:
- A certified copy of the court order for the name change. The order must direct that the birth certificate be amended.
- An affidavit of the person seeking the change.

Statutes and Regulations: S.C. CODE ANN. REGS. 61–19
   State Agency Contact Information:
   Office of Vital Records
   South Carolina Dept. of Health and Environmental Control
   2600 Bull Street
   Columbia, SC 29201
   (803) 898–3630
   http://www.scdhec.gov/administration/vr/birth.htm

South Dakota

South Dakota has no statute or regulation governing name or sex changes on birth certificates. However, the South Dakota Department of Health's website states:

Name Changes
   To change a surname (last name) on a vital record, one must provide a certified copy of a court order that directs that the record be amended AND provide the following information:
   (a) information to identify the certificate;
   (b) the incorrect data as it is listed on the certificate; and
   (c) the correct data as it should appear.

Authority: South Dakota Department of Health website at http://doh.sd.gov/VitalRecords/Amendments.aspx accessed on 07/31/2011
   State Agency Contact Information:
   Vital Records

South Dakota Department of Health
207 East Missouri Avenue, Suite 1-A
Pierre, SD 57501
(605) 773–4961
http://doh.sd.gov/VitalRecords/Amendments.aspx

Tennessee

Tennessee will not change the sex designation on a birth certificate. Tennessee will issue an amended birth certificate for a name change.

Documents needed:

• A certified copy of the court order for the name change

Statutes and Regulations: TENN. CODE ANN. § 68–3–203 and TENN. COMP. R. & REGS. 1200–07–01–.10
    State Agency Contact Information:
    Tennessee Vital Records
    1st Floor, Central Services Building
    421 5th Avenue, North
    Nashville, TN 37243
    (615) 741–1763
    http://health.state.tn.us/vr/index.htm

Texas

Texas will change the **name** and will issue an amended certificate. An adult whose name "is changed by court order . . . may request that the state registrar attach an amendment showing the change to the person's original birth record."

Documents needed:

• A certified copy of the court order for the name change

Statutes and Regulations: TEX. HEALTH & SAFETY CODE ANN. § 192.010
    State Agency Contact Information:
    Vital Statistics Unit

Texas Department of Health
P.O. Box 12040
Austin, TX 78711–2040
(512) 458–7111
http://www.dshs.state.tx.us/vs/reqproc/amendment.shtm

Utah

Utah will issue an amended certificate, changing both **name** and **sex**. "When a person born in this state has a name change or sex change approved by an order of a Utah district court or a court of competent jurisdiction of another state or a province of Canada, a certified copy of the order may be filed with the state registrar with an application form provided by the registrar."

Documents needed:

*   An original or certified copy of a court order for the name change
*   A court order for the change of sex designation

Statutes and Regulations: UTAH CODE ANN. § 26–2–11 and UTAH ADMIN. CODE Rule 436–3

State Agency Contact Information:
Office of Vital Records and Statistics
Utah Department of Health
288 North 1460 West
P.O. Box 141012
Salt Lake City, UT 84114–1012
(801) 538–6105
http://www.health.utah.gov/vitalrecords/certificates/certificates.htm

Vermont

Vermont has an unusual procedure to change one's **name** and to change it on the birth certificate. The statute is set out in full below:

"Whenever a person changes his or her name, as provided in this chapter, he or she shall provide the probate division of the superior court with a copy of his or her birth certificate and, if married, a copy of his or her civil marriage certificate, and a copy of the birth certificate of each minor child, if any. The register of probate with whom the change of name is filed and recorded shall transmit the certificates and a certified copy of such instrument of change of name to the supervisor of vital records registration. The supervisor of vital records registration shall forward such instrument of change of name to the town clerk in the town where the person was born within the state, or wherein the original certificate is filed, with instructions to amend the original certificate and all copies thereof in accordance with the provisions of Title 18, Chapter 101. Such amended certificates shall have the words "Court Amended" stamped, written or typed at the top and shall show that the change of name was made pursuant to this chapter."

Documents needed:

- See above.

Statutes and Regulations: VT. STAT. ANN. tit. 15 § 816
  State Agency Contact Information:
  Vermont Department of Health
  Vital Records Section
  P.O. Box 70
  108 Cherry Street
  Burlington, VT 05402–0070
  (802) 863–7275
  http://healthvermont.gov/research/records/vital_records.aspx

Virginia

Virginia will change both the **name** and **sex** and will issue a new birth certificate rather than amend the old one.

Documents needed:
- A certified copy of an order of a court of competent jurisdiction indicating that the sex of an individual has been changed by medical procedure

- A certified copy of the court order for the name change

Statutes and Regulations: VA. CODE ANN. § 32.1–269 and 12 VA. ADMIN. CODE § 5–550–320

State Agency Contact Information:
State of Virginia
Division of Vital Records
Attn: Special Services Dept.
P.O. Box 1000
Richmond, VA 23218–100
(804) 662–6200
http://www.vdh.virginia.gov/vital_Records/index.htm

Washington

Washington has no statute or regulation for change of name or sex on a birth certificate. There is an indication on the website of the Washington Department of Health that a name change can be recorded, but there is no definitive guidance.

Documents needed:
- It is assumed a certified copy of the name change order would be needed.

Statutes and Regulations: None

State Agency Contact Information:
Washington Department of Health
Center for Health Statistics
P.O. Box 47814
Olympia, WA 98504–7814
(360) 236–4300
http://www.doh.wa.gov/EHSPHL/CHS/cert.htm#OrderingThroughCHS

West Virginia

West Virginia will change the **name** and will issue an amended birth certificate.

Documents needed:
- A certified copy of the court order for the name change

Statutes and Regulations: W. VA. CODE ANN. § 16–5–25 and W. VA. CODE R. § 64–32–12
   State Agency Contact Information:
   State of West Virginia
   Vital Registration Office
   Room 165
   350 Capitol Street
   Charleston, WV 25301–3701
   (304) 558–2931
   http://www.wvdhhr.org/bph/hsc/vital/changes.asp

Wisconsin

Wisconsin will change both **name** and/or **sex**, and will issue a new birth certificate.

Documents needed:
- A certified "court or administrative order issued in this state, in another state or in Canada or under the valid order of a court of any federally recognized Indian tribe, band or nation if "the order provides for an ..., name change or name change with sex change...."
- A certified copy of the court order for the name change

Statutes and Regulations: WIS. STAT. ANN. § 69.15
   State Agency Contact Information:
   Wisconsin Vital Records Office
   1 West Wilson Street
   P.O. Box 309
   Madison, WI 53701–0309
   http://www.dhs.wisconsin.gov/vitalrecords/birth.htm

Wyoming

Wyoming will issue an amended certificate for a change in **name, sex** or **both.**

Documents needed:

- A certified copy of a court order directing an amendment of the birth certificate due to a sex change
- A certified copy of a court order changing the name

Statutes and Regulations: Wyo. Stat. Ann. § 35–1–424 and 10 Wyo. Code R. § 4

State Agency Contact Information:
State of Wyoming
Vital Statistics Services
Hathaway Building
Cheyenne, WY 82002
(307) 777–7591
http://health.wyo.gov/rfhd/vital_records/index.html

Persons Born Outside the United States but Are Now Citizens

One can change his or her name and possibly sex or gender on one's U.S. Department of State-issued birth certificate.

On January 3, 2011, the Department of State began issuing a new Consular Report of Birth Abroad (FS-240). As of December 31, 2010, the Certificate of Report of Birth (DS-1350) is no longer issued. All previously issued FS-240 and DS-1350 documents are still valid for proof of identity, citizenship, and other legal purposes.

Mail documents and check or money order to:
Department of State
Passport Services
Vital Records Section
Room 510
1111 19th Street, NW
Washington, DC 20036

Documents needed:

- A notarized written (or typed) request detailing the amendment or correction needed

- Certified copies of documents justifying the amendment requested (e.g., foreign birth certificate, certified copy of court order for the name change, affidavits)
- The original FS-240, a replacement FS-240, or a notarized affidavit stating the whereabouts of the original FS-240
- A copy of requester's valid identification
- Check or money order for $50.00 (as of 07/25/2011). Check website to make sure it has not changed.

Authority: U.S. Dept. of State, Bureau of Consular Affairs' website accessed 11/21/2011 at http://travel.state.gov/passport/get/first/first_825.html accessed on 07/31/2011

State Department Contact Information:

U.S. Dept. of State
1111 19th Street N.W., Suite 510
Washington, DC 20036
(202) 955–0307

State Laws Relating to Changing Driver's Licenses and Non-Driver Identification Cards

State	Procedure	Authority
Alabama	The Department of Public Safety, Driver License Division must be notified of the change within thirty days of a name change.	ALA. ADMIN. CODE Rule 760-X-1-.07
Alaska	A person who changes his or her name must notify the Department of Adminstration's Division of Motor Vehicles within thirty days of a name change.	ALASKA STAT. §§ 28.05.071 and 28.35.135
Arizona	If a person's name changes after receiving a driver's license or nonoperating ID, the person shall notify the department within ten days. A substitute can be obtained with new photo for a fee.	ARIZ. REV. STAT. §§ 28–448 and 28–3170
Arkansas	Application by a licensee to change licensee's name must be accompanied by court order that provides evidence of the change of name.	ARK. CODE ANN. § 27–16–506

State	Procedure	Authority
California	Applicant for change of name driver license or ID card to produce ID to ensure the name on application is his or her true full name by original or certified copy of document issued by a competent jurisdiction that contains the applicant's legal name, date of birth, if available, and government seal, stamp or other official imprint including a name change document that contains the individual's legal name both before and, as a result of, the name change.	Cal. Code Regs. tit. 13 § 20.04
Colorado	Any "court-ordered name change entered by any state or federal court may be used to modify the full legal name of the applicant."	1 Colo. Code Regs. § 204–13:2.0 ¶ 2.3.5
Connecticut	The commissioner will accept "order of the superior court, or other court of competent jurisdiction, pertaining to a change of the applicant's name."	Conn. Agencies Regs. § 14–137–63(a)
Delaware	When the name of a holder of a commercial driver's license changes, an application for a corrected license must be made. Regular driver's licenses are not addressed.	Del. Code Ann. tit. 21 § 2610(b)
District of Columbia	When the holder of a commercial driver's license changes his or her name, he or she shall file an application for a duplicate commercial driver's license with the Department of Motor Vehicles within thirty days.	D.C. Mun. Regs. tit. 18 § 1307.2
Florida	A person must obtain a replacement license within ten days after a name change. Upon the surrender of the original license and the payment of fee, the department shall issue a replacement license "reflecting the necessary changes such as name, . . . and physical description." [The change in physical description may apply to sex changes.]	Fla. Code Ann. § 322.19 and Fla. Admin. Code Ann. Rule 15A-1.020(b)(2)
Georgia	Those whose names have changed for any other reason may obtain a driver's license or identification card in the new name upon submission of a certified copy of the court order granting the change of name. A person must do so within sixty days.	Ga. Comp. R. & Regs. 375–3–1–.24(4) Ga. Code Ann. § 40–5–33
Hawaii	A person must notify the examiner of drivers within thirty days of name change. The examiner may require "satisfactory proof of the change of name."	Haw. Rev. Stat. § 286–116.5(b)

State	Procedure	Authority
Idaho	The name on the birth certificate will be used unless a name changes due to court order.	IDAHO ADMIN. CODE Rule 39.02.75.200
Illinois	A person must apply for a corrected card within thirty days after a name change.	625 ILL. COMP. STAT. 5/6–116
Indiana	A person must apply for a corrected card within thirty days after a name change.	IND. CODE § 9–24–13–4
Iowa	A replacement license can be obtained with a new name with an affidavit of the name change on Form 430043 and a court order containing the full name, date of birth, and court seal. For a sex change, the "licensee shall submit court documentation of the sex change."	IOWA ADMIN. CODE § 761–605.11(321)
Kansas	A person must furnish an affidavit stating the circumstances of the name change.	KAN. CODE ANN. § 8–246
Kentucky	When the name of a licensee is changed, by marriage or otherwise, the person must apply to the circuit clerk in his or her county of residence for the issuance of a corrected license within ten days after the change.	KY. REV. STAT. ANN. § 186.540
Louisiana	There is no statutory or administrative authority for a name or sex change on a license.	
Maine	A person must notify the secretary of state in writing within thirty days of a name change.	ME. REV. STAT. ANN. tit. 29-A § 1407
Maryland	A person must notify the Motor Vehicle Administration in writing within thirty days of a name change and can obtain a corrected license.	MD. ANN. CODE. TRANSP. § 16–116
Massachusetts	A person has thirty days to report a name change to the Registrar of Motor Vehicles for a driver's license. No deadline was stated for an ID card.	MASS. GEN. LAWS ch. 90 §§ 8G and 26A

State	Procedure	Authority
Michigan	There is no express statutory authority to change name on driver's license. In 2003, the secretary of state had a practice of issuing a license in a new name upon submission of written verification of current usage of the common law name for at least six months before application. The attorney general issued an opinion stating that the secretary of state may, but is not required to, accept an affidavit alone as sufficient legal proof to effectuate a common law name change on a person's driver's license.	Op. Mich. Atty. Gen. 2003 Mich. OAG No. 7142, 2003 WL 22405340, citing MICH. COMP. LAWS § 257.209
Minnesota	A person must apply for a duplicate license on the form provided by the Department of Public Safety and present a certified copy of the name change court order within thirty days of a name change.	MINN. STAT. § 171.11 and MINN. Rule 7410.0500
Mississippi	A person must apply for a duplicate license on the form provided by the Department of Public Safety and present a certified copy of the name change court order within thirty days of a name change.	MISS. ANN. CODE § 63–1–9
Missouri	A name change for a driver's license or non-driver ID will be supported by a court order or amended birth certificate.	MO. CODE REGS. ANN. tit. 12 § 10–24.448
Montana	A name change for a driver's license will be supported by a court order.	MONT. ADMIN. Rule 23.3.128
Nebraska	A person must apply for a duplicate license with the county treasurer within sixty days of a name change.	NEB. REV. STAT. § 60–4,120
Nevada	A person must apply for a duplicate license on the form provided by the Department of Public Safety and present a certified copy of the name change court order within thirty days of a name change.	NEV. REV. STAT. §§ 483.390 and 483.870 and NEV. ADMIN. CODE § 483.055
New Hampshire	A person must notify the director of the division of motor vehicles within ten days of a name change.	N.H. REV. STAT. ANN. § 263:9
New Jersey	A person must notify the director of the division of motor vehicles within two weeks of a name change. A person can be fined for failure to so notify. The same applies to name change for an ID card.	N.J. STAT. ANN. §§ 39:3–9a and 39:3–29.6

State	Procedure	Authority
New Mexico	A replacement license or ID card for a name change can be obtained upon furnishing proof satisfactory to Tax and Revenue Department, Motor Vehicle Division.	N.M. STAT. ANN. §§ 66–5–20 and 66–5–404
New York	To change the name or sex on a driver's license or non-driver ID card, use N.Y. Dept. of Motor Vehicles Form MV-44 (Application for Driver License or Non-Driver ID Card). Go to a DMV office. A certified copy of a court order is needed for a name change. To change the sex, one must present proof of a sex change, which is "a written statement from a physician, a psychologist, or a psychiatrist that is printed on letterhead. The statement must certify that one's gender is one's main gender (male or female)."	New York Dept. of Motor Vehicles website.1 No statute or regulation on point.
North Carolina	A person must notify the Division of Motor Vehicles within sixty days of a name change. A duplicate license or new card will be issued.	N.C. GEN. STAT. §§ 20–7.1, 20–14, and 20–37.9
North Dakota	A person must notify the director of the department of transportation within ten days of a name change. A duplicate or substitute license will be issued.	N.D. CENT. CODE §§ 39–06–18 and 39–06–20
Ohio	A person can obtain a duplicate license or replacement ID card from the Registrar of Motor Vehicles upon proof of a name change. A certified copy of the court order is required as proof.	OHIO REV. CODE ANN. §§ 4507.06 and 4507.52 OHIO ADMIN. CODE 4501:1–1–21
Oklahoma	For both citizens and noncitizens, the name on the driver's license or identification card must be same as the name on the document presented, unless the applicant also presents a court order of name change.	No statute or regulation found. Oklahoma Dept. of Public Safety website.2
Oregon	A person must apply for a duplicate license on the form provided by the Department of Public Safety within thirty days of a name change. A license is invalid without the change, and it is an offense to not report it.	ORE. REV. STAT. ANN. §§ 807.400, 807.420 and 807.560

State	Procedure	Authority
Pennsylvania	A person must notify the Department of Transportation within fifteen days of a name change.	75 Pa. Cons. Stat. § 1515
Rhode Island	A person must notify the Division of Motor Vehicles within ten days of a name change. "In order to prove a name change from the name contained on a primary identity document, a government issued Marriage Certificate/License is required)." There is no mention of accepting a court order.	R.I. Gen. Laws §§ 31–3–35 and 31–10–32 and R.I. Code R. § 47–1–36 APPENDIX A
South Carolina	A person must notify the Division of Motor Vehicles within ten days of a name change.	S.C. Code Ann. § 56–1–230
South Dakota	The statute has no policy for change but imposes a fee for a duplicate license or "name change."	S.D. Codified Laws § 32–12–16
Tennessee	A person must notify the Division of Safety within ten days of a name change.	Tenn. Code Ann. § 55–50–333
Texas	A person must notify the Department of Public Safety within thirty days of a name change.	27 Tex. Admin. Code § 15.36
Utah	Utah Dept. of Public Safety, Driver License Division will issue substitute license upon proof of a change of full legal name by a certified copy of a Utah court order or other acceptable proof.	Utah Code Ann. § 53–3–216 and Utah Admin. Code Rule 708–41.3(4)
Vermont	A person must notify the commissioner of motor vehicles "forthwith."	Vt. Stat. Ann. tit. 23 § 4110
Virginia	Does not mention a name change but allows for a duplicate license when "there are good reasons why a duplicate should be issued."	Va. Code Ann. § 46.2–343
Washington	A person must notify the Department of Licensing within ten days of a name change. A copy of the court order or an affidavit is required.	Wash. Rev. Code § 46.20.205 and Wash. Admin. Code § 308–93–500
West Virginia	No statutory or regulatory procedure was found.	

State	Procedure	Authority
Wisconsin	Secretary of Transportation will issue substitute license upon change of name by licensee.	WIS. CODE ANN. § 343.19
Wyoming	A person must apply for a duplicate license within ten days. Changes of name because of a legal proceeding may be made by the original copy of the court order and the applicant's certification that the requested name change is not for any wrongful or fraudulent purpose, does not and shall not infringe on the interest, rights, or privacy of any other person, and is not prohibited by or in violation of any judicial or administrative adjudication.	WYO. STAT. ANN. § 31-7-137 and 1 WYO. CODE RULES § 5

1. New York Dept. of Motor Vehicles website accessed on 07/22/2011 at http://nys-dmv.custhelp.com/app/answers/detail/a_id/405/kw/name%20change/related/1.

2. Oklahoma Dept. of Public Safety website accessed on 07/22/2011 at http://www.dps.state.ok.us/dls/dlid.htm.

State Laws Relating
to Marriage

State	Recognizes Same Sex Marriage	Authority
Alabama	Yes?[1]	ALA. CODE § 30–1–19, and ALA. CONST. art. I § 36.03
Alaska	Yes[2]	ALASKA CONST. art. I § 25
Arizona	Yes[3]	ARIZ. REV. STAT. §§ 25–101 and 25–112
Arkansas	Yes?[4]	ARK. CODE ANN. §§ 9–11–208 and 9–11–107
California	Yes[5]	

---

1. The Alabama's ban on same sex marriages was declared unconstitutional on January 23, 2015. See: Searcy v. Strange, 2015 WL 328825 (S.D. Ala. 2015)

2. ALASKA CONST. Art. 1, § 25 and ALASKA STAT. § 25.05.011, *et seq.* were declared unconstitutional by the U.S. District Court in Hamby v. Parnell, ___ F.Supp.3d ___, 2014 WL 5089399 (D. Alaska 2014)

3. The court in Majors v. Horne, 14 F.Supp.3d 1313 (D. Ariz. 2014) declared ARIZ. REV. STAT. § 25-101(c) and § 25-125 to be unconstitutional.

4. The Pulaski County, Arkansas Circuit Court in Case No. 60CV–13–2662 on May 9, 2014 entered an order that read in pertinent part as follows: "THIS COURT HEREBY FINDS the Arkansas Constitutional and Legislative ban on same-sex marriage through Act 144 of 1997 and Amendment 83 is unconstitutional." The case is on appeal to the Arkansas Supreme Court. See: Smith v. Wright, Not Reported in S.W.3d, 2014 Ark. 222, 2014 WL 2021834 (2014)

5. CAL. CONST. art. 1, § 7.5 (Proposition 8 adopted 2008), declared unconstitutional by *Perry v. Schwarzenegger*, 671 F.3d 1052 (9ᵗʰ Cir. 2012), *aff'g* 704 F. Supp. 2d 921 (N.D. Cal. 2010), *reh. en banc den.* 681 F.3d 1065 (9ᵗʰ Cir. 2012), cert. den., *sub nom* Hollingsworth v. Perry, 133 S.Ct. 786, 184 L.Ed.2d 526 (2014); and CAL. FAM. CODE § 308.5, declared unconstitutional by *In re Marriage Cases*, 43 Cal.4ᵗʰ 757, 183 P.3d 384, 76 Cal. Rptr. 3d 683 (2008). CAL. FAM. CODE § 308(a) passed in 2009 declared that same-sex marriages legally entered into on or before November 4, 2008, in other states or countries will be recognized as marriages under California law. Same-sex marriages taking place in other states or countries after November 4, 2008, will only be recognized as domestic partnerships.

State	Recognizes Same Sex Marriage	Authority
Colorado	Yes[6]	COLO. CONST., art. II, §31 and COLO. REV. STAT. §§ 14–2–104 and
Connecticut	Yes	*Kerrigan v. Commissioner of Public Health*, 289 Conn. 135, 957 A.2d 407 (2008) which declared CONN. GEN. STAT. § 46b-38aa, *et seq.* unconstitutional on state law grounds.
Delaware	Yes	DEL. CODE ANN. tit. 13 § 129
District of Columbia	Yes	D.C. CODE § 46–401
Florida	Yes?[7]	
Georgia	No?[8]	GA. CONST. art. 1, §4, ¶ 1 and GA. CODE ANN. § 19–3–3.1
Hawaii	Yes	HAW. REV. STAT. § 572–1, *et seq.*
Idaho	Yes[9]	
Illinois	Yes[10]	750 ILL. COMP. STAT. 5/201, *et seq.*
Indiana	Yes[11]	IND. CODE § 31–11–1–1
Iowa	Yes	Varnum v. Brien, 763 N.W.2d 862 (Iowa 2009), which declared IOWA CODE § 595.2 unconstitutional
Kansas	Yes?[12]	
Kentucky	Yes[13]	KY. REV. STAT. ANN. §§ 402.005 and 402.020

6. Burns v. Hickenlooper, Not reported in F.Supp.3d, 2014 WL 5312541 (D. Col. 2014) declared COL. CONST. Art. 2, § 31 and COL. REV. STAT. ANN. § 14-2-104 unconstitutional

7. Florida's ban on same sex marriages was declared unconstitutional on August 21, 2014. See: Brenner v. Scott, 999 F.Supp.2d 1278 (N.D. Fla. 2015), stay pending appeal denied by Armstrong v. Brenner, 135 S.Ct. 890 (2014)

8. The U.S. District Court has declined to dismiss a challenge to the Georgia ban on same sex marriages, but has yet to rule on the merits of the case. See: Inniss v. Aderhold, ___F. Supp.3d ___, 2015 WL 300593 (N.D. Ga. 2015)

9. Idaho's ban on same sex marriages was declared unconstitutional by Latta v. Otter, 771 F.3d 456 (9th Cir. 2014), stay vacated by 135 S.Ct. 345, 190 L.Ed.2d 245 (2014)

10. In Lee v. Orr, Not reported in F.Supp.2d, 2014 WL 683680 (N.D. Ill. 2014) the court declared 750 ILL. COMP. STAT. 5/201, 750 ILL. COMP. STAT. 5/212, and 750 ILL. COMP. STAT. 5/213.1 (repealed June , 2014) to be unconstitutional.

11. Baskin v. Bogan, 766 F.3d 648 (7th Cir. 2014) , cert. den. 135 S.Ct. 316, 190 L.Ed.2d 142 (2014) declared IND. CODE § 31-11-1-1 to be unconstitutional

12. Idaho's ban on same sex marriages was declared unconstitutional on November 14, 2014 by Marie v. Moser, ___ F.Supp.3d ___, 2014 WL 5598128 (D. Kan. 2014), stay denied 135 S.Ct. 511 (2014)

13. The court in Love v. Beshear, 989 F.Supp.2d 536 (W.D. Ky. 2014) declared KY. CONST. § 233A and KY. REV. STAT. § 402.005 unconstitutional.

State	Recognizes Same Sex Marriage	Authority
Louisiana	No	LA. CONST. art. 12, § 15 and LA. CIV. CODE ANN. art. 86
Maine	Yes	ME. REV. STAT. ANN. tit. 19-A § 701
Maryland	Yes?[14]	Maryland Civil Marriage Protection Act, 2012 Md. Laws Ch. 2, which amends MD. CODE ANN. FAM. LAW §§ 2–201 and 2–202 (effective Jan. 1, 2013)
Massachusetts	Yes	*Goodridge v. Department of Public Health*, 440 Mass. 309, 798 N.E.2d 941 (2003) which reformulated the definition of "marriage," as employed in MASS. GEN. LAWS ch. 207 §§ 19 and 20 to mean voluntary union of two persons as spouses, to exclusion of all others regardless of sex
Michigan	No?[15]	MICH. COMP. LAWS § 551.1, *et seq.*
Minnesota	Yes	MINN. STAT. § 517.01 (2013)
Mississippi	Yes/No[16]	MISS. CONST. art. 14, § 263A and MISS. ANN. CODE § 93–1–1, *et seq.*
Missouri	Yes?[17]	
Montana	Yes?[18]	
Nebraska	No?[19]	NEB. CONST. art. I, § 29
Nevada	Yes[20]	

14. Maryland is in the Fourth Circuit which declared Virginia's ban on same sex marriages unconstitutional. So, it is very likely that Maryland's ban would be declared unconstitutional. See: Bostic v. Schaefer, 760 F.3d 352 (4th Cir. 2014), cert. den. 135 S.Ct. 308, 190 L.Ed.2d 140 (2014).

15. Michigan's ban on same sex marriages was declared unconstitutional by DeBoer v. Snyder, 973 F.Supp.2d 757 (E.D. Mich. 2014), rev'd by DeBoer v. Snyder, 772 F.3d 388 (6th Cir. 2014), cert. granted ___ U.S. ___, 2015 WL 213650 (Jan 16, 2015), and Caspar v. Snyder, ___ F.Supp.3d ___, 2015 WL 224741 (E.D. Mich. 2015)

16. Campaign for Southern Equality v. Bryant, ___ F.Supp.3d ___, 2014 WL 6680570 (S.D. Miss. 2014), stay granted 773 F.3d 55 (5th Cir. 2014)

17. Missouri's ban on same sex marriages was declared unconstitutional on November 7, 2014 by Lawson v. Kelly, ___ F.Supp.3d ___, 2014 WL 5810215 (W.D. Mo. 2014)

18. Montana's ban on same sex marriages was declared unconstitutional. See: Rolando v. Fox, 23 F.Supp.3d 1227 (D. Mont. 2014)

19. Nebraska's ban on same sex marriages has been challenged but the challenge has not been ruled upon. Waters v. Heineman, Not Reported in F.Supp.3d, 2015 WL 106377 (D. Neb. 2015)

20. Nevada's ban on same sex marriages was declared unconstitutional. See: Latta v. Otter, 771 F.3d 456 (9th Cir. 2014), which reversed Sevcik v. Sandoval, 911 F.Supp.2d 996 (D. Nev. 2012).

State	Recognizes Same Sex Marriage	Authority
New Hampshire	Yes	N.H. Rev. Stat. Ann. § 457:1, *et seq.*
New Jersey	Yes	New Jersey's ban on same sex marriages was declared unconstitutional. See: Garden State Equality v. Dow, 216 N.J. 314, 79 A.3d 1036 (2013)
New Mexico	Yes	New Mexico's ban on same sex marriages was declared unconstitutional. See: Griego v. Oliver, 316 P.3d 865 (N.M. 2013)
New York	Yes	Marriage Equality Act, 2011 N.Y. Sess. Law Ch. 95, which amends N.Y. Dom. Rel. Law §§ 10–a and 10–b
North Carolina	No/Yes[21]	N.C. Gen. Stat. § 51–1.2
North Dakota	No	N.D. Cent. Code § 14–03–01
Ohio	Yes[22]	Ohio Rev. Code Ann. § 3101.01
Oklahoma	Yes[23]	Okla. Const. art. 2, §35 and Okla. Stat. tit. 43 § 3.1
Oregon	Yes?[24]	
Pennsylvania	Yes[25]	23 Pa. Cons. Stat. § 1704
Rhode Island	Yes	R.I. Gen. Laws § 15–1–1
South Carolina	Yes?[26]	

21. The Fourth Circuit held that N.C. Const. Art. XIV, § 6 and N.C. Gen. Stat. Ann. § 51-1, *et seq* unconstitutional in Bostic v. Schaefer, 760 F.3d 352 (4th Cir. 2014), cert. den. 135 S.Ct. 308, 190 L.Ed.2d 140 (2014) See also: Fisher–Borne v. Smith, 14 F.Supp.3d 695 (M.D. N.C. 2014)

22. Ohio Const. Art. XV, § 11 and Ohio Rev. Code § 3101.0 were declared unconstitutional by the court in Henry v. Himes, 14 F.Supp.3d 1036 (S.D. Ohio 2014).

23. Okla. Const. Art. 2, § 35 was declared unconstitutional by Bishop v. Smith, 760 F.3d 1070 (10th Cir. 2014) , cert. den. 135 S.Ct. 271, 190 L.Ed.2d 139 (2014)

24. Oregon's ban on same sex marriages was declared unconstitutional. See: Geiger v. Kitzhaber, 994 F.Supp.2d 1128 (D. Or. 2014), stay denied by National Organization for Marriage v. Geiger, 134 S.Ct. 2722, 189 L.Ed.2d 760 (2014)

25. In Whitewood v. Wolf, 992 F.Supp.2d 410 (M.D. Pa. 2014) the court declared that 23 Pa. Consol. Stat. Ann. §§ 1102 and 1704 was unconstitutional.

26. Condon v. Haley, 21 F.Supp.3d 572 (D. S.C. 2014), stay denied by Wilson v. Condon, 135 S.Ct. 702 (2014)

State	Recognizes Same Sex Marriage	Authority
South Dakota	Yes?[27]	
Tennessee	No?[28]	TENN. CONST. art. 11, §18 and TENN. CODE ANN. § 36–3–113
Texas	Yes[29]	TEX. CONST. art. 1, § 32 and TEX. FAM. CODE ANN. § 2.001
Utah	Yes[30]	UTAH CONST. art. 1, §29 and UTAH CODE ANN. § 30–1–2
Vermont	Yes	VT. STAT. ANN. tit. 15 § 8
Virginia	Yes[31]	VA. CONST. art. 1, §15-A and VA. CODE ANN. §§ 20–45.2 and 20–45.3
Washington	Yes	WASH. REV. CODE § 26.04.010
West Virginia	Yes?[32]	
Wisconsin	Yes[33]	WIS. CONST. art. 13 § 13 and WIS. CODE ANN. § 765.001
Wyoming	Yes?[34]	

---

27. South Dakota's ban on same sex marriages was declared unconstitutional. See: Rosenbrahn v. Daugaard, ___ F.Supp.3d ___, 2015 WL 144567 (D. S.D. 2015)

28. Tennessee's ban on same sex marriages was declared unconstitutional and then upheld on appral. See: Tanco v. Haslam, 7 F.Supp.3d 759 (M.D. Tenn. 2014), rev'd by DeBoer v. Snyder, 772 F.3d 388 (6th Cir. 2014), cert. granted by Tanco v. Haslam, ___ U.S. ___, 2015 WL 213648 (2015)

29. Texas' ban on same sex marriages was declared unconstitutional. See: De Leon v. Perry, 975 F.Supp.2d 632 (W.D. Tex. 2014)

30. UTAH CODE ANN. 1953 § 30-1-2 was declared unconstitutional in Kitchen v. Herbert, 755 F.3d 1193 (10th Cir. 2014) , cert. den. 135 S.Ct. 265, 190 L.Ed.2d 138 (2014)

31. VA. CODE ANN. § 20-45.2 was declared unconstitutional in Bostic v. Schaefer, 760 F.3d 352 (4th Cir. 2014), cert. den. 135 S.Ct. 308, 190 L.Ed.2d 140 (2014).

32. West Virginia's ban on same sex marriages was declared unconstitutional. See: McGee v. Cole, ___ F.Supp.3d ___, 2014 WL 5802665 (S.D. W.Va. 2014)

33. Wisconsin's ban on same sex marriages was declared unconstitutional. See: Wolf v. Walker, 986 F.Supp.2d 982, subsequent determination, 26 F.Supp.3d 866 (W.D. Wis. 2014), aff'd 766 F.3d 648 (7th Cir. 2014), cert. den. 135 S.Ct. 316, 190 L.Ed.2d 142 (2014)

34. Wyoming's ban on same sex marriages was declared unconstitutional. See: Guzzo v. Mead, Not Reported in F.Supp.3d, 2014 WL 5317797 (D. Wyo. 2014)

Cities and Counties with Housing Nondiscrimination Ordinances and Laws That Include Gender Identity or Expression

State	City or County	Authority
Arizona	City of Tucson	CITY OF TUCSON CODE, art. VII, §§ 17–12 and 17–50
California	City of Los Angeles	LOS ANGELES MUN. CODE § 49.70, *et seq.*
	City of Oakland	OAKLAND CODE OF ORDINANCES § 9.44.020
	City of San Diego	SAN DIEGO MUN. CODE, art. 2, § 52.9604
	City and County of San Francisco	S.F. POLICE CODE §3304
	City of Santa Cruz	SANTA CRUZ MUN. CODE 9.83.010, *et seq.*
	County of Santa Cruz	SANTA CRUZ COUNTY CODE 8.52.010, *et seq.*
	City of West Hollywood	WEST HOLLYWOOD MUN. CODE, chap. 9.28.010, *et seq.*

State	City or County	Authority
Colorado	City of Boulder	CITY OF BOULDER REV. CODE, chap. 12–1
	City and County of Denver	DENVER REV. MUN. CODE § 28–91, *et seq.*
Florida	County of Broward	BROWARD COUNTY CODE OF ORDINANCES §§16 ½ – 3 and 16 ½ – 23.1
	City of Gainesville	CITY OF GAINESVILLE CODE OF ORDINANCES § 8–88
	City of Gulfport	CITY OF GULFPORT CODE OF ORDINANCES § 26–32
	City of Key West	CITY OF KEY WEST CODE OF ORDINANCES § 38–28
	County of Leon	LEON COUNTY CODE OF ORDINANCES § 9–50, *et seq.*
	City of Miami Beach	CITY OF MIAMI BEACH CODE OF ORDINANCES §§ 62–33 and 62–88
	County of Monroe	MONROE COUNTY CODE OF ORDINANCES § 14–73, *et seq.*
	County of Palm Beach	PALM BEACH COUNTY CODE OF ORDINANCES § 15–36, *et seq.*
	City of Tampa	CITY OF TAMPA CODE OF ORDINANCES § 12–71, *et seq.*
	County of Volusia	VOLUSIA COUNTY CODE OF ORDINANCES § 36–51, *et seq.*
	City of West Palm Beach	CITY OF WEST PALM BEACH CODE OF ORDINANCES § 42–31, *et seq.*
Georgia	City of Atlanta	CITY OF ATLANTA CODE OF ORDINANCES § 94–91, *et seq.*
Illinois	City of Champaign	CITY OF CHAMPAIGN CODE OF ORDINANCES §§ 17–1 to 17–3 and 17–71, *et seq.*
	City of Chicago	MUN. CODE OF CHICAGO, ch. 5–8–010 *et seq.*
	County of Cook	COOK COUNTY CODE OF ORDINANCES § 42–31, *et seq.*
	City of Decatur	DECATUR MUN. CODE, ch. 28, art. 2

State	City or County	Authority
	City of DeKalb	DeKalb Mun. Code §§ 49.02, *et seq.*
	City of Evanston	Evanston Code of Ordinances § 5–5–1, *et seq.*
	City of Peoria	Peoria Code of Ordinances § 17–71, *et seq.* and 17–96, *et seq.*
	City of Springfield	Springfield Code of Ordinances § 93.01, *et seq.*
	City of Urbana	Urbana Mun. Code §§ 12–39 and 12–64
Indiana	City of Bloomington	Bloomington Mun. Code § 2.21.020
	City of Evansville	Evansville Mun. Code § 2.30.010
	City of Indianapolis and County of Marion	Rev. Code of Consolidated City and County of Indianapolis/Marion §§ 581–101, 581–103 and 581–403
	County of Monroe	Monroe County Code, chap. 520
Iowa	City of Council Bluffs	Council Bluffs Code of Ordinances §§ 1.40.030 and 1.40.100
	City of Iowa City	Iowa City Code §§ 2–5–1, *et seq.*
	County of Johnson	Johnson County Ordinance No. 12–28–06–01
	City of Waterloo	Waterloo City Code § 5–3A–1, *et seq.*
Kansas	City of Lawrence	Code of the City of Lawrence § 10–101, *et seq.*
Kentucky	City of Covington	Covington Code of Ordinances § 37.05
	Lexington-Fayette County	Lexington-Fayette County Code of Ordinances § 2–33
	Louisville-Jefferson County Metro Government	Louisville-Jefferson County Code of Ordinances § 92.01, *et seq.*

State	City or County	Authority
Louisiana	City of New Orleans	NEW ORLEANS CODE OF ORDINANCES § 86–26, *et seq.*
Maryland	County of Howard	HOWARD COUNTY CODE OF ORDINANCES § 12–200, *et seq.*
Massachusetts	City of Boston	BOSTON MUN. CODE 10–3.1, *et seq.*
	City of Cambridge	CAMBRIDGE MUN. CODE §§ 2.76.030 and 2.76.120
	City of Northampton	NORTHAMPTON MUN. CODE §§ 22–100, *et seq.*
Maryland	City of Baltimore	BALTIMORE CITY CODE, art. 4, § 3–5
	County of Montgomery	MONTGOMERY COUNTY CODE § 27–12, *et seq.*
Michigan	City of Ann Arbor	ANN ARBOR CODE OF ORDINANCES § 9:150, *et seq.*
	City of Detroit	DETROIT CODE OF ORDINANCES § 27–1–1, *et seq.*
	City of East Lansing	EAST LANSING CODE OF ORDINANCES §§ 22–31, *et seq.*
	City of Ferndale	FERNDALE CODE OF ORDINANCES § 28–3, *et seq.*
	City of Lansing	LANSING CODE OF ORDINANCES § 295.01, *et seq.*
	Saugatuck Township	SAUGATUCK TOWNSHIP CODE OF ORDINANCES § 2–251, *et seq.* (exempts housing with no more than two families with one occupied by the owner)
	City of Traverse	CODIFIED ORDINANCES OF TRAVERSE CITY § 605.01, *et seq.*
	City of University City	UNIVERSITY CITY CODE OF ORDINANCES § 9.08.260, *et seq.*
	City of Ypsilanti	YPSILANTI CODE OF ORDINANCES § 58–61, *et seq.*, and 58–91, *et seq.*
Minnesota	City of Minneapolis	MINNEAPOLIS CODE OF ORDINANCES § 139.10, *et seq.*

State	City or County	Authority
	City of St. Paul	St. Paul Code of Ordinances § 183.01, *et seq.*
Missouri	City of Clayton	Mun. Code of City of Clayton § 225.030, *et seq.*
	City of Kansas City	Kansas City Code of Ordinances § 38–1, *et seq.*
	City of University City	University City Code of Ordinances § 9.08.260, *et seq.*
Montana	City of Missoula	Missoula Mun. Code § 9.64.010, *et seq.*
New York	City of Albany	Albany Mun. Code § 48–23, *et seq.*
	City of Buffalo	Code of the City of Buffalo § 154–12 , *et seq.*
	City of Ithaca	Ithaca Mun. Code § 215–1, *et seq.*
	City of New York	N.Y.C. Admin. Code § 8–101, *et seq.*
	City of Rochester	Rochester Mun. Code § 63–1, *et seq.*
	County of Suffolk	Suffolk County Code § 89–11, *et seq.*
	County of Tompkins	Tompkins County Code § 92–1, *et seq.*
Ohio	City of Akron	Akron Code of Ordinances § 139.12
	City of Bowling Green	Bowling Green Code of Ordinances § 153.01, *et seq.*
	City of Cincinnati	Cincinnati Code of Ordinances § 914–1, *et seq.*
	City of Cleveland	Cleveland Codified Ordinances § 665.01, *et seq.*
	City of Columbus	Columbus Code of Ordinances § 2331.01, *et seq.*
	City of Dayton	Dayton Code of Ordinances § 32.01, *et seq.*
	City of Oxford	Oxford Codified Ordinances § 143.01, *et seq.*

State	City or County	Authority
	City of Toledo	Toledo Mun. Code 554.01, *et seq.*
	Village of Yellow Springs	Yellow Springs Code of Ordinances § 626.01, *et seq.*
Oregon	City of Beaverton	Beaverton City Code § 5.16.025
	City of Bend	Bend Code, tit. V, ch. 5.25.015
	County of Benton	Benton County Code, ch. 28, ¶ 28.110
	City of Corvallis	Corvallis Mun. Code, ch. 1.23, § 1.23.060
	City of Hillsboro	Hillsboro Mun. Code § 7.28.030
	City of Lake Oswego	Lake Oswego Mun. Code § 34.22.060
	City of Lincoln City	Lincoln City Mun. Code § 9.14.010, *et seq.*
	County of Multnomah	Multnomah County Ordinance No. 969, § 15.340, *et seq.*
	City of Portland	Portland City Code § 23.01.060
	City of Salem	Salem Rev. Code § 97.040
Pennsylvania	City of Allentown	Allentown Mun. Code § 181.01, *et seq.*
	City of Easton	Easton City Code 79–1, *et seq.*
	County of Erie	Erie County Human Relations Commission Ordinance 39 (2007)
	City of Harrisburg	Code of City of Harrisburg §§ 4–101.1 and 4–105.2
	Borough of Lansdowne	Lansdowne Borough Code § 38.1, *et seq.*
	Township of Lower Merion	Lower Merion Mun. Code § 93–1, *et seq.*
	Borough of New Hope	New Hope Borough Code § 129–1, *et seq.*

State	City or County	Authority
	City of Philadelphia	PHILADELPHIA CODE §9–1101, *et seq.*
	City of Pittsburgh	PITTSBURGH CODE OF ORDINANCES § 651.01, *et seq.,* and § 659.03
	City of Scranton	SCRANTON CITY CODE § 296–1, *et seq.*
	Township of Springfield	SPRINGFIELD MUN. CODE § 47–1, *et seq.*
	Township of Susquehanna	SUSQUEHANNA ORDINANCE No. 11–17
	Borough of Swarthmore	SWARTHMORE CODIFIED ORDINANCES, ch. 207.01, *et seq.*
	Borough of West Chester	WEST CHESTER CODE OF ORDINANCES § 37A-1, *et seq.*
	Township of Whitemarsh	WHITEMARSH ORDINANCE No. 901
	City of York	YORK CITY CODIFIED ORDINANCES ,tit. 5, art. 185.01, *et seq.*
South Carolina	City of Charleston	CHARLESTON CODE OF ORDINANCES § 16–16, *et seq.*
	City of Columbia	COLUMBIA CODE OF ORDINANCES § 11–391, *et seq.*
Texas	City of Austin	AUSTIN CODE OF ORDINANCES § 5–1–1, *et seq.*
	City of Dallas	DALLAS CODE OF ORDINANCES § 46–1, *et seq.*
	City of Fort Worth	FT. WORTH CODE OF ORDINANCES § 17–86, *et seq.*
Utah	County of Grand	GRAND COUNTY ORDINANCE No. 494
	City of Harrisville	HARRISVILLE MUN. CODE § 4.62.010, *et seq.*
	City of Logan	LOGAN CITY CODE § 2.64.010, *et seq.*
	City of Midvale	MIDVALE MUN. CODE § 26.12.010

State	City or County	Authority
	City of Murray	MURRAY CITY CODE § 5.48.010, *et seq.*
	City of Ogden	OGDEN CITY CODE § 12–20–1, *et seq.*
	City of Park City	PARK CITY CODE OF ORDINANCES, tit. 4, ch. 17, § 4–17–1, *et seq.*
	City of Salt Lake	SALT LAKE CITY CODE § 10.04.010, *et seq.*
	County of Salt Lake	SALT LAKE COUNTY CODE OF ORDINANCES § 10.14.010, *et seq.*
	County of Summit	SUMMIT COUNTY CODE OF ORDINANCES § 1–15A-1, *et seq.*
	City of Taylorsville	TAYLORSVILLE CITY CODE § 19.03.010, *et seq.*
	City of West Valley	WEST VALLEY CODE OF ORDINANCES § 26–3–101, *et seq.*
Washington	City of Burien	BURIEN CODE OF ORDINANCES § 8.50.010, *et seq.*
	County of King	KING COUNTY CODE § 12.20.010, *et seq.*
	City of Olympia	OLYMPIA MUN. CODE § 5.80.040
	City of Seattle	SEATTLE MUN. CODE § 14.08.010, *et seq.*
	City of Tacoma	TACOMA MUN. CODE § 1.29.010, *et seq.*
West Virginia	City of Charleston	CHARLESTON CODE OF ORDINANCES § 62–1, *et seq.*
Wisconsin	City of Madison	MADISON CODE OF ORDINANCES § 39.03
	City of Milwaukee	MILWAUKEE CODE OF ORDINANCES § 109–41

Cities and Counties with Employment Nondiscrimination Ordinances and Laws That Include Gender Identity or Expression

State	City or County	Authority
Arizona	City of Tucson	CITY OF TUCSON CODE, art. III, §17–12
California	City of Los Angeles	LOS ANGELES MUN. CODE § 49.70, *et seq.*
	City of Oakland	OAKLAND CODE OF ORDINANCES § 9.44.020
	City of San Diego	SAN DIEGO MUN. CODE, art. 2, § 52.9604
	City and County of San Francisco	S.F. POLICE CODE §3303
	City of San Jose	SAN JOSE MUN. CODE § 2.08.3030
	City of Santa Cruz	SANTA CRUZ MUN. CODE 9.83.010, *et seq.*
	County of Santa Cruz	SANTA CRUZ COUNTY CODE 8.52.020, *et seq.*
	City of West Hollywood	WEST HOLLYWOOD MUN. CODE, chap. 9.28.010, *et seq.* (applies only to those who contract with the city)

State	City or County	Authority
Colorado	City of Boulder	CITY OF BOULDER REV. CODE chap. 12–1
	City and County of Denver	DENVER REV. MUN. CODE § 28–92, *et seq.*
Florida	County of Broward	BROWARD COUNTY CODE OF ORDINANCES §§ 16 ½ – 3 and 16 ½ – 21
	City of Gainesville	CITY OF GAINESVILLE CODE OF ORDINANCES § 8–48
	City of Gulfport	CITY OF GULFPORT CODE OF ORDINANCES § 26–22
	City of Key West	CITY OF KEY WEST CODE OF ORDINANCES § 38–221
	City of Lake Worth	CITY OF LAKE WORTH CODE OF ORDINANCES § 20–2
	County of Leon	LEON COUNTY CODE OF ORDINANCES § 9–25, *et seq.*
	City of Miami Beach	CITY OF MIAMI BEACH CODE OF ORDINANCES §§ 62–33 and 62–86
	County of Monroe	MONROE COUNTY CODE OF ORDINANCES § 14–40, *et seq.*
	City of Oakland Park	CITY OF OAKLAND PARK CODE OF ORDINANCES § 2–158 (applies only to city employment)
	County of Palm Beach	PALM BEACH COUNTY CODE OF ORDINANCES § 2–261
	City of Tampa	CITY OF TAMPA CODE OF ORDINANCES § 12–16, *et seq.*
	County of Volusia	VOLUSIA COUNTY CODE OF ORDINANCES § 36–26, *et seq.*
	City of West Palm Beach	CITY OF WEST PALM BEACH CODE OF ORDINANCES § 42–31, *et seq.*
Georgia	City of Atlanta	CITY OF ATLANTA CODE OF ORDINANCES § 94–110, *et seq.*
Illinois	City of Carbondale	CARBONDALE CITY CODE § 7–6–1, *et seq.* (applies only to city employment and employment related to all contracts with the city)
	City of Champaign	CITY OF CHAMPAIGN CODE OF ORDINANCES § 17–1, *et seq.*

State	City or County	Authority
	City of Chicago	MUN. CODE OF CHICAGO, ch. 2–160–020, *et seq.*
	County of Cook	COOK COUNTY CODE OF ORDINANCES § 42–31, *et seq.*
	City of Decatur	DECATUR MUN. CODE, ch. 28, art. 2
	City of DeKalb	DEKALB MUN. CODE § 49.02, *et seq.*
	City of Evanston	EVANSTON CODE OF ORDINANCES §1–12–3, *et seq.* (applies only to city employees, contractors and vendors)
	City of Peoria	PEORIA CODE OF ORDINANCES § 17–116, *et seq.*
	City of Springfield	SPRINGFIELD CODE OF ORDINANCES § 93.01, *et seq.*
	City of Urbana	URBANA MUN. CODE §§ 12–39 and 12–62
Indiana	City of Bloomington	BLOOMINGTON MUN. CODE § 2.21.020
	City of Evansville	EVANSVILLE MUN. CODE § 2.30.010
	City of Indianapolis and County of Marion	REV. CODE OF CONSOLIDATED CITY AND COUNTY OF INDIANAPOLIS/MARION §§ 581–101, 581–103 and 581–403
	County of Monroe	MONROE COUNTY CODE, chap. 520
Iowa	City of Council Bluffs	COUNCIL BLUFFS CODE OF ORDINANCES §§ 1.40.030 and 1.40.080
	City of Iowa City	IOWA CITY CODE §§ 2–1–1, *et seq.*
	County of Johnson	JOHNSON COUNTY ORDINANCE No. 12–28–06–01
	City of Waterloo	WATERLOO CITY CODE § 5–3–3
Kansas	City of Lawrence	CODE OF THE CITY OF LAWRENCE § 10–101, *et seq.*
Kentucky	City of Covington	COVINGTON CODE OF ORDINANCES § 37.08
	Lexington-Fayette County	LEXINGTON-FAYETTE COUNTY CODE OF ORDINANCES § 2–33
	Louisville-Jefferson County Metro Government	LOUISVILLE-JEFFERSON COUNTY CODE OF ORDINANCES § 92.01, *et seq.*
Louisiana	City of New Orleans	NEW ORLEANS CODE OF ORDINANCES § 86–22, *et seq.*
Maryland	City of Baltimore	BALTIMORE CITY CODE, art. 4, § 3–1

State	City or County	Authority
	County of Howard	HOWARD COUNTY CODE OF ORDINANCES § 12–200, *et seq.*
	County of Montgomery	MONTGOMERY COUNTY CODE § 27–19
Massachusetts	City of Boston	BOSTON MUN. CODE 12–9.1, *et seq.*
	City of Cambridge	CAMBRIDGE MUN. CODE §§ 2.76.030 and 2.76.120
	City of Northampton	NORTHAMPTON MUN. CODE § 22–100, *et seq.*
Michigan	City of Ann Arbor	ANN ARBOR CODE OF ORDINANCES § 9:150, *et seq.*
	City of Detroit	DETROIT CODE OF ORDINANCES § 27–3–1
	City of East Lansing	EAST LANSING CODE OF ORDINANCES § 22–32, *et seq.*
	City of Ferndale	FERNDALE CODE OF ORDINANCES § 28–3, *et seq.*
	City of Lansing	LANSING CODE OF ORDINANCES § 297.01, *et seq.*
	Saugatuck Township	SAUGATUCK TOWNSHIP CODE OF ORDINANCES § 2–251, *et seq.*
	City of Traverse	CODIFIED ORDINANCES OF TRAVERSE CITY § 605.01, *et seq.*
	City of Ypsilanti	YPSILANTI CODE OF ORDINANCES § 58–61, *et seq.*
Minnesota	City of Minneapolis	MINNEAPOLIS CODE OF ORDINANCES § 139.10, *et seq.*
	City of St. Paul	ST. PAUL CODE OF ORDINANCES § 183.01, *et seq.*
Missouri	City of Kansas City	KANSAS CITY CODE OF ORDINANCES § 38–1, *et seq.*
	City of University City	UNIVERSITY CITY CODE OF ORDINANCES § 9.08.260, *et seq.*
Montana	City of Missoula	MISSOULA MUN. CODE § 9.64.010, *et seq.*
New York	City of Albany	ALBANY MUN. CODE § 48–23, *et seq.*
	City of Buffalo	CODE OF THE CITY OF BUFFALO § 154–9, *et seq.*
	City of Ithaca	ITHACA MUN. CODE § 215–1, *et seq.*

State	City or County	Authority
	City of New York	N.Y.C. ADMIN. CODE § 8–101, *et seq.*
	City of Rochester	ROCHESTER MUN. CODE § 63–1, *et seq.*
	County of Suffolk	SUFFOLK COUNTY CODE § 89–11, *et seq.*
	County of Tompkins	TOMPKINS COUNTY CODE § 92–1, *et seq.*
Ohio	City of Akron	AKRON CODE OF ORDINANCES § 34.03 (applies only to those contracting with city)
	City of Bowling Green	BOWLING GREEN CODE OF ORDINANCES § 39.01, *et seq.*
	City of Cincinnati	CINCINNATI CODE OF ORDINANCES § 914–1, *et seq.*
	City of Cleveland	CLEVELAND CODIFIED ORDINANCES § 663.01, *et seq.*
	City of Columbus	COLUMBUS CODE OF ORDINANCES § 2331.01, *et seq.*
	City of Dayton	DAYTON CODE OF ORDINANCES § 32.01, *et seq.*
	City of Oxford	OXFORD CODIFIED ORDINANCES § 143.01, *et seq.*
	County of Summit	SUMMIT COUNTY CODIFIED ORDINANCES § 169.01, *et seq.* (applies only to county employees)
	City of Toledo	TOLEDO MUN. CODE 554.01, *et seq.*
	Village of Yellow Springs	YELLOW SPRINGS CODE OF ORDINANCES § 632.01, *et seq.*
Oregon	City of Beaverton	BEAVERTON CITY CODE § 5.16.020
	City of Bend	BEND CODE tit. V, ch. 5.25.005
	County of Benton	BENTON COUNTY CODE, ch. 28, ¶ 28.105
	City of Corvallis	CORVALLIS MUN. CODE, ch. 1.23, § 1.23.050
	City of Hillsboro	HILLSBORO MUN. CODE § 7.28.020
	City of Lake Oswego	LAKE OSWEGO MUN. CODE § 34.22.050
	City of Lincoln City	LINCOLN CITY MUN. CODE § 9.14.010, *et seq.*
	County of Multnomah	MULTNOMAH COUNTY ORDINANCE No. 969, § 15.340, *et seq.*, and MULTNOMAH COUNTY CODE § 9.010, *et seq.* (county employees only)

State	City or County	Authority
	City of Portland	PORTLAND CITY CODE § 23.01.050
	City of Salem	SALEM REV. CODE § 97.005
Pennsylvania	City of Allentown	ALLENTOWN MUN. CODE § 181.01, *et seq.*
	City of Easton	EASTON CITY CODE 79–1, *et seq.*
	County of Erie	ERIE COUNTY HUMAN RELATIONS ORDINANCE 39 (2007)
	City of Harrisburg	CODE OF CITY OF HARRISBURG §§ 4–101.1 and 4–105.1
	Borough of Lansdowne	LANSDOWNE BOROUGH CODE § 38.1, *et seq.*
	Township of Lower Merion	LOWER MERION MUNICIPAL CODE § 93–1, *et seq.*
	Borough of New Hope	NEW HOPE BOROUGH CODE § 129–1, *et seq.*
	City of Philadelphia	PHILADELPHIA CODE §9–1101, *et seq.*
	City of Pittsburgh	PITTSBURGH CODE OF ORDINANCES § 651.01, *et seq.,* and § 659.02
	City of Scranton	SCRANTON CITY CODE § 296–1, *et seq.*
	Township of Springfield	SPRINGFIELD MUNICIPAL CODE § 47–1, *et seq.*
	Borough of State College	STATE COLLEGE CODE OF ORDINANCES, ch. V, part I, § 901, *et seq.*
	Township of Susquehanna	SUSQUEHANNA ORDINANCE No. 11–17
	Borough of Swarthmore	SWARTHMORE CODIFIED ORDINANCES, ch. 207.01, *et seq.*
	Borough of West Chester	WEST CHESTER CODE OF ORDINANCES § 37A-1, *et seq.*
	City of York	YORK CITY CODIFIED ORDINANCES, tit. 5, art. 185.01, *et seq.*
Texas	City of Austin	AUSTIN CODE OF ORDINANCES § 5–3–1, *et seq.*
	City of Dallas	DALLAS CODE OF ORDINANCES § 46–1, *et seq.*
	County of Dallas	DALLAS COUNTY CODE OF ORDINANCES § 86–221, *et seq.* (county employment only)

State	City or County	Authority
	City of Fort Worth	FT. WORTH CODE OF ORDINANCES § 17–66, *et seq.*
Utah	County of Grand	GRAND COUNTY ORDINANCE No. 494
	City of Harrisville	HARRISVILLE MUN. CODE § 4.60.010, *et seq.*
	City of Logan	LOGAN CITY CODE § 2.62.010, *et seq.*
	City of Midvale	MIDVALE MUN. CODE § 26.08.010
	City of Murray	MURRAY CITY CODE § 5.44.010, *et seq.*
	City of Park City	PARK CITY CODE OF ORDINANCES, tit. 4, ch. 16, § 4–16–1, *et seq.*
	City of Salt Lake	SALT LAKE CITY CODE § 10.04.010, *et seq.*
	County of Salt Lake	SALT LAKE COUNTY CODE OF ORDINANCES § 10.13.010, *et seq.*
	County of Summit	SUMMIT COUNTY CODE OF ORDINANCES § 1–15B-1, *et seq.*
	City of West Valley	WEST VALLEY CODE OF ORDINANCES § 26–2–101, *et seq.*
Washington	City of Burien	BURIEN CODE OF ORDINANCES § 8.50.010, *et seq.*
	County of King	KING COUNTY CODE § 12.16.010, *et seq.* (only applies to county contractors, subcontractors and vendors)
	City of Seattle	SEATTLE MUN. CODE § 14.04.040, *et seq.*
	City of Tacoma	TACOMA MUN. CODE § 1.29.010, *et seq.*
West Virginia	City of Charleston	CHARLESTON CODE OF ORDINANCES § 62–1, *et seq.*
Wisconsin	County of Dane	DANE COUNTY CODE OF ORDINANCES § 19.01, *et seq.* (applies only to county employees and county contractors)
	City of Madison	MADISON CODE OF ORDINANCES § 39.03
	City of Milwaukee	MILWAUKEE CODE OF ORDINANCES § 109–45

U.S. Companies That Provide Health Insurance Coverage for Sex Reassignment Surgery*

- 3M Co.
- A.T. Kearney, Inc.
- AAA Northern California, Nevada & Utah
- Insurance Exchange
- Abercrombie & Fitch Co.
- Accenture Ltd.
- Aetna, Inc.
- Akin, Gump, Strauss, Hauer & Feld, L.L.P.
- Alcatel-Lucent
- Alcoa, Inc.
- Alston & Bird, L.L.P.
- American Express Co.
- Ameriprise Financial Inc.
- AMR Corp. (American Airlines)
- Aon Corp.
- Apple, Inc.
- AT&T, Inc.
- Automatic Data Processing, Inc.
- Avaya, Inc.

* Human Rights Campaign, Corporate Equality Index, p. 20 (2012) at http://sites.hrc.org/documents/CorporateEqualityIndex_2012.pdf (last visited December 8, 2011).

- Avon Products Inc.
- Bain & Co. Inc.
- Baker & McKenzie, L.L.P.
- Bank of America Corp.
- Bank of New York Mellon Corp., The (BNY Mellon)
- Barclays Capital
- Barnes & Noble Inc.
- Best Buy Co., Inc.
- Bingham McCutchen, L.L.P.
- BlackRock
- Blue Cross Blue Shield of Florida, Inc.
- Blue Cross Blue Shield of Minnesota
- BMO Bankcorp, Inc.
- Booz Allen Hamilton, Inc.
- Boston Consulting Group
- Bristol-Myers Squibb Co.
- Broadridge Financial Solutions, Inc.
- Brown Rudnick, L.L.P.
- Brown-Forman Corp.
- Bryan Cave, L.L.P.
- Caesars Entertainment Corp.
- Campbell Soup Co.
- Capital One Financial Corp.
- Cardinal Health, Inc.
- CareFusion Corp.
- Cargill Inc.
- Carlton Fields, P.A.
- Chapman and Cutler, L.L.P.
- Charles Schwab Corp., The
- Chevron Corp.
- Choate, Hall & Stewart, L.L.P.
- Choice Hotels International Inc.
- Chrysler L.L.C.
- Chubb Corp.
- Cisco Systems Inc.

- Citigroup Inc.
- Clifford Chance US, L.L.P.
- Clorox Co.
- Coca-Cola Co., The
- Comerica Inc.
- Corning Inc.
- Covington & Burling LLP
- Credit Suisse USA, Inc.
- Crowell & Moring, L.L.P.
- Cummins Inc.
- Davis Wright Tremaine, L.L.P.
- Debevoise & Plimpton, L.L.P.
- Delhaize America Inc.
- Dell Inc.
- Deloitte L.L.P.
- Deutsche Bank
- Dewey & LeBoeuf, L.L.P.
- Diageo North America
- DLA Piper
- Dorsey & Whitney, L.L.P.
- Dow Chemical Co., The
- Dykema Gossett, P.L.L.C.
- E. I. du Pont de Nemours and Co. (DuPont)
- Eastman Kodak Co.
- eBay Inc.
- Edwards Angell Palmer & Dodge, L.L.P.
- Eli Lilly & Co.
- EMC Corp.
- Ernst & Young, L.L.P.
- Exelon Corp.
- Faegre & Benson, L.L.P.
- Federal Home Loan Mortgage Corp. (Freddie Mac)
- Fenwick & West, L.L.P.
- Ford Motor Co.
- Fried, Frank, Harris, Shriver & Jacobson, L.L.P.

- Gap Inc.
- Genentech Inc.
- General Mills Inc.
- General Motors Co.
- Gibson, Dunn & Crutcher, L.L.P.
- GlaxoSmithKline plc
- Goldman Sachs Group Inc., The
- Google, Inc.
- Group Health Cooperative
- Group Health Permanente
- Herman Miller Inc.
- Hewlett-Packard Co.
- Hinshaw & Culbertson, L.L.P.
- Hogan Lovells US, L.L.P.
- Hyatt Hotels Corp.
- ING North America Insurance Corp.
- Intel Corp.
- International Business Machines Corp. (IBM)
- Intuit Inc.
- Jenner & Block, L.L.P.
- Johnson & Johnson
- JPMorgan Chase & Co.
- K&L Gates, L.L.P.
- Kellogg Co.
- Kimpton Hotel & Restaurant Group, Inc.
- Kirkland & Ellis, L.L.P.
- KPMG, L.L.P.
- Kraft Foods, Inc.
- Levi Strauss & Co.
- Limited Brands, Inc.
- Littler Mendelson, P.C.
- Lockheed Martin Corp.
- Marsh & McLennan Companies, Inc.
- McDermott Will & Emery, L.L.P.
- McKinsey & Co., Inc.

- Medtronic, Inc.
- MetLife, Inc.
- Microsoft Corp.
- MillerCoors, L.L.C.
- Mitchell Gold + Bob Williams
- Morgan Lewis & Bockius, L.L.P.
- Morgan Stanley
- Morrison & Foerster, L.L.P.
- Nationwide
- Navigant Consulting, Inc.
- Nike Inc.
- Nixon Peabody, L.L.P.
- Nordstrom, Inc.
- Northern Trust Corp.
- Office Depot, Inc.
- Oracle Corp.
- Orbitz Worldwide, Inc.
- Orrick, Herrington & Sutcliffe, L.L.P.
- Owens Corning
- Patterson Belknap Webb & Tyler, L.L.P.
- Paul Hastings, L.L.P.
- Paul, Weiss, Rifkind, Wharton & Garrison, L.L.P.
- Pearson, Inc.
- PepsiCo, Inc.
- Perkins Coie, L.L.P.
- Pfizer, Inc.
- PG&E Corp.
- Pillsbury Winthrop Shaw Pittman, L.L.P.
- PricewaterhouseCoopers, L.L.P.
- Prudential Financial, Inc.
- Raytheon Co.
- Replacements Ltd.
- Robins, Kaplan, Miller & Ciresi, L.L.P.
- Rockwell Automation, Inc.
- Ropes & Gray, L.L.P.

- Schiff Hardin, L.L.P.
- Sears Holdings Corp.
- Sedgwick, Detert, Moran & Arnold, L.L.P.
- Sempra Energy
- Seyfarth Shaw, L.L.P.
- Shearman & Sterling, L.L.P.
- Sheppard, Mullin, Richter & Hampton, L.L.P.
- Shook, Hardy & Bacon, L.L.P.
- Sidley Austin, L.L.P.
- Simpson, Thacher & Bartlett, L.L.P.
- Sodexo, Inc.
- Southern California Edison Co.
- Sprint Nextel Corp.
- Squire, Sanders & Dempsey, L.L.P.
- Staples, Inc.
- Starwood Hotels & Resorts Worldwide
- State Farm Group
- Sun Life Financial, Inc. (U.S.)
- Supervalu, Inc.
- Sutherland Asbill & Brennan, L.L.P.
- Symantec Corp.
- TD Bank, N.A.
- Teachers Insurance and Annuity Association College Retirement Equities Fund
- Tech Data Corp.
- Thompson Coburn, L.L.P.
- Thomson Reuters
- Tiffany & Co.
- Time Warner, Inc.
- TJX Companies, Inc., The
- Toyota Financial Services Corp.
- Toyota Motor Sales USA, Inc.
- Troutman Sanders, L.L.P.
- U.S. Bancorp
- UBS AG

- Unilever
- United Continental Holdings Inc.
- United Parcel Service, Inc. (UPS)
- United Technologies Corp.
- UnitedHealth Group Inc.
- Volkswagen Group of America, Inc.
- Wachtell, Lipton, Rosen & Katz, L.L.P.
- Walt Disney Co., The
- Wells Fargo & Co.
- Whirlpool Corp.
- White & Case, L.L.P.
- Wilmer Cutler Pickering Hale & Dorr, L.L.P.
- Winston & Strawn, L.L.P.
- Xerox Corp.
- Yahoo! Inc.

Cities and Counties with Public Accommodations Nondiscrimination Ordinances and Laws That Include Gender Identity or Expression

State	City or County	Authority	Bathroom, etc. Provisions
Arizona	City of Tucson	CITY OF TUCSON CODE, art. III, §17–12	None
California	City of Los Angeles	LOS ANGELES MUN. CODE § 49.70, *et seq.*	None
	City of Oakland	OAKLAND CODE OF ORDINANCES § 9.44.020	The city ordinance prohibits the denial of access to "facilities, including dressing and bathroom facilities, consistent with the person's gender identity." Sub § E.
	City of San Diego	SAN DIEGO MUN. CODE, art. 2, § 52.9605	None

State	City or County	Authority	Bathroom, etc. Provisions
	City and County of San Francisco	S.F. Police Code §3305	None
	City of Santa Cruz	Santa Cruz Mun. Code 9.83.010, *et seq.*	None
	County of Santa Cruz	Santa Cruz County Code 8.52.010, *et seq.*	None
	City of West Hollywood	West Hollywood Mun. Code, chap. 9.28.010, *et seq.*	None
Colorado	City of Boulder	City of Boulder Rev. Code, chap. 12–1	"[T]ransitioned transsexuals may use the locker rooms and shower facilities of their new sex and shall be protected by" the law "from any discrimination in their use of such locker rooms and shower rooms," and "transitioning transsexuals shall be granted reasonable accommodation in access to locker rooms and shower facilities." 12–1–4(c) and (d)
	City and County of Denver	Denver Rev. Mun. Code § 28–91, *et seq.*	"[T]ransitioned transsexuals may use the locker rooms and shower facilities of their new sex and shall be protected . . . from discrimination in their use of such locker rooms and shower rooms," and "transitioning transsexuals shall be granted reasonable accommodation in access to locker rooms and shower facilities." § 28–96(c) and (d)
Florida	County of Broward	Broward County Code of Ordinances §§16 ½ – 22	§ 16½-22 does "not prohibit discrimination on the basis of sex in: [r]estrooms, shower rooms, bathhouses, and similar facilities, which are by their nature distinctly private, or YMCA, YWCA, and similar type dormitory lodging facilities."

State	City or County	Authority	Bathroom, etc. Provisions
	City of Dunedin	DUNEDIN CODE OF ORDINANCES § 43–31, *et seq.*	None
	City of Gainesville	CITY OF GAINESVILLE CODE OF ORDINANCES § 8–67, *et seq.*	None
	City of Gulfport	CITY OF GULFPORT CODE OF ORDINANCES § 26–40, *et seq.*	The city ordinance does "not prohibit discrimination on the basis of sex in restrooms, shower rooms, bathhouses, and similar facilities" or "dormitory lodging facilities." §26–43(b)
	City of Key West	CITY OF KEY WEST CODE OF ORDINANCES § 38–225	The city ordinance does "not apply to any facility, as to discrimination based on sex, which is distinctly private in nature, such as restrooms, shower rooms, and dressing rooms." § 38–225
	County of Leon	LEON COUNTY CODE OF ORDINANCES § 9–40, *et seq.*	The city ordinance does "not prohibit discrimination on the basis of sex or gender in restrooms, shower rooms, bathhouses, and similar facilities which are by their nature simply private, or dormitory lodging facilities." § 9–43(c)
	City of Miami Beach	CITY OF MIAMI BEACH CODE OF ORDINANCES §§ 62–33 and 62–87	None
	County of Monroe	MONROE COUNTY CODE OF ORDINANCES § 14–43	"Shall not apply to any facility, as to discrimination based on sex, that is distinctly private in nature, such as restrooms, shower rooms, and dressing rooms."

State	City or County	Authority	Bathroom, etc. Provisions
	County of Palm Beach	PALM BEACH COUNTY CODE OF ORDINANCES § 15–36, *et seq.*	None
	City of Tampa	CITY OF TAMPA CODE OF ORDINANCES § 12–61, *et seq.*	Does not apply to discrimination "on the basis of sex in restrooms, shower rooms, bath houses, health spas, or similar facilities which are by their nature distinctly private, or dormitory-lodging facilities." § 12–66(a)(1)
	County of Volusia	VOLUSIA COUNTY CODE OF ORDINANCES § 36–40, *et seq.*	Shall not prohibit a "restriction or use in restrooms, shower rooms, bathhouses, and similar facilities consistent with the facility user's actual anatomical gender, except that if the facility user has undergone and completed gender transition surgical procedures, either before or during employment, then said user shall be allowed to utilize restrooms, shower rooms and similar facilities consistent with his or her transsexual status." § 36–42(3)
	City of West Palm Beach	CITY OF WEST PALM BEACH CODE OF ORDINANCES § 42–31, *et seq.*	The city ordinance does not apply to discrimination "on the basis of sex in restrooms, shower rooms, bathhouses, health spas or similar facilities, which are by their nature distinctly private, or dormitory-lodging facilities." § 43–38(1)
Georgia	City of Atlanta	CITY OF ATLANTA CODE OF ORDINANCES § 94–66, *et seq.*	None

State	City or County	Authority	Bathroom, etc. Provisions
Illinois	City of Champaign	CITY OF CHAMPAIGN CODE OF ORDINANCES § 17–56, *et seq.*	"It shall not be unlawful to discriminate on the basis of sex in the provision of facilities which are distinctly private in nature, such as restrooms, shower rooms, bath houses, health clubs or other similar facilities." § 17–57(b)
	City of Chicago	MUN. CODE OF CHICAGO, ch. 2–160–010, *et seq.*	"[A]ny person may use a public accommodation or any of its products, facilities or services that are open to persons of the sex or gender reflected on any government issued identification of that individual including a driver's license, a state identification card or passport." § 2–160–070(e)
	County of Cook	COOK COUNTY CODE OF ORDINANCES § 42–31, *et seq.*	The city exempts from discrimination "Any facility that is distinctly private in nature, such as restrooms, shower rooms, bath houses, dressing rooms, or health clubs" [§ 42–37(b)(1)a.] and "[a]ny facility that restricts rental of residential or sleeping rooms to individuals of one sex." § 42–37(b)(1)b. But it provides that: "the determination of an individual's sex or gender shall be based upon the sex or gender of that individual as reflected on any official identification of that individual recognized by the State of Illinois, including a driver's license or state identification card." § 42–37(b)(1)d.
	City of Decatur	DECATUR MUN. CODE, ch. 28, art. 2	The city exempts "discrimination based on sex, which is distinctly private in nature such as restrooms, shower rooms, bath houses, health clubs and other similar facilities." § 10–3.B.

State	City or County	Authority	Bathroom, etc. Provisions
	City of Peoria	PEORIA CODE OF ORDINANCES § 17–141, *et seq.*	None
	City of Springfield	SPRINGFIELD CODE OF ORDINANCES § 93.01, *et seq.*	The city exempts "discrimination based on sex, which is distinctly private in nature such as restrooms, shower rooms, bath houses, health clubs and other similar facilities." § 93.12(c)(1_b)
	City of Urbana	URBANA MUN. CODE §§ 12–39 and 12–63	None
Indiana	City of Evansville	EVANSVILLE MUN. CODE § 2.30.010	"It shall not be discriminatory practice to maintain separate restrooms or dressing rooms for men and women." § 2.30.010.B. – definition of "Discriminatory Practice" ¶ (1)(a)
	City of Indianapolis and County of Marion	REV. CODE OF CONSOLIDATED CITY AND COUNTY OF INDIANAPOLIS/ MARION §§ 581–101, 581–103 and 581–403	It is not a violation to "maintain separate restrooms or dressing rooms for the exclusive use of either sex." § 581–404(d)(1)
	County of Monroe	MONROE COUNTY CODE, chap. 520	"[I]t shall not be a discriminatory practice to maintain separate restrooms or dressing rooms." ch. 520-3(23)
Iowa	City of Council Bluffs	COUNCIL BLUFFS CODE OF ORDINANCES §§ 1.40.030 and 1.40.090	None
	City of Iowa City	IOWA CITY CODE §§ 2-5-1, *et seq.*	None

State	City or County	Authority	Bathroom, etc. Provisions
	County of Johnson	JOHNSON COUNTY ORDINANCE No. 12–28–06–01	The city ordinance does "not apply to sex discrimination to any facility that is distinctly private in nature, such as restrooms, shower rooms, bath houses, dressing rooms, or health clubs." ¶ V.(B)
	City of Waterloo	WATERLOO CITY CODE § 5–3A-1, *et seq.*	None
Kansas	City of Lawrence	CODE OF THE CITY OF LAWRENCE § 10–101, *et seq.*	None
Kentucky	City of Covington	COVINGTON CODE OF ORDINANCES § 37.05	The city ordinance does not apply to "Restrooms, shower rooms, bath-houses, and similar facilities, which are, by their nature, distinctly private" and "YMCA, YWCA, and similar dormitory-type lodging facilities." § 37.07(C)(2)
	Lexington-Fayette County	LEXINGTON-FAYETTE COUNTY CODE OF ORDINANCES § 2–33	Employers may designate "appropriate gender specific restroom or shower facilities." § 2–33(6)(b)
	Louisville-Jefferson County Metro Government	LOUISVILLE-JEFFERSON COUNTY CODE OF ORDINANCES § 92.01, *et seq.*	The city ordinance does not apply to: "Restrooms, shower rooms, bath houses and similar facilities which are by their nature distinctly private;" and "YMCA, YWCA and similar type dormitory lodging facilities." § 92.05(C)(1)

State	City or County	Authority	Bathroom, etc. Provisions
Louisiana	City of New Orleans	NEW ORLEANS CODE OF ORDINANCES § 86–33, *et seq.*	The city does not "prohibit the placement of persons in a separate restroom, bath, locker, room, shower, physical or medical examination or treatment facility, dressing area, or dormitory or sleeping room used by more than one party of persons at a time, if such placement is reasonable and based on the person's sex or sexual orientation or gender identification." § 86–33(c)
Maryland	City of Baltimore	BALTIMORE CITY CODE, art. 4, § 3–2	None
	County of Howard	HOWARD COUNTY CODE OF ORDINANCES § 12–200, *et seq.*	The county exempts from discrimination places with less than two "rental rooms or apartments."
	County of Montgomery	MONTGOMERY COUNTY CODE § 27–10, *et seq.*	None
Massachusetts	City of Boston	BOSTON MUN. CODE 12–9.7	"[N]othing contained herein shall permit the use of restrooms, baths, showers, dressing rooms, or other private accommodations which are separated by sex to be used by the opposite sex, except it shall be an unlawful and discriminatory practice to prevent or prohibit the use of restrooms, baths, showers, dressing rooms, or other private accommodations based on the gender identity publicly and exclusively expressed or asserted by the person seeking to use such restrooms, baths, showers, dressing rooms, or other private accommodations."
	City of Cambridge	CAMBRIDGE MUN. CODE §§ 2.76.030 and 2.76.120	It is not unlawful to designate "a restroom of a privately owned athletic or exercise facility for the exclusive or preferential use of members of a single sex." § 2.76.120.M.3,c.

State	City or County	Authority	Bathroom, etc. Provisions
	City of Northampton	NORTHAMPTON MUN. CODE §§ 22–100, *et seq.*	None
Michigan	City of Ann Arbor	ANN ARBOR CODE OF ORDINANCES § 9:150, *et seq.*	None
	City of Detroit	DETROIT CODE OF ORDINANCES § 27–6–1, *et seq.*	It is not a discriminatory "practice for the owner or authorized agent of a public accommodation or public service facility to restrict the use of a lavatory of such facility on the basis of the sex of the proposed user." § 27–6–2
	City of East Lansing	EAST LANSING CODE OF ORDINANCES §§ 22–31, *et seq.*	None
	City of Ferndale	FERNDALE CODE OF ORDINANCES § 28–3, *et seq.*	None
	City of Lansing	LANSING CODE OF ORDINANCES § 297.01, *et seq.*	"It is permissible to restrict the use of shower or changing areas in health clubs or recreational facilities on the basis of sex when separate and private shower or changing areas do not exist." § 297.08(b)(1)
	Saugatuck Township	SAUGATUCK TOWNSHIP CODE OF ORDINANCES § 2–251, *et seq.*	The township ordinance exempts from discrimination all boy and girl schools.
	City of Traverse	CODIFIED ORDINANCES OF TRAVERSE CITY § 605.01, *et seq.*	None

State	City or County	Authority	Bathroom, etc. Provisions
	City of Ypsilanti	YPSILANTI CODE OF ORDINANCES § 58–61, *et seq.*	It is permitted to "restrict use of lavatories and locker room facilities on the basis of sex." § 58–71(13)
Minnesota	City of Minneapolis	MINNEAPOLIS CODE OF ORDINANCES § 139.10, *et seq.*	None
	City of St. Paul	ST. PAUL CODE OF ORDINANCES § 183.01, *et seq.*	None
Missouri	City of Clayton	MUN. CODE OF CITY OF CLAYTON § 225.030, *et seq.*	The city exempts from discrimination any "private club, a place of accommodation owned by or operated on behalf of a religious corporation, association or society or other establishment which is not in fact open to the public." § 225.060.C.
	City of Kansas City	KANSAS CITY CODE OF ORDINANCES § 38–1, *et seq.*	None
	City of University City	UNIVERSITY CITY CODE OF ORDINANCES § 9.08.260, *et seq.*	None
Montana	City of Missoula	MISSOULA MUN. CODE § 9.64.010, *et seq.*	None
New York	City of Albany	ALBANY MUN. CODE § 48–23, *et seq.*	None
	City of Buffalo	CODE OF THE CITY OF BUFFALO § 154–4 , *et seq.*	None

State	City or County	Authority	Bathroom, etc. Provisions
	City of Ithaca	ITHACA MUN. CODE § 215–1, *et seq.*	None
	City of New York	N.Y.C. ADMIN. CODE § 8–101, *et seq.*	None
	City of Rochester	ROCHESTER MUN. CODE § 63–1, *et seq.*	The city allows maintenance of "separate bathrooms, locker rooms, and bathing facilities for males and females." § 63–9.M.(1)
	County of Suffolk	SUFFOLK COUNTY CODE § 89–11, *et seq.*	None
	County of Tompkins	TOMPKINS COUNTY CODE § 92–1, *et seq.*	None
Ohio	City of Bowling Green	BOWLING GREEN CODE OF ORDINAN CES § 39.01, *et seq.*	None
	City of Cincinnati	CINCINNATI CODE OF ORDINANCES § 914–1, *et seq.*	None
	City of Cleveland	CLEVELAND CODIFIED ORDINANCES § 667.01, *et seq.*	"Nothing . . . shall be construed to establish unlawful discrimination based on actual or perceived gender identity or expression due to the denial of access to bathrooms, showers, locker rooms or dressing facilities, provided reasonable access to adequate facilities is available." § 667.01(g)
	City of Columbus	COLUMBUS CODE OF ORDINANCES § 2331.01, *et seq.*	None
	City of Dayton	DAYTON CODE OF ORDINANCES § 32.01, *et seq.*	None

State	City or County	Authority	Bathroom, etc. Provisions
	City of Oxford	OXFORD CODIFIED ORDINANCES § 143.01, *et seq.*	None
	City of Toledo	TOLEDO MUN. CODE 554.01, *et seq.*	None
	Village of Yellow Springs	YELLOW SPRINGS CODE OF ORDINANCES § 632.01, *et seq.*	None
Oregon	City of Beaverton	BEAVERTON CITY CODE § 5.16.030	"Reasonable and appropriate accommodations shall be made to permit all persons access to restrooms consistent with their expressed gender." However, the prohibitions "against discriminating on the basis of gender identity do not prohibit: [h]ealth or athletic clubs or other entities that operate gender-specific facilities involving public nudity, such as showers and locker rooms, from requiring an individual to document their gender or transitional status. Such documentation can include but is not limited to a court order, letter from a physician, birth certificate, passport, or driver's license." §15.16.040.E.
	City of Bend	BEND CODE, tit. V, ch. 5.25.020	None
	County of Benton	BENTON COUNTY CODE, ch. 28, ¶ 28.115	None
	City of Corvallis	CORVALLIS MUN. CODE, ch. 1.23, § 1.23.050	None

State	City or County	Authority	Bathroom, etc. Provisions
	City of Hillsboro	HILLSBORO MUN. CODE § 7.28.040	"Reasonable and appropriate accommodations must be made to allow access for a person to a restroom that is consistent with an individual's expressed gender." § 7.28.040.C.
	City of Lake Oswego	LAKE OSWEGO MUN. CODE § 34.22.070	None
	City of Lincoln City	LINCOLN CITY MUN. CODE § 9.14.010, et seq.	None
	County of Multnomah	MULTNOMAH COUNTY ORDINANCE No. 969, § 15.340, et seq.	The county does not prohibit "Health or athletic clubs or other entities that operate gender-specific facilities involving public nudity, such as showers and locker rooms, from requiring an individual to document their gender or transitional status. Such documentation can include but is not limited to a court order, letter from a physician, birth certificate, passport, or driver's license." § 15.340(C)(1)
	City of Portland	PORTLAND CITY CODE § 23.01.070	None

State	City or County	Authority	Bathroom, etc. Provisions
	City of Salem	Salem Rev. Code § 97.0060	The prohibitions against gender identity discrimination do not prohibit "Health or athletic clubs or other entities that operate gender-specific facilities involving public nudity, such as showers and locker rooms, from requiring an individual to document their gender or transitional status. Such documentation can include, but is not limited to, a court order, letter from a physician, birth certificate, passport, or driver's license." These exceptions do "not excuse a failure to provide reasonable and appropriate accommodations permitting all persons access to restrooms consistent with their expressed gender." § 97.080(c)
Pennsylvania	City of Allentown	Allentown Mun. Code § 181.01, et seq.	None
	City of Easton	Easton City Code 79–1, et seq.	None
	County of Erie	Erie County Human Relations Commission Ordinance 39 (2007)	None
	City of Harrisburg	Code of City of Harrisburg §§ 4–101.1 and 4–105.3	None
	Borough of Lansdowne	Lansdowne Borough Code § 38.1, et seq.	None
	Township of Lower Merion	Lower Merion Mun. Code § 93–1, et seq.	None

State	City or County	Authority	Bathroom, etc. Provisions
	Borough of New Hope	New Hope Borough Code § 129–1, et seq.	None
	City of Philadelphia	Philadelphia Code §9–1101, et seq.	None
	City of Pittsburgh	Pittsburgh Code of Ordinances § 651.01, et seq., and § 659.04	None
	City of Scranton	Scranton City Code § 296–1, et seq.	None
	Township of Springfield	Springfield Mun. Code § 47–1, et seq.	None
	Township of Susquehanna	Susquehanna Ordinance No. 11–17	None
	Borough of Swarthmore	Swarthmore Codified Ordinances, ch. 207.01, et seq.	None
	Borough of West Chester	West Chester Code of Ordinances § 37A-1, et seq.	None
	Township of Whitemarsh	Whitemarsh Ordinance No. 901	None
	City of York	York City Codified Ordinances tit. 5, art. 185.01, et seq.	None

State	City or County	Authority	Bathroom, etc. Provisions
South Carolina	City of Charleston	CHARLESTON CODE OF ORDINANCES § 16–28, *et seq.*	None
	City of Columbia	COLUMBIA CODE OF ORDINANCES § 11–501, *et seq.*	None
Texas	City of Austin	AUSTIN CODE OF ORDINANCES § 5–2–1, *et seq.*	None
	City of Dallas	DALLAS CODE OF ORDINANCES § 46–1, *et seq.*	None
	City of El Paso	EL PASO CODE OF ORDINANCES § 10.16.010, *et seq.*	None
	City of Fort Worth	FT. WORTH CODE OF ORDINANCES § 17–46, *et seq.*	None
Washington	City of Burien	BURIEN CODE OF ORDINANCES § 8.50.010, *et seq.*	None
	County of King	KING COUNTY CODE § 12.22.010, *et seq.*	None
	City of Seattle	SEATTLE MUN. CODE § 14.06.010, *et seq.*	None
	City of Tacoma	TACOMA MUN. CODE § 1.29.010, *et seq.*	None

State	City or County	Authority	Bathroom, etc. Provisions
West Virginia	City of Charleston	CHARLESTON CODE OF ORDINANCES § 62–1, *et seq.*	Public accommodations discrimination is not specifically outlawed in the Charleston Code but is declared a human and civil right in § 62–2, and the Human Rights Commission is empowered to receive complaints about discrimination in public accommodations. § 62–45(3). Restrooms are not mentioned.
Wisconsin	City of Madison	MADISON CODE OF ORDINANCES § 39.03	None

Cities and Counties with Education Nondiscrimination Ordinances and Laws That Include Gender Identity or Expression

State	City or County	Authority
Arizona	City of Tucson	The city ordinance does not specifically ban discrimination in education but includes "educational institutions" in its public accommodations ban. CITY OF TUCSON CODE, art. III, §§ 17–11 and 17–12
California	City of Los Angeles	LOS ANGELES MUN. CODE § 49.70, et seq.
	City of San Diego	SAN DIEGO MUN. CODE, art. 2, § 52.9607
	City of Santa Cruz	SANTA CRUZ MUN. CODE 9.83.010, et seq.
	County of Santa Cruz	SANTA CRUZ COUNTY CODE 8.52.010, et seq.
Colorado	City and County of Denver	DENVER REV. MUN. CODE § 28–91, et seq.

State	City or County	Authority
Florida	City of Gainesville	The city ordinance does not specifically include education, but the CITY OF GAINESVILLE CODE OF ORDINANCES § 8–67(b)(6) on public accommodations includes "schools, library or educational facilities supported in part or whole by public funds, kindergartens, daycare centers."
	City of Tampa	The city ordinance does not specifically apply to education but the public accommodation provision includes "library or educational facilities supported in part or whole by public funds." CITY OF TAMPA CODE OF ORDINANCES § 12–62
Illinois	City of Chicago	The city ordinance has no provision about educational discrimination, but the public accommodation provision exempts "any educational institution, as to discrimination based on sex, which restricts enrollment of students to individuals of one sex." MUN. CODE OF CHICAGO, ch. 5–8–070(d)
	County of Cook	The county ordinance does not specifically address education, but exempts from its public accommodation provisions "[a]ny educational institution that restricts enrollment of students to individuals of one sex." COOK COUNTY CODE OF ORDINANCES § 42–37(b)(1)c. But it provides that: "the determination of an individual's sex or gender shall be based upon the sex or gender of that individual as reflected on any official identification of that individual recognized by the State of Illinois, including a driver's license or state identification card." § 42–37(b)(1)d.
Indiana	City of Evansville	EVANSVILLE MUN. CODE § 2.30.010
	City of Indianapolis and County of Marion	REV. CODE OF CONSOLIDATED CITY AND COUNTY OF INDIANAPOLIS/MARION §§ 581–101, 581–103 and 581–403
	County of Monroe	MONROE COUNTY CODE, chap. 520
Iowa	City of Council Bluffs	COUNCIL BLUFFS CODE OF ORDINANCES §§ 1.40.030 and 1.40.120
	City of Iowa City	IOWA CITY CODE §§ 2–5–1, et seq.

State	City or County	Authority
	County of Johnson	JOHNSON COUNTY ORDINANCE No. 12–28–06–01
	City of Waterloo	WATERLOO CITY CODE § 5–3A-1, *et seq.*
Massachusetts	City of Boston	BOSTON MUN. CODE 12–9.6
	City of Cambridge	CAMBRIDGE MUN. CODE §§ 2.76.030 and 2.76.120
Michigan	City of Detroit	DETROIT CODE OF ORDINANCES § 27–5–1, *et seq.*
	City of East Lansing	EAST LANSING CODE OF ORDINANCES § 22–31, *et seq.* does not specifically state education, but declares it "to be contrary to the public policy" to "deny any other person the enjoyment of his/her civil rights or for any person to discriminate against any other person in the exercise of his/her civil rights" because of "student status. . . . Student status refers to a person enrolled in an educational institution recognized by the State of Michigan in pursuit of a recognized degree." §§ 22–31 and 22–32
	Saugatuck Township	SAUGATUCK TOWNSHIP CODE OF ORDINANCES § 2–251, *et seq.* The township ordinance included gender identity or expressed in its definition of "[p]ublic accommodations and public services." § 2–252
Minnesota	City of Minneapolis	MINNEAPOLIS CODE OF ORDINANCES § 139.10, *et seq.*
	City of St. Paul	ST. PAUL CODE OF ORDINANCES § 183.01, *et seq.*
Montana	City of Missoula	MISSOULA MUN. CODE § 9.64.010, *et seq.*
New York	City of Buffalo	CODE OF THE CITY OF BUFFALO § 154–9, *et seq.*
	City of Ithaca	ITHACA MUN. CODE § 215–1, *et seq.*
	City of New York	N.Y.C. ADMIN. CODE § 8–101, *et seq.*
	County of Tompkins	TOMPKINS COUNTY CODE § 92–1, *et seq.*
Ohio	City of Bowling Green	BOWLING GREEN CODE OF ORDINANCES § 39.01, *et seq.*
Pennsylvania	City of Harrisburg	CODE OF CITY OF HARRISBURG §§ 4–101.1 and 4–105.4

State	City or County	Authority
	Township of Susquehanna	Susquehanna Ordinance No. 11–17

Index